§➤ *Browning's Later Poetry, 1871−1889*

Browning's Later Poetry
❧ 1871–1889

Clyde de L. Ryals

Cornell University Press

ITHACA AND LONDON

First published 1975 by Cornell University Press.
Published in the United Kingdom by Cornell University Press Ltd., 2-4 Brook Street, London W1Y 1AA.

International Standard Book Number 0-8014-0964-0
Library of Congress Catalog Card Number 75–16927
Printed in the United States of America by York Composition Co., Inc.

§∂ *In Memory of*
  Henri Talon, 1909–1972
  and
  Lionel Stevenson, 1902–1973

৯ Contents

Preface	9
Introduction	13
1. *Balaustion's Adventure*	28
2. *Prince Hohenstiel-Schwangau*	42
3. *Fifine at the Fair*	59
4. *Red Cotton Night-Cap Country*	83
5. *Aristophanes' Apology*	101
6. *The Inn Album*	119
7. *Pacchiarotto and Other Poems* and *The Agamemnon of Aeschylus*	132
8. *La Saisiaz: The Two Poets of Croisic*	147
9. *Dramatic Idyls* and *Jocoseria*	165
10. *Ferishtah's Fancies*	190
11. *Parleyings with Certain People of Importance in Their Day*	201
12. *Asolando*	227
Conclusion	241
Bibliography	249
Index	257

ଜ Preface

Like many prefaces this one is defensive. I should like to state forthrightly what I do and do not attempt to do in the following pages. I am primarily interested in the form of Browning's later work, that is, the overall structure of a poem and, in a local way, the manner in which themes and ideas are presented in interweaving and contrapuntal fashions throughout the poems. I do not say very much about language or style. It is not that I think language and style unimportant or that I am uninterested in them; it is just that I am here more interested in questioning why a poem is cast in a certain form. In other words, I do not pretend to say all that could be said about any given poem.

Thanks are due to several in the preparation of this book. I should like to indicate my debt to two former students, Maryanne Caporaletti and Janice Haney, who gave me helpful ideas. Dorothy Roberts proved an impeccable typist, for whose careful work I am most appreciative. Boyd Litzinger and Roma King gave the book a rigorous and sympathetic reading in typescript. I have profited from their many suggestions and, absolving them of responsibility for any errors of fact and judgment, acknowledge their help with gratitude. I should also like to record my appreciation to the John Simon Guggenheim Memorial Foundation for a Fellowship which made the writing of the book possible.

Portions of the book have been previously published. Parts of Chapter 1 appeared in *PMLA* (October 1973); of Chapter 2 in *Nineteenth-Century Literary Perspectives: Essays in Honor of Lionel Stevenson,* ed. Clyde de L. Ryals (Durham: Duke Uni-

10   Preface

versity Press, 1974)'; of Chapter 3 in *Essays in Criticism* (April 1969) and *English Language Notes* (September 1969); of Chapter 4 in *Romantic and Victorian: Studies in Memory of William H. Marshall*, ed. W. Paul Elledge and Richard L. Hoffman (Rutherford: Fairleigh Dickinson University Press, 1971); of Chapter 5 in *Carlyle and His Circle: Essays in Honor of Charles Richard Sanders*, ed. John Clubbe (Durham: Duke University Press, 1975). I thank the various editors of the journals and the university presses for their kind permission to reprint this material.

Lastly, a bibliographical note. All quotations from Browning's later poetry, except as otherwise noted, are taken from the first London edition. Line numbers have been added to correspond with the Camberwell Edition, *Complete Works of Robert Browning*, ed. Charlotte Porter and Helen A. Clarke, 12 vols. (New York: Thomas Y. Crowell, 1898). Quotations from Browning's poetry prior to 1871 and from the *Essay on Shelley* are from the Camberwell Edition.

C. L. R.

London and
Durham, North Carolina

ह≈ *Browning's Later Poetry, 1871–1889*

                                        God, perchance,
Grants each new man, by some as new a mode,
Intercommunication with Himself,
Wreaking on finiteness infinitude;
By such a series of effects, gives each
Last His own imprint: old yet ever new
The process: 't is the way of Deity.
How it succeeds, He knows: I only know
That varied modes of creatureship abound,
Implying just as varied intercourse
For each with the creator of them all.
Each has his own mind and no other's mode.

Prince Hohenstiel-Schwangau, 171–82

❧ Introduction

Writing in 1942, H. B. Charlton summed up the current critical estimate of Browning's later poetry: "Now it is universally agreed by critics of all shades of opinion . . . that after *The Ring and the Book,* though his output of verse was vast, the poetic prerogative had faded before the demands of a more formally philosophic purpose. . . ."[1] This opinion has not changed substantially during the past three decades.[2] It is now time, I believe, to attempt a new appreciation in answer to the question Park Honan posed in his review of Browning scholarship: "Will our generation, or a later one, discover that Browning did not fall asleep in 1869 . . . ?"[3] As there are few critics who would deny

1. "Browning's Ethical Poetry," *Bulletin of the John Rylands Library,* 27 (1942), 40–41.
2. Three quotations will suffice to indicate the general disfavor in which Browning's later poems are still held. The first is from an essay by an important Browning critic: ". . . *Balaustion's Adventure* [1871] ought to be considered as closing . . . Browning's best period" (Robert Langbaum, "Browning and the Question of Myth," *PMLA,* 81 [1966], 582–3). The second is from a widely used anthology of Victorian poetry: "The majority of his poems written before the seventies are free of glib doctrine and of false assurance" (Introduction to the Browning section in *Victorian Poetry and Poetics,* ed. Walter E. Houghton and G. Robert Stange [Boston: Houghton Mifflin, 1968], p. 169). The third is from a recent volume of selections of Browning's poetry: "Most of the poetry written after *The Ring and the Book* . . . is usually considered inferior to Browning's earlier work. It is marked by crabbed argumentation, or by a headlong, undiscriminating verbosity of style" (Introduction to *The Poetry of Robert Browning,* ed. Jacob Korg [Indianapolis and New York: Bobbs-Merrill, 1971], p. xx).
3. "Robert Browning," *The Victorian Poets: A Guide to Research,* ed. Frederic E. Faverty (Cambridge: Harvard University Press, 1968), p. 117.

Browning a place among the major English poets, it is shocking that the poems written during the last twenty years of his life—more than one-third of his corpus—are largely unread and unstudied.[4]

My purpose in this book is to show, mainly by studying individual poems, that Browning's later work is not simply a sprawling, unstructured mass of versified argument written by a man whose artistic gifts had somehow been maimed or dissipated in the late 1860's. Indeed, I wish to demonstrate that the achievements of Browning's later years are remarkable and that their worth is due primarily to his plastic imagination, the shaping power that molds the most disparate ideas and experiences into a unified whole. I want, in other words, to present the later Browning as a poet intent upon discovering forms that would give shape and meaning to thought and feeling, and, further, to suggest incidentally that if the poet was occasionally careless about language or style he was so because his attention was focused largely on the overall design of his poetry. In my investigation of each of the volumes published from 1871 to 1889, my point of departure will be an examination of the form of the poetry, by which I mean both the inner structuring principles and the modal strategy employed by the poet to deal with and thus encompass a certain idea or problem. For it is mainly on the basis of form that Browning's later work is deplored. Benjamin Jowett long ago expressed this dissatisfaction most succinctly: "He has no form, or has it only by accident when the subject is limited. His thought and feeling and knowledge are generally out of all proportion to his powers of expression."[5] And Browning himself, repeating the

4. Of the many recent books on Browning only two pay serious attention to the later poems: Roma A. King, Jr., *The Focusing Artifice* (Athens: Ohio University Press, 1968); Philip Drew, *The Poetry of Browning: A Critical Introduction* (London: Methuen, 1970). I have drawn freely on both these very useful studies.

5. Quoted in Hallam Tennyson, *Alfred Lord Tennyson: A Memoir* (London: Macmillan, 1897), II, 344. In speaking of form, I refer, as does Jowett, to structure, not to "crabbed argument," "unmusicality," and other infelicities with which the later Browning is frequently charged.

strictures on his prolixity and formlessness, jokingly has one of his characters say in reference to the author of a piece of doggerel: "That bard's a Browning; he neglects the form" (*The Inn Album*, I. 17).[6] The most rewarding way to deal with a work of literature, especially one by an author regarded as at least competent in his craft, is, I feel, not to dismiss it as formless but to ask why it assumes such shape as it has.

In his later work as in his earlier, Browning sought for the proper forms to embody the content of his intellect and imagination, that is, to express his idea of reality. He held no belief more firmly than that of growth and development; he insisted that life is not a having and a resting but a growing and a becoming, the organism being dead that ceases to change. And, of course, the man himself changed. Those critics, consequently, who hold that *The Ring and the Book* "is a definitive summing up of Browning's philosophy of life"[7] have, in my opinion, contributed to the confusion concerning Browning's later poetry. I do not wish to

6. Some further characteristic remarks on the supposed formlessness in Browning's later poetry follow.

If Browning's poetic force were allied with a corresponding feeling for poetic form . . . , he would have been beyond dispute the greatest poet England has possessed for many generations. . . . Defects of manner and of form . . . repel the advances of would-be readers. [R. E. Prothero, "On Robert Browning" (1890), reprinted in *Browning: The Critical Heritage,* ed. Boyd Litzinger and Donald Smalley (London: Routledge and Kegan Paul, 1970), pp. 520–21]

His long poems have no structure. . . . Even his short poems have no completeness, no limpidity. [George Santayana, "The Poetry of Barbarism" (1900), reprinted in *The Browning Critics,* ed. Boyd Litzinger and K. L. Knickerbocker (Lexington: University of Kentucky Press, 1967), p. 71]

His art, seldom altogether sure or perfectly sustained in poems of any length, underwent surprising fluctuations in the years following *The Ring and the Book.* [Introduction to the Browning section in *Victorian Poetry,* ed. E. K. Brown and J. O. Bailey (New York: Ronald Press, 1962), p. 168]

He wrote too much [in the 1870's] and frequently ignored form. [John M. Hitner, "Browning's Grotesque Period," *Victorian Poetry,* 4 (1966), 12]

Much of his poetry, with the exception of the best of his dramatic monologues, lacks unity, it is crowded with non-essentials. [Barbara Melchiori, *Browning's Poetry of Reticence* (Edinburgh and London: Oliver and Boyd, 1968), p. 17]

7. William O. Raymond, *The Infinite Moment, and Other Essays in Robert Browning,* 2nd ed. (Toronto: University of Toronto Press, 1965), p. 4.

claim that his last thoughts were his best or that they more accurately represent the "real" Browning. For the "real" Browning is the whole man, the poet who wrote the *Parleyings* as well as the poet who composed *Men and Women*. My point is that Browning's thoughts and feelings changed and, moreover, that as they changed so did his forms. To see the truth of this, we have only to examine his religious views, particularly those on the Incarnation. It is, perhaps, not an overstatement to say that the chief problem with which Browning deals is a theological one and that his theological concern in large part determines the form of his work.

In his first published poem the poet spoke, through a thin disguise, of "a principle of restlessness" within himself, which would "be all, have, see, know, taste, feel, all" (*Pauline*, 287–8). This was, in his second work, spelled out as the desire "to comprehend the works of God, / And God himself, and all God's intercourse / With the human mind" (*Paracelsus*, i. 533–5). The heroes of Browning's early works seek to leap to the infinite in a single motion of the soul, and fail, discovering instead of an intensification of life only a dissipation of their energies. Recognizing God's infinitude in contrast to their own finite condition, they learn, especially in the dramas, that they must work within human limitations. The soul must find a body, the ideal must be expressed in terms of the real. Sordello hopes that,

> though I must abide
> With dreams now, I may find a thorough vent
> For all myself, acquire an instrument
> For acting . . . ; my soul
> Hunting a body out may gain its whole
> Desire some day! [i. 832–7]

For he knows: "I must, ere I begin to Be, / Include a world, in flesh, I comprehend / In spirit now" (iii. 172–4). Yet, unable to face up to the demands of reality that require him to temper ambition, Sordello ends his life unfulfilled both as man and poet. The reasons for his failure are complex, but ultimately his problem was his inability to find a ground of values which would permit him to resolve the conflict between the infinite and the finite. Browning wrestled with *Sordello* for seven years and finally concluded it in a state of obvious frustration. Yet he had made gains since *Pauline,* for he had learned that Romantic idealism offers no ground for action in either art or society. Where such a ground was to be discovered still eluded him. Although with the writing of *Sordello* he put aside as vain any attempt to comprehend fully God and all his works, he nevertheless retained the desire to discover how the finite is related to the infinite. If, he appears to have reasoned, one cannot reach Ultimate Truth by a single leap, perhaps one can approach it in steps. This seems to have been Browning's strategy in his short dramatic poems, devised to render different perspectives on life. If somehow he could enter into a sufficient number of points of view, then perhaps he could achieve something approaching full vision. For life has many facets. As Sordello says:

> Since
> One object, viewed diversely, may evince
> Beauty and ugliness . . .
> Why must a single of the sides be right?
> What bids choose this and leave the opposite?   [vi. 441–6]

No, "the real way seemed made up of all the ways" (vi. 36). And for almost thirty years Browning in his dramatic monologues proceeded to give as many ways of seeing life as he possibly could. He would, of course, favor certain points of view to the exclusion of others, because he found some kinds of speakers more congenial than others, but in using these special vantage points he would attempt to survey life in its infinite variety.

As all the world knows, the dramatic monologue was the mode that proved best suited to Browning's needs at this time. He more or less perfected it. And he did so because it permitted him for the most part to begin without assumptions as to moral and religious values.[8] But even this mode broke down as an instrument when

8. For a study of the development of the dramatic monologue and

Browning turned his attention to certain subjects. There is, for example, the famous case of "Saul," which the poet printed in an unfinished version in 1845 because he could find no satisfactory solution to the speaker's problem.

Part of the problem of "Saul" was solved when Browning turned to the Incarnation of Christ as the source of values that had previously eluded him. This seems to have happened shortly after his marriage to Elizabeth Barrett in 1846.[9] We first see Browning's Incarnational theology reflected in a reissue of *Paracelsus* in 1849[10] and in *Christmas-Eve and Easter-Day* in 1850, and then in the *Men and Women* volume of 1855 containing the completed "Saul," wherein the King is permitted the saving vision of Christ as the embodiment of power and love.

The structuring of life on the basis of a transcendental vision of God Browning had come to recognize as an impossibility. Without this vision, however, the universe appears to be void and formless, without purpose or direction. As the poems of his middle years unfold, they show that in a world characterized by multitudinousness and fragmentation a pattern is needed to impose order on the chaotic nature of existence. For Browning the pattern is to be found in the mystery of the Incarnation, which vouchsafes to

---

Browning's use of it, see Robert Langbaum's epochal *The Poetry of Experience: The Dramatic Monologue in Modern Literary Tradition* (New York: Random House, 1957).

9. In the 1849 reissue of *Paracelsus* Browning added to the original lines, "God is the PERFECT POET, / Who in his person acts his own creations" (II. 610–11), the following passage:

> Shall man refuse to be aught less than God?
> Man's weakness is his glory—for the strength
> Which raises him to heaven and near God's self,
> Came spite of it: God's strength his glory is,
> For thence came without our weakness sympathy
> Which brought God down to earth, a man like us.

In the 1863 edition he deleted the added passage and returned to the original reading.

10. An excellent discussion of Browning's changing views and the reorientation of his art during his early career may be found in Thomas C. Collins, *Robert Browning's Moral-Aesthetic Theory, 1833–1855* (Lincoln: University of Nebraska Press, 1967).

the phenomenal world creative, organizing, and redemptive powers. The Incarnation is not, however, an event that occurred many years ago once and for all but, on the contrary, is an ongoing process by which God manifests Himself in the lives of all men who wish to make sense out of existence. The poet would have us see that underlying all the ambiguities and impenetrabilities of life is the basic pattern of sin and redemption, for which the Incarnation is the archetype.[11]

To Browning, moreover, the Incarnation of Christ offered an analogy to the practice of poetry. Just as God makes plain the central truth of life by means of the Incarnation, so does the poet through his imaginative vision impart value to disordered phenomena by penetrating the illusions of existence and revealing the true nature of things. With Christ the poet shares in the work of redeeming men from error and bondage, making them focus on the true and the eternal. As Browning observed in "Old Pictures at Florence," the artist tries "to bring the invisible full into play."

The analogy between the Incarnation and the practice of poetry is suggested in the *Essay on Shelley* of 1852, which is of considerable interest for the light it throws on Browning's own poetic theory. According to the literary criticism of his day, there are, says Browning, two kinds of poets. On the one hand there is the objective poet, who reproduces "things external . . . with an immediate reference, in every case, to the common eye and apprehension of his fellow men. . . . Such a poet is properly the *poietés*, the fashioner; and the thing fashioned, his poetry, will of necessity be substantive, projected from himself and distinct." On the other hand there is the subjective poet, who "is impelled to embody the thing he perceives, not so much with reference to the many below as to the One above him, the supreme Intelligence which apprehends all things in their absolute truth. . . . Not what man sees, but what God sees, . . . —it is toward these that he struggles" (*Works*, XII. 282–3). We can discern that in de-

---

11. See William Whitla, *The Central Truth: The Incarnation in Browning's Poetry* (Toronto: University of Toronto Press, 1963). Whitla, however, deals with the later poetry in a cursory fashion.

scribing two different kinds of poets Browning is, in effect, describing the two strains in his own work—one transcendental and upward toward the infinite, the other descendental and downward toward the finite; the first is most evident in his poetry through 1840, the second, most readily discoverable in the monologues of his middle years. And he goes one step farther and presents his own (veiled) aspiration when he says: "Nor is there any reason why these two modes of poetic faculty may not issue hereafter from the same poet in successive perfect works, examples of which . . . we have hitherto possessed in distinct individuals only" (*Works,* XII. 285). This much of the *Essay* is not overtly Christian; indeed, it may well owe its analysis of the two strains of poetic genius to Carlyle.[12] But at the close Browning presents Shelley as a Christian poet malgré lui: "I call him a man of religious mind, because every audacious negative cast up by him against the Divine was interpenetrated with a mood of reverence and adoration,—and because I find him everywhere taking for granted some of the capital dogmas of Christianity, while most vehemently denying their historical basement" (XII. 296–7). Shelley was a great (and, Browning would have it, Christian) poet because, like the author of the completed "Saul," he perceived simultaneously "Power and Love in the absolute" and "Beauty and Good in the concrete," because ultimately his poetry is an essay "towards a presentment of the correspondency of the universe to Deity, of the natural to the spiritual, and of the actual to the ideal" (XII. 299), all of which, Browning implies, is figured in the Incarnation.

During the years of his marriage Browning seems to have ac-

12. The opposing ideas of the "objective" and "subjective" complement and interplay with each other in somewhat the same manner as those of the "descendental" and "transcendental" are interwoven in *Sartor Resartus*. After completing the *Essay on Shelley,* Browning wrote to Carlyle, ". . . I have put down a few thoughts that presented themselves—one or two, in respect of opinions of your own (I mean, that I was thinking of those opinions while I wrote)" (*Letters of Robert Browning, Collected by Thomas J. Wise,* ed. Thurman L. Hood [London: John Murray, 1933], p. 36; hereafter cited as Hood, *Letters*).

cepted the Incarnation without denying its "historical basement."
After Mrs. Browning's death in 1861, however, he appears to have
entertained doubts as to its historicity. Throughout the 1860's
Browning was preoccupied with the assaults constantly being
made on Christianity, and his concern is manifested in the poems
of *Dramatis Personae* (1864). The publication of *Essays and Reviews,* the Bishop Colenso case, the publication of Renan's *La Vie
de Jésus*—these, in addition to the work of the "Higher Critics"
in Germany, caused the poet great uneasiness, not because he
found them unsettling to his own faith but because they served to
diminish the popular belief in Christianity. "The candid incline
to surmise of late / That the Christian faith proves false, I find,"
he wrote in "Gold Hair," apparently speaking *in propria persona.*
But "I still, to suppose it true, for my part, / See reasons and reasons." What matters, he says, through the mouth of St. John in
"A Death in the Desert," is not the importance of historical proofs
but the realization and appropriation of the divine love of God
by men as taught by the Christian faith; or, to put it another way,
the sovereign credential of Christianity is its truth to human experience. "Why, where's the need of Temple," the speaker asks
in the Epilogue to *Dramatis Personae,* "when the walls / O' the
world are that?" God is eternally manifesting Himself throughout
the whole creation and in the heart of man. No need then to
insist upon special revelation in a particular place to elect individuals, since every man, imperfect as he may be, can, by opening
himself to the power of God, become temporarily God-like. In
spite of the questioning of the historical Jesus, the essence of
Christianity remains above controversy:

> That one Face, far from vanish, rather grows,
> Or decomposes but to recompose,
> Become my universe that feels and knows.

From the poems of *Dramatis Personae* we learn that for Browning the historicity of the Incarnation is not of prime importance.
As Roma King observes, "It serves intitially, he proposes, as a
hypothesis, an imaginative projection, to which man commits

himself. It becomes the motive and the tentative shaping pattern for self-creating action. The result of man's commitment, the experience which ensues, is its own meaning."[13] In other words, a man believes and acts as if it were historically true. The Incarnation is a necessary fiction that assumes a mythic reality.

Browning's changing views concerning history and historical evidence, particularly as related to the Incarnation, contributed greatly to his increasing dissatisfaction with the dramatic monologue. Initially, he conceived of the dramatic monologue as a means of seeing aspects of life, that is, of producing "testimony" from different points of view. But more and more he came to distrust all human testimony. We note this particularly in the casuistic monologues of *Dramatis Personae*—"A Death in the Desert" especially, which, says Elinor Shaffer, exhibits "the process by which the claim to ocular witness was transformed into the claim to valid Christian experience."[14] Thus recognizing the failure of the dramatic monologue as a poetic strategy, he hit upon a new strategy: to relate various perspectives by a common theme and action, as Hillis Miller says, to "use point of view to transcend point of view."[15] By providing a large number of perspectives centered on one event, the poet could at last escape the unreliability, the special pleading, which characterizes human speech, and could perhaps at last approximate God's own infinite and "objective" vision. This at any rate was Browning's hope in writing *The Ring and the Book*. Yet with the composition of this

13. "The Necessary Surmise: The Shaping Spirit of Robert Browning's Poetry," *Romantic and Victorian: Studies in Memory of William H. Marshall*, ed. W. Paul Elledge and Richard L. Hoffman (Rutherford, Madison, and Teaneck, N.J.: Fairleigh Dickinson University Press, 1971), p. 349.

14. "Browning's St. John: The Casuistry of the Higher Criticism," *Victorian Studies*, 16 (1972), 216. This essay brilliantly explores Browning's ways of interpreting history. In showing that St. John in "A Death in the Desert" is "Browning's archetypal casuist" (p. 221), this article calls into question the notion of "Browning the Simple-Hearted Casuist," which is the title of an essay by Hoxie N. Fairchild first printed in the *University of Toronto Quarterly*, 48 (1949), 234–40.

15. *The Disappearance of God: Five Nineteenth-Century Writers* (rpt. New York: Schocken Books, 1965), p. 148.

poem of epic scope Browning was to discover again what he had already known, namely, that there is no such thing as "objective truth." What man is left with finally, in his determination of truth, is himself: in his search for "objective reality" he discovers that he always confronts himself alone.

This is the final statement of *The Ring and the Book*. Toward it all the poem's chief themes point—the unceasing conflict of testimony, the constant reminders that appearances are often more plausible than reality, the demonstration that language is more frequently a vehicle of falsehood than of truth. The Pope is aware of these vagaries of life when he makes his determination of Pompilia's innocence and Guido's guilt. He also bears them in mind when he addresses himself to the Incarnation, accepting it not as indisputable historical fact or as infallible dogma but as a truth tested on the pulses. In the figure of the Pope Browning would have us see that the crucial consideration of any creed is not so much what men believe as how they respond, any belief being a meaningless abstraction which neither occasions action nor results from it. The point the Pope makes is that in all questions of judgment, whether of things finite or infinite, love—sympathy, commitment—must be anterior to reason. Hence he does not weigh argument against argument or fact against fact but cuts through them to a sympathetic apprehension of their truth. Thus endowed with the power of love, a man "may tell a truth / Obliquely, do the thing shall breed the thought, / Nor wrong the thought, missing the mediate word" (xii. 855–7).

In *The Ring and the Book* Browning tried to overcome the barrier of language through form. Earlier, in *Sordello,* he had acknowledged the difficulty—indeed the impossibility—of communicating the immediacy of perception in language:

> Because perceptions whole, like that he sought
> To clothe, reject so pure a work of thought
> As language: thought may take perceptions's place
> But hardly co-exist in any case,
> Being its mere presentment—of the whole
> By parts, the simultaneous and the sole
> By the successive and the many. [ii. 589–95]

The tools one has to work with are not adequate to expression of
the wholeness of man's being—his transcendental as well as his
descendental impulses, his soul as well as his body, his fancy as
well as his facts. In the *Essay on Shelley,* however, Browning
posited the poet who could see and show both the high and the
low "in successive perfect works," although "of the perfect shield,
with the gold and the silver side set up for all comers to chal-
lenge, there has yet been no instance" (xII. 285). But it was not
through language alone that such a shield was to be forged. "I
know that I don't make out my conception by my language," he
told Ruskin in an often-quoted letter. All poetry is "a putting the
infinite within the finite. You would have me paint it all plain
out, which can't be." Yet, he goes on, "by various artifices I try
to make shift with touches and bits of outlines which *succeed* if
they bear the conception from me to you." Which is to say that
not by language alone but by discontinuities and manipulation of
perspective he hopes to communicate "the whole [which] is all
but a simultaneous feeling with me." Therefore, he tells Ruskin,
"in asking for more *ultimates* you must accept less *mediates,* nor
expect that a Druid stone-circle will be traced for you with as
few breaks to the eye as the North Crescent and South Crescent
that go together so cleverly in many a suburb."[16] With the perspectivist art of *The Ring and the Book* Browning sought to give
form to the formless—a paradox expressed in the central ring
metaphor of the poem. As the Pope says, "Truth, nowhere, lies
yet everywhere in these [different perspectives]— / Not absolutely in a portion, yet / Evolvible from the whole" (x. 228–30).
Through the efficacy of form the poet wished, to use the terms of
his letter to Ruskin, to arrive at ultimates with fewer mediates, to
"tell a truth / Obliquely, do the thing shall breed the thought,
/ Nor wrong the thought, missing the mediate word." Through
form he aspired to express the disparate elements of man's nature
in a work that "shall mean beyond the facts, / Suffice the eye and
save the soul beside" (xII. 862–3).

16. Quoted in *The Works of John Ruskin,* ed. E. T. Cook and Alexander Wedderburn (London: Allen, 1909), XXXVI, xxxiv.

However successful Browning may have found his formal inno-
vations in *The Ring and the Book,* the fact remains that he never
again turned to this particular kind of perspectivist art. For he
knew that the fullness of his own being could be apprehended
only through a process of creative action, which means constant
experimentation and breaking bounds. He could realize himself
only in the acts in which he assumed the most contradictory elements of his nature; he could become a person only when, in a
manner of speaking, he authorized himself.

> Man,—as befits the made, the inferior thing,—
> Purposed, since made to grow, not make in turn,
> Yet forced to try and make, else fail to grow,—
> Formed to rise, reach at, if not grasp and gain
> The good beyond him,—which attempt is growth,—
> Repeats God's process in man's due degree,
> Attaining man's proportionate result,—
> Creates, no, but resuscitates, perhaps.
> . . . man, bounded, yearning to be free,
> May so project his surplusage of soul
> In search of body, so add self to self
> By owning what lay ownerless before,—
> So find, so fill full, so appropriate forms . . .
> [*The Ring and the Book,* I. 705-19]

In the chapters that follow I assume a high degree of identification between the man and the author. As he said in speaking of
Shelley, "Greatness in a work suggests an adequate instrumen-
tality" (*Works,* XII. 287). In every work a drama is enacted between the man and himself; and it is in the drama that the truth
of his being resides. Without form there is no drama. By examining the testimony of forms, therefore, I shall try to perceive the
spiritual tensions that dictated those forms that became "Browning."

My interest is not primarily biographical. I sometimes simply
look to the man to find the poet, realizing full well that in the
poems may also be found the man. To discern the unique distinc-
tion of Browning's later work, I believe that we must examine,
though briefly, evidence of those singular tensions working within

him. This requires us to inspect the events of his life, to acknowledge his cares and concerns, to discover and vicariously re-enact
his program. In short, we shall try to get at the truth of Browning
through a sympathetic understanding. On this point I can do no
better than quote the man himself: "I am heartily glad," he tells
an admirer of the first two volumes of *The Ring and the Book,*
"I have your sympathy for what I write. Intelligence, by itself, is
scarcely the thing with respect to a new book—as Wordsworth
says (a little altered), 'you must like it before it be worthy of your
liking' " (Hood, *Letters,* p. 128).

I do not believe that *The Ring and the Book* represents the
culmination of Browning's art and thought any more than I believe that there are "two Robert Brownings."[17] I maintain that
there is a unity in his life, which is to be discovered in his constant quest to apprehend the relationship of the finite to the infinite. If, for instance, in his later years he put aside a literal belief
in the Incarnation, it was, as the Pope says in *The Ring and the
Book,* only to "correct the portrait by the living face, / Man's
God, by God's God in the mind of man" (x. 1867–8). During
the quest of his later years there were, to quote a maxim from
Rimbaud's *Une Saison en Enfer,* "no violent salvation games."
Browning suffered few of the lacerations of those who abandon
themselves to the blessed violences of the storm. For he advanced
deliberately and even defensively, step by step, carefully balancing
his transcendental aspirations with a firmly grounded descendentalism. Many of his contemporaries might laugh at his formal
manners, his almost agressive *bonhomie,* his willingness to be
mistaken for a successful financier, his solemn banalities iterated
to his admirers in the Browning Society. Yet behind it all was a

17. This hypothesis was first proposed by Henry James (see *William
Wetmore Story and His Friends* [Boston: Houghton, Mifflin, 1903], II, 69)
and then dramatized in his story "The Private Life." More recently, it has
been advanced by Richard D. Altick in his essay "The Private Life of
Robert Browning," *Yale Review,* 41 (1951), 247–62. The second volume
of Maisie Ward's biography, *Robert Browning and His World* (London:
Cassell, 1969), is subtitled *Two Robert Brownings?*

poet desiring to inquire ever more deeply into the nature of things.[18] His chief problem was to discover the proper forms that would permit him to approach ever closer to Ultimate Reality.[19]

18. Two of Browning's letters of the sixties are interesting in their revelation of the poet's concern to get to the truth of a matter. To Julia Wedgwood he wrote in July 1864: "I live more and more—what am I to write? —for God not man—I don't care what men think now, knowing they will never think my thoughts; yet I need increasingly to tell *the truth*—for whom? Is it that *I* shall be the better, the larger for it, have the fairer start in next life, the firmer stand? Is it pure selfishness, or the obedience to a natural law?" (*Robert Browning and Julia Wedgwood: A Broken Friendship*, ed. Richard Curle [London: John Murray and Jonathan Cape, 1937], p. 53; hereafter cited as *Wedgwood Letters*).

And to Isabella Blagden he confided in September 1867 that he and his wife would argue about their "profoundly different estimates of thing and person": "And I am glad I maintained the truth on each of these points, did not say, 'what matter whether they be true or no?—Let us only care to love each other' " (*Dearest Isa: Robert Browning's Letters to Isabella Blagden*, ed. Edward C. McAleer [Austin: University of Texas Press, 1951], p. 282; hereafter cited as *Dearest Isa*).

19. Donald S. Hair's *Browning's Experiments with Genre* (Toronto: University of Toronto Press, 1972) is a study of the poems through *The Ring and the Book* somewhat along the lines I pursue in this book. Mr. Hair is frank to admit that a study of Browning's experiments "should not, ideally, come to an end with *The Ring and the Book*. Browning experimented relentlessly throughout the 1870s and 1880s, and many of the poems are fascinating puzzles for the critic . . ." (p. 183).

1 &~ Balaustion's Adventure

Between early 1869, when the final volumes of *The Ring and the Book* appeared, and 1871 Browning published nothing. Apparently he was resting from the extraordinary labor required for the writing of his Roman murder story. By 1871 his wife had been dead ten years, and it is possible that his thoughts turned in the spring of that year to a poem commemorating her death. As he recalled his happy years with Elizabeth Barrett Browning, he seems to have been reminded of Euripides, the poet whom she loved and revered as pre-eminently human. What better way to memorialize her than a poem dealing with the Greek dramatist? Whether this was Browning's intention is a matter of conjecture; in any case, however, practically all commentators see in the character of Balaustion, the central figure of the poem, a reflection of Mrs. Browning.

Balaustion's Adventure, Including a Transcript from Euripides, written in May and published in August 1871, is largely given over to a retelling of Euripides' *Alkestis*. Many critics have wondered whether it should be considered anything more than a mere translation. Browning himself made few claims for it. In the dedication to the Countess Cowper he referred to it as a task which "proved the most delightful of May-month amusements," and to Isabella Blagden he spoke of it as "my little new Poem, —done in a month,—and I think a pretty thing in its way" (*Dearest Isa,* p. 362). Rossetti, however, found "the structure of the work . . . beyond all conception perverse" and the Euripidean *Alkestis* "interlarded with Browningian analysis to an extent beyond all reason or relation to things by any possibility Greek in any way." Swinburne thought that "the pathos of the subject is too simple and downright for Browning's analytic method."[1] Later commentators have likewise been worried by the question of its faithfulness to the Greek spirit.[2] In my opinion, such a consideration is irrelevant to an estimation of the poem.

Balaustion's Adventure is the poet's message to his age that, at a time when civilization seems on the verge of complete disruption, the spirit, if not the forms, of the past can enliven the present and redeem the individual from despair. By means of the young girl from Rhodes who narrates the poem Browning presents a parable of personal salvation gained through love and the creative powers. The poem is thus a further exploration of the major themes of *The Ring and the Book*.[3]

In *The Ring and the Book,* it will be recalled, the Pope allows that in pre-Christian times some did attain to truly Christian lives without the benefit of a specifically Christian revelation. Such a

---

1. *Letters of Dante Gabriel Rossetti,* ed. Oswald Doughty and J. R. Wahl (Oxford: Oxford University Press, 1967), III, 981; *The Letters of Algernon Charles Swinburne,* ed. Cecil Y. Lang (New Haven: Yale University Press, 1959), II, 155–6.

2. See Thurman L. Hood, "Browning's Ancient Classical Sources," *Harvard Studies in Classical Philology,* 33 (1922), 79–81; Edmund D. Cressman, "The Classical Poems of Robert Browning," *Classical Journal,* 23 (1927), 198–207; Robert Spindler, *Robert Browning und die Antike* (Leipzig, 1930), I, 59–77; Douglas Bush, *Mythology and the Romantic Tradition* (1937; Norton Edition, New York, 1963), pp. 366–75; William C. DeVane, "Browning and the Spirit of Greece," *Nineteenth-Century Studies,* ed. H. Davis, W. C. DeVane, and R. C. Bald (Ithaca: Cornell University Press, 1940), pp. 183–4.

3. See Robert Langbaum, "Browning and the Question of Myth," *PMLA,* 81 (1966), 575–84, for a treatment of *Balaustion* as a successful poem employing the mythical method. Langbaum has a very high opinion of the poem: "It is actually more successful than *The Ring and the Book* in achieving what it sets out to do. If I hesitate to rank it above or even with *The Ring and the Book,* it is only because the poem is after all mainly Euripides. Yet I am not sure this matters. We probably ought to understand the poem as we understand Ezra Pound's translations—as a creative appropriation of ancient material, a way of giving an ancient poet a historical consciousness he himself could not have had" (p. 583).

one was Euripides, whom the Pope fancies he hears asking why men possessing the light denied to him in "a tenebrific time" (x. 1756) are not morally better. The Greek dramatist intuited something of the nature of God and exhibited in his plays that which the experience of God had taught him. He saw, the Pope implies, that the "perfection fit for God" is "love without a limit" (x. 1362, 1364); he knew that if there is "strength" and "intelligence" and love "unlimited in its self-sacrifice / Then is the tale true and God shows complete" (x. 1364–7). Ruminating on the instance of Euripides and the life of Pompilia, the Pope gives voice to his understanding that in each man there can be "first things made new" when there is "repetition of the miracle, / The divine instance of self-sacrifice / That never ends and aye begins for man" (x. 1649–52).

The Ring and the Book, especially the Pope's monologue, presents a full statement of Browning's belief that to be "creative and self-sacrificing too" is to be "God-like" (x. 1377–8). Yet impressive as "The Pope" is in its humanity and philosophical profundity, the poet barely manages to hide behind his *persona.* In a manner of speaking, "The Pope" is a revelation. But Browning, like Yeats, believed that poetry not only is revelation but also should have the effect of revelation. For years Browning had pursued a poetic method by which he sought, as he says in the Preface to *Strafford,* to display "Action in Character, rather than Character in Action." He had placed characters, historical as well as fictional ones, in various situations and caused them to reveal themselves in moments of lyric intensity; and with the elaborate design of *The Ring and the Book* he evidently felt that, through the interior method of character analysis, he had fully explored the potentialities of the dramatic monologue. For almost forty years he had worked in the same mode; he had taken a part of the actual world, a personage, and made that individual show himself for what he really was. As he wrote to Julia Wedgwood upon completion of *The Ring and the Book,* "The question with me has never been 'Could not one, by changing the factors work out the sum to better result?,' but declare and prove the actual result, and there an end." Apparently, he felt the need to try yet other methods, for he adds in this letter to Miss Wedgwood: "Before I die, I hope to purely invent something,—here [in *The Ring and the Book*] my pride was concerned to invent nothing: the minutest circumstance that denotes character is *true:* the black is so much—the white, no more" (*Wedgwood Letters,* p. 144). To be sure, the poet remained interested in "the incidents in the development of a soul" (Preface to the 1863 edition of *Sordello*). But was it not possible for this development to be investigated by an exterior as well as by an interior means, which is the method of the dramatic monologue? Furthermore, by an exterior method might he not also show the effect of a "soul" as well as its development, display character in action as well as action in character? These possibilities must certainly have been running through the poet's mind. When he undertook his next work, he turned his back on the dramatic monologue as he had perfected it; he elected to explore a mode that was not only an attempt to enlarge the possibilities of the dramatic monologue but, by comparison with his established form, was also an entirely new method. After *The Ring and the Book* there evidently remained a great deal which Browning wanted to say about both art and religion, the subjects always of deepest interest to him. In his long poem of twelve books he had come to more or less settled conclusions about both. But still he had to make his perceptions accessible through a proper symbolizing process, without which earth's verities remain only abstractions to be capitalized as Power, Knowledge, Love, and Will. "A myth may teach," the poet was later to say in "Bernard de Mandeville" in the *Parleyings:* "Only, who better would expound it thus / Must be Euripides not Aeschylus" (204–6).

As only a scant record of Browning's own account of *Balaustion's Adventure* exists, we can only speculate as to the origin and germination of the poem. No doubt his wife's long affection for Euripides and his own intensive study of the dramatist during the middle sixties suggested the use of Euripidean material. Secondly, in *The Ring and the Book* the fancied questioning of the Pope by the Greek tragedian indicates that in Browning's mind the dramatist was associated with the idea of the Incarnation, of which Pompilia is shown to be an avatar. Euripides and Pompilia, the creator and self-sacrificer, the very attributes of Godhead defined in *The Ring and the Book*—what if both were to be brought together in a poem in which their essential qualities were combined in one person? Moreover, what if the personality of this character were revealed by her interpretation of a play by Euripides? In *Balaustion's Adventure* Browning created a heroine very much like Pompilia, who possesses the characteristics of both the poet and the person whose love is redemptive and whose moral and poetic powers are sharpened by acquaintance with a Euripidean drama.[4]

Doubtless the pathos and simplicity of the *Alkestis* appealed to Browning, but evidently he wondered that Euripides did not condemn the man whose moral weakness permitted the death of his beloved wife. It was probably this questioning of the morality of the play that led him to make the *Alkestis* part of his poem. Also, he must have remembered Plutarch's telling of how some captive Greeks were rescued in Syracuse by recitation of the play, and, with his constantly iterated belief that art inspires action, he no doubt envisioned a way to make Euripides' drama the center of a poem that would have as its main concern the relation between art and the mythopoeic power.

Balaustion's Adventure is a poem about salvation, first through art and then through love. The world of the poem is, as was

4. The authors of the latest biography of Browning speculate on the biographical significance of Balaustion.

She combines the gaiety and girlish grace of a lyric Pippa with the readiness to act and the wit of a tragic Pompilia, except that she is not tragic. Threatened by pirates, she inspires her oarsmen . . . by singing them a song from Aeschylus, and then, debarred from safety by Syracusans, she promptly recites her way into their hearts by remembering Euripides. . . . Symbolically her prologue reconstructs the key events in Elizabeth Barrett's life—at least as Browning wished to understand them. . . . Threatened by the encroaching will of an overbearing parent, she too had saved herself by turning to Aeschylus and then Euripides. Frail and beautiful as Balaustion, Elizabeth also had won over the hearts of the populace by offering them exquisite poetry. [William Irvine and Park Honan, *The Book, the Ring, & the Poet* (New York: McGraw-Hill, 1974), pp. 457–8]

previously suggested, very much like Browning's own—a world in process of radical change, a civilization almost in wreck. Athens has been defeated by Sparta at Syracuse, and her allies and dependencies, like Rhodes, are preparing to forswear their allegiance to Athens and join the Spartan league in order to "share the spoil" (15). The young Rhodian girl Balaustion, however, refuses to turn her back on the civilization that is "the life and light / Of the whole world worth calling world at all" (25–6). She will choose "the sacred grove" (33) and "the great Dionusiac theatre" (37)—that is, religion and poetry—in preference to the "spoil" of a purely materialistic culture. The poem, which is entirely her own narrative, shows how Balaustion manages not only to cling to the values that Athens epitomizes for her but also to transform those values so that they remain viable in a "Spartan" world. In brief, *Balaustion's Adventure* is the young woman's (and Browning's) way of exemplifying for a younger, crasser world that it can be enriched and enlivened when the essence of the culture of the past is imaginatively re-created in the present.

In this altered world, Balaustion relates, poetry no longer holds its accustomed sway. Only a "certain few" (156) are responsive to the new kind of poetry such as practiced by Euripides, who, along with his friend Socrates, is misprized and scorned by the populace. Only "some foreigner uncouth" (300), whose mind and ears are not bound by traditional drama, appreciates the genius of Euripides, who, unheeded, lives almost totally isolated from the community for which he writes. Yet, "because Greeks are Greeks, and hearts are hearts, / And poetry is power" (235–6), poetry may still have its value in these changing times. Although Euripides appears, at least among his fellow citizens, to work totally without effect, his poetry saves Balaustion from captivity and perhaps death, it brings her a husband, and it eases the lot of those Greeks in Syracuse who are oppressed.

Poetry has this potency because it is "a power that makes" (318), which is to say, when properly apprehended it calls into play the whole man and causes him to perceive the unity of being. For poetry, "speaking to one sense, inspires the rest, / Pressing them all into its service" (319–20), so that the recipient sees, hears, and feels simultaneously, taking in "time, place, and person too" (328). Thus it is like the young Balaustion, whom her shipmates have named "Wild-pomegranate-flower":

> since, where'er the red bloom burns
> I' the dull dark verdure of the bounteous tree,
> Dethroning, in the Rosy Isle, the rose,
> You shall find food, drink, odour, all at once;
> Cool leaves to bind about an aching brow,
> And, never much away, the nightingale.   [208–13]

The first 357 lines of the poem serve as a prologue to what Browning in the title called "A Transcript from Euripides." They are, as indicated above, devoted chiefly to proclaiming the redemptive power of poetry. It would be wrong, however, to suppose that in this passage Browning is setting forth a purely humanistic view of poetry as the proper substitute for religion in a skeptical age. Set against this introductory section exploring the miraculous effect of art is Balaustion's retelling of the *Alkestis,* the whole point of which in the structure of the poem is to show the ability of a sympathetic auditor to transmute art into that higher morality which is closely allied to religious experience.

Although critics have argued that *Balaustion's Adventure* is a misrepresentation of the original, Browning in fact never set out simply to translate the *Alkestis.* What *Balaustion's Adventure* gives us is not a translation but a young woman's interpretation of the play, the significance of which is that her idea of the events related in the play is a morally and spiritually higher idea than that presented by Euripides. In narrating the dramatic events, Balaustion interweaves moral explanations of the characters with Euripides' dramatic colloquies. Whereas Euripides was careless of or indifferent to some of the moral implications of the story, his interest centering on Admetos's self-control, Balaustion focuses her attention on the development of a soul in Admetos. De-emphasizing the whole idea of arbitrary fate, she shifts attention from Admetos's increasing self-pity, as he contemplates the loneliness he must endure and the taunts of his enemies, to his learning the meaning of love and loss. Balaustion also changes the character of Herakles from that of a jovial giant who enjoys his wine and is willing to help his host; she Christianizes him into a god-man whose whole life is dedicated to the alleviation of the suffering of others.

In Balaustion's retelling of the *Alkestis* the power of poetry is strictly limited. Although Apollo, the god of poetry, seeks to save Admetos from death and indeed is successful in urging the Fates to allow a surrogate to die in his place, when faced with Death, Apollo is completely helpless. In such a situation art is impotent; another savior, as we shall see, is needed for the task.

Unwilling to die, Admetos has called upon all possible powers to rescue him, with the result that if he can find someone to give his life for him he will be allowed to live. His wife Alkestis alone is willing to sacrifice herself to such a cause, and, utterly selfish, the king allows her to go to the grave in his stead. Only at the interment of Alkestis, when he realizes the absolute finality of his loss, does Admetos, now "beginning to be like his wife" (2000), realize his wrong, understand that he "ought not live, / But do live, by evading destiny" (2014–15). But by this time it is, so he has every reason to believe, too late to do otherwise.

At this point Herakles comes to his aid. Both "human and divine," "half God, / Half man" (1049–51), Herakles is the "helper of our world" (1917), who comes "at first cry for help" (1731), "all for love of men" (1726), to "save man so" (1734) "and saves the world" (1878). "All faith, love, and obedience to a friend" (1218), he is "truth itself" (1197). To most men, especially Admetos, "of all evils in the world, the worst / Was—being forced to die, whate'er death gain" (1072–3); but Herakles "held his life / Out on his hand, for any man to take" (1076–7). In short, Herakles is a Greek hero made Christlike.

This exemplar of the Incarnation is not, however, the ascetic whom the Puritans fancied Christ to be. A prophet of joy (1738–41, 1759–72), he reminds the children of the world that "good days had been, / And good days, peradventure, still might be" (1253–4). Eager both to partake of earthly pleasures and to help mankind, Herakles is not above a little tipsiness on wine, and indeed his joyfulness, in Balaustion's opinion, helps mark him as an agent of the divine. "I think," she says, "this is the authentic sign and seal / Of Godship, that it ever waxes glad, / And more glad, until gladness blossoms, bursts / Into a rage to suffer for mankind . . ." (1918–21). When he learns of Admetos's bereavement, Herakles immediately sets about to help the grieving king. His harrowing of Hades and return with the veiled Alkestis serve further to impress upon the husband his selfishness in allowing his wife to immolate herself for him. Now aware of his wrong and willing to repent, Admetos is redeemed from egoism by the self-sacrifice of Alkestis and the intervention of the heroic savior. He vows "to begin a fresh / Existence, better than the life before" (2387–8).

In Balaustion's version of the *Alkestis* the center of interest lies, as we have said, in the spiritual development of Admetos. The personality of the narrator informs and indeed transforms the original to the point where we have an almost totally different piece of literature. Unlike the motion picture *Never on Sunday,* in which an ignorant woman completely misunderstands Sophoclean drama, *Balaustion's Adventure* gives us an interpretation of the *Alkestis* in which the moral possibilities of the original are developed and stressed. Browning would have us see that Balaustion's is not a criticism but a "higher criticism," to use the theological term, of the text. Just as a modern Christian may look behind the literal accounts of the Gospels to grasp the essence of the Christian message, Balaustion goes beyond the actual text of the *Alkestis* to seize upon, in the words of Mrs. Browning that serve as epigraph to the poem, "Euripides, the human, / With his droppings of warm tears, / And his touches of things common / Till they rose to touch the spheres."

To be sure, certain literalists will object to such an interpretation. After Balaustion told the play in Syracuse, a "brisk little somebody, / Critic and whippersnapper" objected to the liberties she had taken (306–16),[5] to which the girl replies that poetry is a power which makes sense transcend sense so that all are unified to the point where one is made to "hear, see and feel, in faith's simplicity" (333), and so that "who hears the poem, therefore, sees the play" (335)—another way of saying that he who imaginatively and sympathetically interprets the text truly understands its meaning, whereas the literalists and the "friendly moralists" (2390) entirely miss the point. And, as we have seen, the validity of Balaustion's interpretation is proven by its effect: it saves her and her companions and also "a band / Of captives, whom their lords grew kinder to" (260–61).

"One thing has many sides," Balaustion maintains (2402). Truth has many facets and may be approached in different ways: "No good supplants a good, / Nor beauty undoes beauty" (2403–4). Euripides and Sophocles and perhaps even others like Balaustion can present visions of the central truth, which may "glorify the Dionusiac shrine: / Not clash against this crater, in the place / Where the God put it when his mouth had drained, / To the last dregs, libation life-blood-like . . ." (2407–10). Hence the young woman is able to give her version of the Alkestis story without fear lest she be defiling a sacred myth.

In *The Ring and the Book* the Pope believed that every Christian must refashion the Christian story for himself, putting "the same truth / In a new form" (x. 1392–3). Though not a Christian, Balaustion agrees with the principle enunciated by the Pope, and illuminates the spiritual possibilities in the *Alkestis*. She goes still farther when she embodies the meaning she derives from Euripides' play in a new form. Poetry being a power that makes, it

---

5. Nearly all commentators identify the "brisk little somebody" as Alfred Austin, Browning's most hostile critic, who was to become, after the death of Tennyson, Poet Laureate. (For Browning's further vendettas with Austin see Chapter 7). Irvine and Honan suggest that the "critic and whippersnapper" refers not only to Austin but also to "the archetypal myope who cannot see beyond conventions, all of Elizabeth's hostile critics together" (*The Book, the Ring, & the Poet*, p. 458).

not only gives new perspectives on the truth; it also stimulates
creation in others. "Ah, that brave / Bounty of poets," Balaustion
exclaims,

> the one royal race
> That ever was, or will be, in this world!
> They give no gift that bounds itself and ends
> I' the giving and the taking: theirs so breeds
> I' the heart and soul o' the taker, so transmutes
> The man who only was a man before,
> That he grows god-like in his turn, can give—
> He also: share the poet's privilege,
> Bring forth new good, new beauty, from the old. [2416–25]

So it is with her. She has "drunk" the poem and "quenched" her
thirst, satisfying both heart and soul; "yet more remains" (2431–
2)—namely, the impulse to render her version of the Alkestis
legend.

In her version Balaustion dramatizes the redemption that she
personally has experienced. When Apollo became the servant of
the king, his music tamed the natural lusts and greed in Admetos
to the point where he vowed to rule "solely for his people's sake"
(2450). He would perfect his people, yet a whisper says that the
desire is vain. Why, Admetos asks, does evil prosper and why is
good not allowed time for completion? Why cannot physical reality sustain the soul's longings?

Alkestis supplies the answers to her husband's questions. Aware
of the coming fate, she has begged Apollo to allow Admetos "to
live and carry out to heart's content / Soul's purpose, turn each
thought to very deed" (2501–2). Apollo is unable fully to grant
her request but will allow Admetos to live upon condition that she
die for him. Admetos refuses the bargain; for to agree would
violate the very humanity for which he wishes to live. Let then
some other mortal undertake his work. Enough if he has attained
Zeus's purpose "inalienably mine, to end with me" (2555)—
namely, to love.

Alkestis argues that he cannot forswear his vow to be a right-
eous king. He must live and rule in order to carry out their com-

bined ideal. So entirely are they one being that the choice must be made regardless of each as an individual. And as they lovingly embrace, her soul enters his. She dies and her spirit goes to Hades, where is it refused entrance. "Hence, thou deceiver!" commands the Queen of the Underworld. "This is not to die, / If, by the very death which mocks me now, / The life, that's left behind and past my power, / Is formidably doubled" (2632-5). Before the embrace is relaxed, Alkestis is alive again, and she and Admetos live out their lives long and well.

In Balaustion's version, rendered in the most beautiful poetry of the work, there is no heroic redeemer to reclaim Alkestis as there was in Euripides' play. Indeed, it is precisely the point of her story that love saves Alkestis from death and allows her to work with her husband for the benefit of the kingdom. In the newer world that Balaustion inhabits, when all the traditional beliefs and loyalties have begun to decay, she, like the Pope in *The Ring and the Book*, foresees a time when the old mythology must be reinterpreted to prevent the essence of the myth from being discarded along with its outer trappings. For her as for the Pope the "perfection fit for God" is "love without a limit" (x. 1362, 1364); when there is strength, intelligence, and love "unlimited in its self-sacrifice, / Then is the true tale and God shows complete" (x. 1364-7). No need then for a mythic Herakles or an historical Jesus: the "Christ" is present in the individual's life when he assumes the Christian attributes and re-enacts the Christian story. If the instincts be right, if love be complete, the miracle of the Incarnation is repeated. Whatever the attacks made on traditional faith, the substance of that faith is ever available to him who would accept it. By his own spirit is man deified.

Such salvation as love offers is, however, purely personal. Balaustion emphasizes this truth by ending her story with the statement that, concerning "the Golden Age, / [for which] Our couple, rather than renounce, would die," she never heard that "ever one first faint particle came true" (2656-8). While endorsing what she understands to be the spiritual theme of Euripides' play, salvation through love, and indeed exploring it further in her own version, she reveals the limit of that love as a redemptive process. For she presents a world impregnable to the values generated by that love. The Golden Age does not come, nor is it likely to come. In her story only the savior is saved.

Implicit in her version is this question, why work for the good of the world if that goal must be constantly frustrated? Although the question is never fully answered, Balaustion suggests possibilities of an answer. Her Apollo tells Alkestis that even though the world appears to be utterly recalcitrant to morality there are nevertheless "seeds of good asleep / Throughout the world" (2537–8), which can be awakened, so that "no fruit, man's life can bear, will fade" (2532). This is, however, only a hope, and in spite of the evidence of his senses man should act on this hope. As for herself, Balaustion believes that he "who venerates the Gods, i' the main will still / Practise things honest though obscure to judge" (1295–6). Good will not necessarily prevail, but a person must act as if it will. And the surest guide for human action is love.

Balaustion's version is proof of her belief that poetry can "bring forth new good, new beauty, from the old" (2425). And her theory of the efficacy of poetry is further vindicated by the poetess and the painter who, at the end of her narrative, are said to produce works of art in response to Euripides' play. Like the Incarnation, artistic creation is not accomplished and forever done with when it is set down in a certain form; rather, it continues to reverberate and stimulate new impulses toward creation in others. Although Euripides is scorned by the Athenians and his drama failed to win the prize at the festival, his *Alkestis* is to be cherished not only for aesthetic and moral qualities but also as an afflatus: it inspired the poetess, the Kaunian painter, and Balaustion to create new works of art, and, moreover, it saved Balaustion and her companions in Syracuse—"It all came of this play that gained no prize!" (2704). What matter, then, whether it win acclaim or not? Like the Christian story, Euripides' poetry expresses the greatest values of human life and, further, by urging to self-possession and fresh creation, offers salvation to all who would open their ears to hear and their eyes to see. This is surely prize enough: "Why crown whom Zeus has crowned in soul before?" (2705). Ultimately, *Balaustion's Adventure* is the embodiment of Browning's idea of Christian love and of what it means to be a poet. In the essay on Shelley he had insisted that "the misapprehensiveness of his age is exactly what a poet is sent to remedy." By "looking higher than any manifestation yet made of both beauty and good," the poet renders his vision of the "ideal of a future man" which may be realized in "the forthcoming stage of man's being" (*Works,* XII. 292–4). This is precisely what Balaustion does, and at a time when society has lost sight of the ideals by which it should live. She takes an example of beauty and good in her culture, shows its essential meaning, and then proceeds to demonstrate how the virtue of the past can be the stepping-stone to higher good. In herself as in her art Balaustion manifests the salvation to be attained through love and the creative powers. She sums up all that Browning had previously tried to say about both his artistic creed and his religious faith. Finally, she probably epitomizes all those qualities the poet had cherished in his wife.[6] She is one of Browning's loveliest creations.

6. See Joseph H. Friend, "Euripides Browningized: The Meaning of *Balaustion's Adventure," Victorian Poetry,* 2 (1964), 179–86. Friend argues convincingly that the poem is an effort on Browning's part "to deal in his art with the living problem of his marriage to Elizabeth Barrett ten years after her death" (p. 186). He sees reflected in the poem Browning's remorse over the "betrayal" of his wife when he proposed marriage to Lady Ashburton. For details of the proposal see the following chapter, note 5.

2 &~ Prince Hohenstiel-Schwangau

Browning saw *Balaustion's Adventure* through the press and almost immediately upon its publication began work on a new poem. Although in setting and subject matter distantly removed from Athens of the fifth century, both formally and thematically *Prince Hohenstiel-Schwangau, Saviour of Society* bears a certain relationship to the Greek poem. It will be recalled that in Balaustion's version of the *Alkestis* King Admetos, resolved to perfect his kingdom, could not bring into being that Golden Age of which he dreamed. In this next work Browning takes up a modern instance of a ruler who would redeem his people, Napoleon III, and examines why he too fails. Prefaced by a motto from Euripides, which suggests a kinship with *Balaustion*, *Prince Hohenstiel-Schwangau* deals with one who (in Browning's translation of the passage from the *Hercules Furens*)

> from labour pass'd
> To labour—tribes of labours! Till, at last,
> Attempting one more labour, in a trice,
> Alack, with ills [he] *crowned the edifice.*

In his investigation of a would-be savior of society the poet experiments further with the dramatic monologue, which he had expanded to lengthy and complex proportions in *Balaustion*, in an effort to overcome the limitations of that mode.

Browning wrote the poem during a holiday in the late summer of 1871. In the midst of composition he confided to his friend Isa Blagden: "I have written about 1800 absolutely new lines or more, and shall have the whole thing out of hand by the early

winter,—that I can't help thinking a sample of my very best work
. . ." (*Dearest Isa,* p. 367). When the poem was completed he
wrote to another correspondent that he had just sent "a rather
important poem to press" (Hood, *Letters,* p. 151). Yet by the
time the poem appeared in print, in December 1871, his enthusiasm had apparently waned. He told Edith Story ". . . I expect you not to care three straws for what, in the nature of
things, is uninteresting enough, even compared with other poems
of mine which you have been only too good to. What poetry can
be in a sort of political satire . . . ?" (Hood, *Letters,* pp. 151–
2). It is intriguing to ponder why Browning so drastically revised
his estimate of the poem when it was published. An answer to
such a question must necessarily be speculative, but the attempt
to provide one might illuminate some of the problems of the
monologue, which, taking J. M. Cohen's strictures as representative of the critical consensus, is thought to be filled with "inconsistencies, . . . casuistries and tangled argument" resulting from
the poet's lack of control over his material.[1]

On the manuscript of *Prince Hohenstiel-Schwangau* Browning
wrote at the conclusion that a "few lines of the rough draft [were]
written at Rome, 1860";[2] and soon after its publication he confirmed that he "conceived the poem, twelve years ago in the Via
del Tritone—in a little handbreadth of prose" (Hood, *Letters,*
p. 152). The idea of a monologue spoken by a character repre-
senting Napoleon III was, then, not new.[3] Evidently the original
conception of a poem written in the name of the French Emperor
had been of a dramatic monologue more or less along the lines of
those in the *Men and Women* volume of 1855. Yet in the decade

1. *Robert Browning* (London: Longmans, Green, 1952), p. 129.
2. Details regarding manuscripts, dates and places of composition, revisions, and publication of Browning's poems are, unless otherwise indicated, taken from William Clyde DeVane, *A Browning Handbook,* 2nd ed.
(New York: Appleton-Century-Crofts, 1955). Hereafter cited as DeVane,
Handbook.
3. Early in 1871 Browning said: "I wrote, myself, a monologue in his
[Louis Napoleon's] name twelve years ago, and never could bring the
printing to my mind as yet" (Hood, *Letters,* p. 145).

or so after Browning first attempted a poem modeled on Louis Napoleon, the shape of his work had altered a great deal. As we have seen, in *Balaustion's Adventure* Browning sought to widen the scope of the dramatic monologue by combining a purely objective form of literature, Euripidean drama, with the more interior monologue, by filtering the drama through the eyes and mouth of a young girl from Rhodes. Innovative though the *Adventure* was in form, it remained essentially a dramatic monologue expressive of only one point of view. What else could be done with this mode that Browning had always found most congenial? How could it be made to yield a greater overview, so that a blending of the "objective" and "subjective," such as he had spoken of in the *Essay on Shelley,* might be achieved in simultaneous perspectives?

One additional possibility lay in the combination of dramatic monologue with interior dialogue, employed prevously in *Christmas-Eve and Easter-Day.* After all, in a certain sense the monologues are what the speaker in "Christmas-Eve" calls "talking with my mind" (1132). What if he now experimented with an interior dialogue, in which the different voices are clearly not those of the speaker himself, set within the confines of a dramatic monologue? It would be basically the method of *Balaustion's Adventure*—that is, monologue *in propria persona* plus interpolated material, with a return in the final lines to the speaker's own voice.

In his later years Browning was not content to repeat his previous efforts. If this were to be a poem somewhat like *Balaustion's Adventure* in form, it would nevertheless have to be different. It would not be suffice that interior dialogue serve in lieu of a play. The dialogue would provide another point of view so that, somewhat like the later *Parleyings,* the vision of the poem would be almost double.[4] Presumably with such a strategy in mind Brown-

4. In "The Pope" Browning had also experimented with multiple audiences within one monologue. Park Honan counts ten sets of audiences in the poem. "The Pope," says Honan, "speaks to each one of these audiences in a different manner, and each one has the effect of bringing to

ing set out in *Prince Hohenstiel-Schwangau* to test whether he could achieve greater comprehensiveness by using a form which would present differing points of view, not sequentially but almost simultaneously, within one poem.

Aside from purely experimental considerations of form, it was also quite necessary that Browning not be restricted to one point of view when writing about Napoleon III. For the poet had highly ambivalent and constantly changing feelings about the Emperor. During his wife's lifetime he and Mrs. Browning did not often agree on the stature and sincerity of the French ruler, and this division in their opinions was a source of some pain to him. In the 1850's and until her death in 1861 Mrs. Browning regarded Napoleon as the one hope for the liberation of Italy. Browning, however, "thought badly of him at the beginning of his career . . . ; better afterward, on the strength of promises he made, and gave indications of intending to redeem,—I think him very weak in the last miserable year [1870–1871]" (*Dearest Isa,* p. 371). Further, he wrote to another correspondent several days later, "I don't think so much worse of the character as shown us in the last few years, because I suppose there to be a physical and intellectual decline of faculty, brought about by the man's own faults, no doubt—but I think he struggles against these . . ." (Hood, *Letters,* p. 152). In brief, the poet saw in Napoleon III the man who is constantly pulled first one way and then the other by the contradictory thrusts of his personality. This is to say that for Browning the Emperor was a complex personality whose ideals and actions were frequently antithetical.

Napoleon III possessed a character about which the most contradictory statements seem true. Elected President of France as a

---

light something new and different in the Pope's character-complex" (*Browning's Characters* [New York and London: Yale University Press, 1961], p. 151). The technique of *Hohenstiel-Schwangau* is, however, somewhat different. There is an imaginary audience as in "The Pope," but the Prince's interior dialogue represents a dialectical exercise set off sharply from the speaker's monologue in his own voice. In this respect, the dialogue between the shrewd worldly voice and the impulsive, idealistic voice more nearly resembles the drama in *Balaustion.*

political liberal, he soon found his programs thwarted and became a repressive ruler. A youthful advocate of a democratic state, he staged a coup d'état and had himself, as "Savior of Society," proclaimed Emperor, eventually aiming to found a dynasty. In his early years he was dedicated to the idea of a free Italy, but once in power he acted swiftly to suppress the Roman Republic. Yet some years later he joined Cavour and the King of Sardinia in an attempt to drive the Austrians out of Italy, finally, however, coming to terms with Austria and annexing Nice and Savoy for France. A man who declared that the Empire was Peace, he spent most of his time as Emperor making war. His policy was a curious mixture of democratic and imperialistic designs, and it is no wonder that in his day he was commonly referred to as the Sphinx. Louis Napoleon was the very sort of individual to appeal to Browning as subject for a poem.

In his youthful poetry Browning had written of the romantic desire for the ideal untethered to the real and had portrayed characters, like Paracelsus and the lover of Pauline, who sought the infinite without regard to physical and psychological limitations and thus failed. But by and large the poet in his middle years focused instead on those personages who, if idealistic by bent, achieved their goals without compromising with the world's claims, or who, if material-minded, fought for their desiderata without reference to an ideal conception of the way the world might be. In short, he pictured individuals either unbothered by or not subject to contending demands of personality. This is, admittedly, a partially accurate generalization, but we have only to recall the Grammarian, the coda to "The Statue and the Bust," Pompilia, and Guido to see the truth in it.

In 1871 Browning began once again to examine individuals whose actions were to some degree paralyzed by an unhappy blending in their temperaments of conflicting desires.[5] It was,

5. The reason for this renewed interest, which continued with the writing of *Fifine at the Fair* and *Red Cotton Night-Cap Country* in 1872 and 1873, may not be far to find if we remember one particular biographical

then, all the more important that he discover a form that would allow expression of the various sides of man's nature. The solution as to which form would best serve apparently came to him while he was vacationing in Perthshire in the summer of 1871.[6] And he was so pleased with the solution that he declared to Miss Blagden: "I never at any time in my life turned a holiday into such an occasion of work" (*Dearest Isa*, p. 367). It was evidently his pleasure with the form that made him hold so high an opinion of the work which critics have almost universally dispraised and which he himself came later to misprize.

The poem implicitly asks this question, why do men with good intentions fail to attain to what they aspire? And the answer provided is that the human personality is never adequate to the demands made upon it. With imperfect eyes and imperfect speech man never can properly visualize or verbalize the promptings of his soul. Once those aspirations are released from the depths of

fact: Browning's proposal of marriage to Louisa Lady Ashburton in September 1869. Browning made his proposal in the frankest terms and on the most practical grounds, telling the lady that his son needed a mother but that his heart was buried with his dead wife in Florence. Naturally the offer was rejected. The ensuing guilt on the poet's part for his unfaithfulness to the spirit of his beloved wife may well have contributed to the conception and composition of *Prince Hohenstiel-Schwangau*. In this story of a man torn between his highest ideals and the practicalities of life which sully those ideals Browning may have recognized some of his own shortcomings. Betty Miller in her biography, *Robert Browning: A Portrait* (London: John Murray, 1952), sees in *Balaustion's Adventure* the first expression of Browning's remorse for his unfaithfulness to his wife's memory (p. 252). Joseph H. Friend in "Euripides Browningized," 179–86, has vastly expanded and explored Mrs. Miller's point. See also William Whitla, "Browning and the Ashburton Affair," *Browning Society Notes*, 2, No. 2 (July 1972), 12–14.

6. Although he wrote to Edith Story on 1 January 1872 that he had conceived the poem twelve years earlier in Rome, he evidently meant that he had thought of writing a monologue about Napoleon III. It was only in Perthshire that "a little hand-breadth of prose" was "breathed out into this full-blown bubble in a couple of months this autumn that is gone" (Hood, *Letters*, p. 152).

the self into the light of external reality they are, by the very nature of the world, deflected from their true intent. And it is this truth the speaker of the poem learns from his attempted multifaceted examination of himself.

Yet to ask and to answer a question about the nature of man and the world is not the purpose of the Prince's speech. Insofar as the speech has any motivation at all it is simply that which he provides—"Revealment of myself!" (22), talking for the sheer love of it. Commentators have called the monologue "a defence of the doctrine of expediency" and have spoken of the Prince as one of Browning's great casuists.[7] But to the extent that casuistry implies deception the Prince is no casuist at all. Although there is an initial pretence of an auditor—and this mainly to provide a dramatic context in which the monologue might occur—the Prince is speaking solely to himself. Only as the monologue progresses does it become clear that the revelation is to himself, which means justification of himself to himself. As it begins, the monologue evidently has no strategic purpose at all. If Hohenstiel-Schwangau is an unreliable narrator, it is not by design but from lack of self-understanding.

The first part of his monologue is spoken *in propria persona*. Here the Prince attempts to justify his conservative rule:

> To save society was well: the means
> Whereby to save it,—there begins the doubt
> Permitted you, imperative on me;
> Were mine the best means? Did I work aright
> With powers appointed me?—since powers denied
> Concern me nothing.   [701–6]

His defense is that he has acted in a practical manner; if he has not done all that social visionaries would have him do, it is because he has first had to devote himself to the immediate needs of his people. He recognizes the importance of idealism in politics,

7. Mrs. Sutherland Orr, *A Handbook to the Works of Robert Browning*, 6th ed. (London: G. Bell, 1927); hereafter referred to as Orr, *Handbook*. See also William O. Raymond's chapter on "Browning's Casuists" in his *The Infinite Moment*, pp. 129–55.

but he is also aware that he must assure his people sufficient material sustenance:

> No, my brave thinkers, whom I recognize,
> Gladly, myself the first, as, in a sense,
> All that our world's worth, flower and fruit of man!
> Such minds myself award supremacy
> Over the common insignificance,
> When only Mind's in question,—Body bows
> To quite another government, you know.   [1101–7]

But the more he talks the less convincing he finds himself to be, and he commences to perceive that his career may not have been quite so altruistic or even so successful as in the beginning he claimed it was. For in speaking he half realizes that what he consciously thought himself to be may not be what in fact he is.

> you know the thing I tried to do!
> All, so far, to my praise and glory—all
> Told as befits the self-apologist,—
> Who ever promises a candid sweep
> And clearance of those errors miscalled crimes
> None knows more, none laments so much as he,
> And ever rises from confession, proved
> A god whose fault was—trying to be man.
> Just so, fair judge,—if I read smile aright—
> I condescend to figure in your eyes
> As biggest heart and best of Europe's friends,
> And hence my failure. God will estimate
> Success one day; and, in the mean time—you!   [1201–13]

The insight is evanescent but it is signified by the Prince's half-jocular admission that he is a "failure" (1212) and one of life's "losers" (1217). Having so confessed, he immediately shifts perspective from "autobiography" (1220) to biography, from first- to third-person narrative. Human kind can bear only so much reality.

The second part of the poem is what Hohenstiel-Schwangau terms "pure blame, history / And falsehood"—"what I never was, but might have been" (1221–2, 1224). It is offered as a counterbalance to what has already been recounted of his "praise and glory . . . as befits the self-apologist" (1202–3). But we soon see that the second half, which is told from two points of view—those of the Head Servant, the idealized ruler, and Sagacity, the shrewd opportunist—is another strategy in self-apology. The speaker claims always to have acted as the Head Servant and to have turned a deaf ear to the unprincipled pleas of Sagacity.

Here, however, the speaker has as much difficulty in convincing himself that he has followed the highest ideals as he had in the first part in pretending that he acted practically but altruistically:

> thus the life I might have led,
> But did not,—all the worse for earth and me—
> Doff spectacles, wipe pen, shut book, decamp! [2085–7]

The truth is that he has been both idealistic and opportunistic. In other words, Hohenstiel-Schwangau has had no consistent political philosophy; he has acted as it suited him at the moment. This does not mean that he has been an evil ruler; it signifies only that he is a man who has been aware of the right steps to take but has frequently not taken them. This is but one aspect of the Prince's personality that he and we discover. There are still others.

The speaker begins by claiming to be a man of boundless energy, one who must always be doing: "Better to draw than leave undrawn, I think, / Fitter to do than let alone, I hold" (39–40), for " 't is my nature . . . to put a thought . . . Into an act" (80–84). Moreover, it is his "mission" to act (277). We begin to suspect a bit of self-delusion when we learn that all his alleged energy in action was directed toward "sustainment" (710)—this because, he claims, a man has not sufficient time in one life span to put to right the ills of the world. Therefore his enemies, far from accusing him of reckless action, charge him with "indolence, / Apathy, hesitation" (1179–80).

No, his is not the gift to make "what is absolutely new"; rather his talent lies in turning "to best account the thing / That's half-made": "I make the best of the old, nor try for new. / Such will to act . . . Constitute[s] . . . my own / Particular faculty of serving God" (65, 67–8, 268–73). Although things are not better than one could wish, they might well be worse. Although he has not followed the visionary and socially dislocating schemes of humanitarian philosophers, the Prince at least has kept society together. In sum, he has "held the balance straight" (473) by meeting the people's immediate needs.

It is here that the Prince begins to defend himself against the charge of expediency. His justification for his unwillingness or his inability to reform social evils is that he did what, at the time, it was possible to do. Yet what he does not allow or, perhaps, even comprehend is that the feebleness of his actions stemmed, in large part, from his incapacity to decide what he should be undertaking. The longer he talks the more we see in him an uneasy combination of good and ill, of democratic sympathies and imperial designs.   N̶a̶p̶ = K̶i̶n̶g̶

In many cases there can be no doubt that he wants to do the right thing; yet it is difficult for him to act in accordance with his nobler aspirations because he "found earth was not air" (903) : while Mind might advance in one direction, "Body bows / To quite another government" (1106–7). Every time he wants to follow his nobler impulses he feels forced by immediate practical necessity to take a different course. In short, Hohenstiel-Schwangau argues that his ideals have had to yield to realities—the descendental always triumphing over the transcendental. He lives, he dimly realizes, in a complex social order that makes the decisive action of, say, the old Pope in "Iván Ivànovitch" (whom we shall meet later) psychologically impossible. If the world were different, he would act differently. But imperfect nature is ever a bar to the realization of noble hopes. Hence he must discourage a Comte, a Fourier, a Proudhon[8] who would give his people only

8. Auguste Comte, the positivist philosopher, was deprived of his professorship at the Ecole Polytechnique when Louis Napoleon was made Emperor. François Charles Fourier, the socialistic philosopher, advocated communal living. He died in 1837 before Louis Napoleon came to power, but his social schemes were much discussed in Louis Napoleon's day. Pierre Joseph Proudhon, who advocated the abolition of private property, was twice condemned to prison by Louis Napoleon.

beautiful dreams instead of the bread they need to feed their hungry stomachs:

> Mankind i' the main have little wants, not large:
> I, being of will and power to help, i' the main,
> Mankind, must help the least wants first.   [1057–9]

But the truth is that, neither "creator nor destroyer" (299), the Prince has revealed himself akin to Milton's Belial, content with eking out a little life from dried tubers. Better to be, he seems to claim, no matter what the condition, than cease to be.

Although he is sarcastic about the Thiers-Hugo version of his life which occupies more than a third of the poem, this heroic history is a perfect analogue of the Prince's self-justification in the preceding twelve hundred lines and of his whole existence as well. The vacillation between high ideals and the demands of practicality has made him impotent to act. Although he claims to possess abundant energy, he has led a life of constant frustration because, torn by the conflicting claims of his nature, he has not known how to channel that energy in a proper direction.

What we have, then, is an indecisive ruler whose only claim to decent rule has been "sustainment"—and this, given his nature and his time, because he could not do otherwise. Of course, like Fourier he has had his visions, but they have always met with revisions. Between the conception and the creation there fell the shadow of indecisiveness. Thus the monologue ends with what is to be his last great moment of indecision—and, incidentally, the great irony of the poem. Should he forswear the imperialistic idea or not? "Double or quits! The letter goes! Or stays?"[9]

For whatever he did or did not do, however, Hohenstiel-Schwangau refuses to be held accountable. He has acted only in accordance with the "law" enjoined upon him. He tells his fictitious listener that in order to reveal himself he must make plain

---

9. It was Browning's view that the decision to commence the war with Prussia was made by the Emperor's wife, not by the man himself: Napoleon "engaged in this awful war because his wife plagued him" (*Dearest Isa*, p. 371).

"the law by which I lived" (26). This is, he says, the only means by which a man's life can be understood, how all the "facts" of one's existence can be connected: "Rays from all round converge to any point: / Study the point then ere you track the rays" (65–6). His "law" has been to act independently in the service of God —that is, to do God's bidding. Other men, of course, may have "another law" (171). God imposed a duty upon him and he has tried to discharge it in every way possible, even if at times the commission seemed contrary to what his own better nature urged: "Such is the reason why I acquiesced / In doing what seemed best for me to do" (231–2). He did, therefore, not only what "head and heart / Prescribed my hand" but also used "every sort of helpful circumstance, / Some problematic and some nondescript" (235–40). In short, it was his "law" to be what he is and to do what he has done (246–50). His "mission" was "to rule men—men within my reach" and to "order, influence and dispose them so / As render solid and stabilify / Mankind in particles" (277–81)'. If he is pleased to act in a certain way, it is because he takes pleasure in doing God's will; thus he rules men "for their good and my pleasure in the act" (282). Hence all is excused by this "law" divinely mandated.

The circularity of his views is exemplified throughout the poem by the Prince's frequent appeals to law for justification of himself and of the status quo. Just as his "particular faculty of serving God" is to "make the best of the old, nor try for new" (268–73), so to conserve the present order is to work with God. God had a plan in making things as they are, and "my task was to co-operate / Rather than play the rival, chop and change / The order whence comes all the good we know" (620–22). Further, only in an imperfect world—"this same society I save"—can a man prove his devotion to God; and for that reason Hohenstiel-Schwangau has rapped the tampering knuckles of the idealistic reformers for twenty years to prevent them from setting up a society in which pity, courage, and hope could not be experienced. Yes, "Such was the task imposed me, such my end" (639–48).

It would be tedious to point out all the instances in which the speaker justifies himself by appeal to law and too obvious to examine the contradictions of his various appeals. It is sufficient simply to say that the word "law" occurs with greater frequency in *Prince Hohenstiel-Schwangau* than in any other of Browning's poems, as a glance at the Broughton and Stelter Concordance will indicate. In each case the "law" of which the Prince speaks is his interpretation of what he feels God has enjoined upon him. To ask how he knows what God wishes for him is to ask a question that the Prince himself does not pose.

Such rationalization for his lack of deeds is carried on at the conscious level. This is not to say that his design is to deceive, only to state that in excusing himself for inaction he is aware of what he is doing. On a less conscious plane Hohenstiel-Schwangau reveals another aspect of his nature which, even if understood by the speaker, is never openly expressed. In this connection it is instructive to inquire why he chooses such an imaginary auditor for his revelation. Mrs. Sutherland Orr suggests that "his choice of a *confidante* suits the nature of what he has to tell, as well as the circumstances in which he tells it. Politically, he has lived from hand to mouth. So in a different way has she" (*Handbook*, pp. 161–2). But it is not that Hohenstiel-Schwangau finds a fitting analogue for his political prostitution in the imaginary lady of the streets. Rather it is that his choice of listener reflects more than a little about himself.

The Prince is by nature a voluptuary. We have hints in the opening lines, where the "bud-mouth" is fancied to be an Oedipus who lurks "under a pork-pie hat and crinoline, / And, lateish, pounce on Sphinx in Leicester Square" and who "finds me hardly gray, and likes my nose, / And thinks a man of sixty at the prime." We have further intimations as, throughout, he dwells on the delights of cigar-smoking, and, at the close of the monologue spoken in his own (rather than imagined) voice, when he sends "this final puff . . . / To die up yonder in the ceiling-rose" (1215–16). And finally our suspicions tend to be confirmed when we are told that the speaker is not in a London café with a prostitute but is daydreaming in the Residency: "Alone,—no such congenial intercourse!" (2145). It would be a mistake to label the poem an erotic reverie, yet the sensual and specifically sexual elements should not be overlooked.[10] They all point to the Prince as *homme sensuel,* instead of man of action as he initially thinks himself.

Through the monologue the speaker reveals himself to his imaginary listener, Lais, (and to the reader) a different kind of man from that which he believes himself presenting. She and we learn that he is an indecisive voluptuary. But what does he reveal to himself? At the start he promised "revealment of myself" (22) to Lais and, by implication, to himself. Does he achieve his goal? Does he learn anything at all?

What Hohenstiel-Schwangau learns is what the poet himself learns: namely, that no matter how truthful one wishes to be—whether he speak from his own point of view or whether he attempt to gain another perspective on himself—one ultimately is forced to lie. No matter how objective one tries to be, all ratiocination is but rationalization: "Yes, forced to speak, one stoops to say—one's aim / Was—what it peradventure should have been" (2113-14). In the "ghostly dialogue" (2092) that takes place within the self without verbal language there is no need to justify or defend one's self and one's motives, because all claims are put "to insignificance / Beside one intimatest fact—myself / Am first to be considered" (2101-3). But try to express one's aims in words, the result is special pleading: "Somehow the motives, that did well enough / I' the darkness, when you bring them into light / Are found, like those famed cave-fish, to lack eye / And organ for the upper magnitudes" (2106-9). The result is, as the speaker discovers at the end of this monologue, that "one lies oneself / Even in the stating that one's end was truth, / Truth only, if one states as much in words" (2123-5). Yet "words have to come"; language is man's only means for dealing with the world, even though "words deflect / As the best cannon ever rifled will"

10. Browning said of Napoleon III that "when the mask fell . . . we found a lazy and worn-out voluptuary" (*Dearest Isa,* p. 356).

(2133–4). The only truthful statement about oneself that one can make in words is that language is inadequate for apprehension of the self. "Revealment of myself"? Impossible, if one aims to tell what one is and does. If the revelation comes, it will be only by indirection, by clues that one had no notion of.

The disappointment the Prince expresses was doubtless shared by his creator. In his quest for greater objectivity Browning had sought to overcome the most serious limitation of the dramatic monologue by combining the mode with interior dialogue. But the result was the same: the exercise of the dialogue ended in special pleading, with the speaker rationalizing his motives and actions in the same way as in the monologue *in propria persona*. No wonder then that Browning's enthusiasm for the poem flagged with its completion. *Prince Hohenstiel-Schwangau* proved once again that the dramatic monologue was at best a very partial means by which to explore the world. It would require a good many more years of experimentation before the poet arrived at the two-level vision of the *Parleyings*.

But though *Prince Hohenstiel-Schwangau* did not prove to be the formal breakthrough that Browning presumably had hoped, it nevertheless paints a picture of a man who, for the most part knowing and wanting to do right, failed to act in accordance with his noblest aspirations. In his portrait of the character modeled on Napoleon III, Browning showed it to be in the nature of things for one's best intentions frequently to be frustrated. Hopes are born in air; their realization must take place on ground. "Once pedestalled on earth," the Prince, like King Admetos, learns, "I found earth was not air" (902–3).[11] Whatever his situation, a

11. The Prince here echoes a passage in *Balaustion's Adventure*. Admetos too would be the heroic redeemer of his people:

> having learned
> The worth of life, life's worth would he bestow
> On all whose lot was cast, to live or die,
> As he determined for the multitude.
> So stands a statue: pedestalled sublime,
> Only that it may wave the thunder off,
> And ward, from winds that vex, a world below. [2455–61]

But he learns that when "pedestalled on earth" instead of being "pedestalled sublime" he could not work his will.

man is always at the mercy of the world, the devil, and the flesh —of all, in short, that constitutes phenomenal reality. Remembering this, Browning could create a verbal portrait of a complex man whom he did not admire but of whom he could charitably say when the picture was finished: "I think in the main, he meant to do what I say, and, but for the weakness,—grown more apparent in these last years than formerly,—would have done what I say he did not" (*Dearest Isa,* p. 371). The "inconsistencies," "casuistries," and "tangled arguments" are due then not to the poet's lack of control of his material but to the character of the speaker and ultimately, perhaps, to Browning's conception of human nature during his later years.

Most critics have been unsympathetic toward the poem, finding it intolerably long-winded and feeling cheated when it is finally made clear that the Prince has been speaking to himself all along. Park Honan regards it as lacking "in that concentration that seems to be the genius and the condition of the effective dramatic monologue." Roma King objects that the "action is subjective, abstract rather than concrete, intellectual rather than emotional, speculative rather than dramatic."[12] Yet the diffuseness and lack of action are just to the point. Browning wanted to present a character who was all talk, one who, in Honan's words, is "the mechanical chief of a large and complicated machine."[13] Hohenstiel-Schwangau speaks in bureaucratic jargon; he cannot talk, even when he refers to his humanistic ideals, in a human way. As a personality the Prince is a cipher: " 'Who's who?' was aptly asked, / Since certainly I am not I!" (2078–9). Browning drew a good picture of a man whose character was defective because it

12. Honan, *Browning's Characters,* p. 239; King, *The Focusing Artifice,* p. 169. G. K. Chesterton appears to be a minority of one in praising it as "one of the finest and most picturesque of all Browning's apologetic monologues" (*Robert Browning* [New York: Macmillan, 1903], p. 121). A good discussion of the topical nature of the poem and of the demands it makes on the reader for necessary historical knowledge may be found in Philip Drew, *The Poetry of Browning,* pp. 291–303.
13. *Browning's Characters,* p. 238; see pp. 237–40 for an analysis of the diction of the poem.

had no center. Perhaps, as the poet admitted, there can be no *poetry*, if by such we mean beauty of verse, in this sort of political satire (Hood, *Letters*, p. 151), but there can be an excellent presentation of character.

3 ❧ *Fifine at the Fair*

Prince Hohenstiel-Schwangau ends with the speaker not only wondering how truth can be grasped but also and more immediately how even the self can be realized as a defined entity: " 'Who's who?' was aptly asked, / Since certainly I am not I!" (2078–9)¦. How, in other words, can one know anything, oneself included? This epistemological problem intrigued Browning so he could not rest until he examined it more fully. With amazing energy and prodigious speed he took up his pen and began another poem immediately upon publication of *Hohenstiel-Schwangau,* writing half of it in less than a month and finally finishing it—2,355 rhymed alexandrines, with Prologue and Epilogue of 108 lines— about five months later, the poem, he wrote to Isa Blagden, *"growing* under me" (*Dearest Isa,* p. 376). Hohenstiel-Schwangau had deluded himself that he lived by a "law," only to find in the end that this "law" was ever changing, dependent on various times and settings as well as different moods. He came to recognize that without a law he was free but that freedom meant little; he finally perceived, dimly to be sure, that true liberty could come only within the context of an unvarying law. But what might this law be? And where was it to be found? This was the problem Browning wished to explore in writing *Fifine at the Fair* and, in dealing with it, also to consider again the question of why men with good intentions fail to live up to their highest potentialities.

The form Browning chose for his endeavor was again the monolgue, but one almost totally different from anything attempted previously. I can describe it only as cinematic, its shifting perspectives in time and space recalling Bergman's or, more nearly because lighter, Buñuel's dreamy films. It is a narrative, but the story hardly matters. The landscape and the people in it crowd the various scenes, yet they too are comparatively unimportant. What is significant is the internal action, the plunge into the depths of personality to discover what, if anything, is there *au fond*. The progression is not logical; everything seems to fade into something else by chance suggestion. It is an unreal world into which we are carried, and only with greatest difficulty do we follow the kaleidoscopic movement in which nothing appears substantial. The poem grows, as the poet told Miss Blagden. And it ends only when the speaker has completed "this experiment / Of proving . . . that we ourselves are true!" (LXXXII). *Fifine* is, I believe, a poem Baudelaire would have admired enormously.

Since Browning is, as it were, working out a problem in *Fifine*, it is appropriate to consider the genesis of the poem. Critics have long suspected a relationship between *Fifine at the Fair* and its author's biography. Mrs. Sutherland Orr, for example, speculated that "some leaven of bitterness" must have been working within the poet when he wrote the poem. It is probably true that, as W. O. Raymond theorizes, *Fifine* stems, at least in part, from the guilt aroused by Browning's proposal of marriage to Lady Ashburton and her subsequent refusal. It is probably also true that, as Barbara Melchiori states, the poem owes something to the author's repressed sex drive.[1] Quite possibly, the poem should be regarded in an even wider biographical context. The problem of conjugal inconstancy was a cause for the poet's revulsion not only toward himself but also toward the two most influential men in his life.

The first was his father. Only a little more than a year after his beloved wife died, Robert Browning, senior, was looking to an-

1. Mrs. Sutherland Orr, *Life and Letters of Robert Browning,* rev. by Frederick G. Kenyon (Boston: Houghton, Mifflin, 1908), p. 282; hereafter cited as Orr, *Life.* William O. Raymond, *The Infinite Moment,* pp. 105–28; Barbara Melchiori, *Browning's Poetry of Reticence,* pp. 158–87.

other woman for consolation and was, in fact, proposing to marry her. The younger Browning considered his father's new love affair, which was soon terminated, an affront to the memory of his mother. The second instance concerned Percy Bysshe Shelley. From early youth Browning had admired the great Romantic both as man and poet almost to the point of idolatry. When, therefore, he learned in 1851 that Shelley had deserted his wife and child without providing for them, and had fled with another woman, the revelation came as a great shock. Here in the two men he honored most he discoverd only fickleness where he had expected to find fidelity. If such is the case among the best of men, what couldn't one suspect of ordinary males? Is a man so composed that he is always at the mercy of the flesh? Is lifelong faithfulness to one woman only a dream and a mockery?

In "Any Wife to Any Husband," written apparently soon after his discoveries about Shelley and his father, Browning turned his attention to the subject. The dying wife, who is the speaker, knows that, while her husband will prove true to her in spirit, he will not remain so in body. She anticipates the arguments he will make to justify his actions, and she sees them all as mere rationalizations of weakness. In its analysis of the man's attitude the poem was prophetic of Browning's affair with Lady Ashburton. What had happened to the father also happened to the son. In an ill-considered moment Browning the widower proposed marriage to another woman. His action proved what previously he had suspected: man is indeed lacking in constancy, is indeed the slave of flesh. Although he prides himself on his beautiful spirit, man is nevertheless always at the mercy of the senses.

It is not unreasonable, then, to suppose that *Fifine at the Fair,* a poem whose central theme or, rather, point of departure, is marital constancy, had a biographical genesis. It owes its setting to Browning's three visits to Brittany in the 1860's after the death of his wife.

Fifine consists of three parts: Prologue, main monologue, and Epilogue. We cannot thoroughly appreciate the work if we do not see its unity. While a number of critics have found the Prologue charming, none has explained its relationship to the rest of the poem. At the risk of being tedious, let us consider the identity of the speaker in the introduction. Although many critics refer to him as "the poet,"[2] by which they seem to mean Browning, there is absolutely no warrant for doing so. He refers to himself only in the first person, and if indeed Elizabeth Barrett Browning is, as some commentators suggest (e.g. DeVane, *Handbook*, p. 369), the "certain soul / Which early slipped its sheath" alluded to in lines 33–4, the speaker does not call her so by name. Whether the speaker of the Prologue is the same as the speaker of the main monologue—this is another question and one which will at present be deferred.

Because biography has so frequently interfered with interpretation of the text, let us, again risking tediousness, quickly paraphrase the Prologue ("Amphibian"). The speaker, who is apparently the amphibian of the title, is floating far out in the bay when a butterfly passes between him and the sun. Each is alone, each seems to own the element in which it is buoyed, and each is foreign to the medium of the other. Thinking on the impossibility of their exchanging supporting elements, the speaker wonders whether the butterfly can "feel the better" watching a human creature pretend that he is not a land creature, for he certainly rejoices that the air "comports so well" with the insect which once had choice of land. This speculation leads him further to wonder whether "a certain soul," having slipped its earthly sheath and now dwelling in heaven, does, like the butterfly, look down on "one" (evidently the speaker) who still lives on earth and has no desire to slip his sheath.

Nevertheless, worldling though he be, there are times when the world is too much with him and when to escape from it, into a sphere overbrimming with passion and thought, he leaves the land for the sea: "Unable to fly, one swims!" In these moments when he is borne up by passion and thought, he smugly says that creatures of the air fare scarcely better than those of the sea.

2. See, for example, Charlotte C. Watkins, "The 'Abstruser Themes' of Browning's *Fifine at the Fair*," *PMLA*, 74 (1959), 426–37.

"Emancipate through passion / And thought," the swimmer sub-
stitutes poetry for heaven; and in this ecstasy the swimmer seems
like the "spirit-sort" who live in air, imagining what they know
and dreaming what they do.

Meanwhile, if one tires of retreat into a quasi-heavenly sphere,
there is always land in sight. Indeed after a long swim it is always
pleasant to return to "land the solid and safe": a mortal can bear
just so much of heaven. Truly amphibian, indeed belonging (by
nature and desire) far more to land than to the ersatz heaven,
the "I" wonders whether the soul previously alluded to looks at,
pities, and wonders at him who mimics flight.

This much of the Prologue seems perfectly clear. The only
caveat to bear in mind is that Browning uses the word "poetry,"
as he frequently does, in its widest sense, more or less as Shelley
employs it in *A Defense of Poetry* to mean "the expression of the
imagination." To understand it in its more limited meaning will
perhaps mislead us.

The obscure part of the Prologue is the opening two lines:
"The fancy I had to-day, / Fancy which turned a fear!" The
crux lies in the word "turned": does it mean "turned into" or
"turned away"? Browning probably uses it ambiguously. The
"fancy"—the musing on the relationship between the swimmer
and the butterfly—turned *into* a "fear" because it led him to
wonder whether the beloved soul in heaven looks with sympathy
on his worldly life, on one who finds the sensible world more congenial than the spiritual. The "fancy" turned *away* a "fear" because, as we shall see, it led to the main monologue and to the
answer in the final lines of the Epilogue.

The body of the poem is an attempt to deal with the nature of
an "amphibian"—with one who belongs to phenomenal reality
but who, capable of emancipation from the physical through exercise of the imagination, also can partake, partially at any rate,
of the spiritual realm. In working out the implications of the
Prologue, the main monologue renders a poetic statement about
the nature of man. It shows him placed on the isthmus of a middle state, seeing that his home is earth but also perceiving that

his true home is elsewhere, his real values different; and it depicts man held in tension by a polarity of opposing thrusts, one transcendental or upward toward the infinite and one descendental or downward toward the palpable. Thus the monologue is structured on an interplay between the desire for change and lawlessness on the one hand and the wish for constancy and law on the other.

To probe the amphibian nature most thoroughly, Browning elected to explore the whole contradictory makeup of man by examining him as a creature capable of love. He would show his amphibian ever striving with a hungry heart to reach the infinite but always falling back into the merely sensible. He would portray him assuming the stance of metaphysician and idealist on the subject of love but, in spite of his aspirations, constantly prevented by his biological nature from reaching the state that he feels, in his heart, he should attain. Ultimately, his concern would be essentially the same as that which preoccupied Tennyson in *Idylls of the King,* where man is shown properly bound "by such vows as is a shame / A man should not be bound by, yet the which / No man can keep" ("Gareth and Lynette").

But who was to be the speaker? There is no record of when Browning read Molière's *Don Juan,* a quotation from which serves as motto to *Fifine.* It would not be surprising, however, to learn that he was perusing the play in the late sixties and early seventies. If such speculation is correct, then during the germinal stages of *Fifine,* Browning was reading about a hero who was obviously a man after his own heart. This is the way his servant describes Don Juan in the play: "Vous tournez les choses d'une manière qu'il semble que vous avez raison, et cependant il est vrai que vous ne l'avez pas" (I. ii).

It was doubtless this aspect of Molière's Don Juan—the ability to talk, to make the false appear true and vice versa—that intrigued Browning in molding his conception of his speaker and caused him to prefix a quotation from *Don Juan* to his poem. It was certainly not the libertine of legend that appealed to the poet as appropriate speaker for his monologue. As W. H. Auden describes the figure, "Don Juan of the myth is not promiscuous by nature but by will; seduction is his vocation. Since the slightest trace of affection will turn a number on his list of victims into a name, his choice of vocation requires the absolute renunciation of love. It is an essential element in the legend, therefore, that Don Juan be, not a sinner out of weakness, but a defiant atheist."[3] Quite obviously, Browning's hero is not of this stamp.

There were also other appealing possibilities that the figure of Don Juan must have presented to Browning's imagination. By using Don Juan as his speaker he could in effect suggest that there is something of the Don in every man. Moreover, Browning could show, as it were, that just as the "Byron de nos jours" is not the Romantic Byron ("Dis Aliter Visum"), so the Victorian Don Juan is not the Don of legend: the great seducer would become a husband merely talking about seduction. Finally, by naming his protagonist Don Juan, Browning, with his predilection for undercutting his speakers' arguments, could intimate that while in the beginning of the monologue the speaker had few, if any, similarities with the Don of popular tradition, in the end he would prove to be a voluptuary after all. The possibilities for irony were practically unending.[4]

The monologue begins with the speaker inviting his wife to visit the fair of St. Gilles. It is a holiday, and the narrator adopts the mood of the day: "O trip and skip, Elvire! Link arm in arm with me! / *Like* husband and *like* wife . . ." (italics added). As we shall see, it is metaphorically the beginning of a quest in which the seeker explores various aspects and meanings of life. It must be noted that the poem begins with a consideration of the fair, not with Fifine. The speaker is concerned primarily with the fair as a whole, which we soon see is made emblematic of life, and

3. *The Dyer's Hand and Other Essays* (London: Faber and Faber, 1962), p. 392.
4. Because there is only one speaker, the narrator is necessarily nameless. But there is strong evidence that his name is Don Juan: the epigraph, to which the monologue is apparently a reply, is from Molière's *Don Juan* and is addressed to Don Juan; his wife is named Elvire; he quotes his friends addressing him as "Don" (e.g. xxxv).

he expounds on its appearance and meaning before he mentions
Fifine. Although he speaks of her in passing in section III, Fifine
is not specifically considered until section XV, when the narrator
makes clear that he is merely using her as the ground of his argument: "This way, this way, Fifine! / Here's she, shall make my
thoughts be surer what they mean!" Regarded in this way, Fifine
is less an object of seductive charm than a representation of a
particular trend of thought which the monologist wishes to pursue. Mainly, she is an excuse for the speaker to talk.

Like so many of Browning's characters, Don Juan speaks
chiefly because he likes to hear himself talk. As Robert Langbaum
has shown, many of Browning's monologists achieve no good by
speaking—which is to say, their utterance serves no strategic purpose.[5] In the case of Don Juan it would have been far easier to
steal away from Elvire on some simple pretext than to explain at
such great length his desire for Fifine. But deception of Elvire is
not his purpose: insofar as he is attracted to the gipsy girl at all,
he speaks in order to defend his desire for her not only to his wife
but to himself as well. Don Juan cannot understand why, as a
man of reason, he should actually want Fifine, realizing as he
does that she is inferior to Elvire, that she indeed is only "this
fizgig called Fifine" (XXXIII). In effect, therefore, the argument is
a dialogue of the mind with itself: his utterance is both apology
and self-analysis, an attempt to explain himself to himself and to
formulate, once and for all, the "law" which he would like to
live by.

Critics speak of Juan's sophistry.[6] But insofar as sophistry implies deception there is little that is sophistical in Don Juan's
monologue. Because he has so little design on his wife in his argument, the Don, caught up in his own rhetoric, probably believes
most of what he says. Throughout the entire poem Elvire never

5. *The Poetry of Experience*, pp. 182–209.
6. For example, John T. Nettleship, *Robert Browning*, 2nd ed. (London: E. Matthews, 1890), pp. 221–67, paraphrases *Fifine* and indicates
which sections are truthful and which sophistical. See also DeVane, *Handbook*, p. 368.

utters a word. To be sure, the husband puts words into her mouth, but she remains silent. It may be that Elvire is not even present. It may even be that Elvire is the "certain soul / Which early slipped its sheath," alluded to in the Prologue. Particularly in the closing sections the Don seems to conceive of Elvire as a mere "ghost" or "phantom": "Suppose you are a ghost!" he says, "A memory, a hope, / A fear, a conscience" (cxxx). "Be but flesh and blood," he invokes more than once (cxxxi), only, in the last section, to admonish her to "slip from flesh and blood, and play the ghost again" if he does not soon return from his meeting (either real or fancied) with Fifine. The point to be made is that Don Juan, so little conscious of his wife as a flesh-and-blood human being, cannot be said to speak in order to impress her with the validity of his line of reasoning. If it eventuates that his argument is sophistical, that argument none the less does not issue from a desire to deceive.

For the speaker the two women who are ostensibly the subject of his musings become almost allegorical figures, mere ghosts and phantoms as he calls them. On his quest Don Juan becomes unmindful of his immediate world. What is more important to him than either lady, what in fact preoccupies him throughout the poem is the subject of change in a world characterized by illusion. If, as Mrs. Melchiori says, the imagery is largely sexual, it is used not so much to discuss the problem of sexual relationships as to illuminate the great problem of constancy and commitment in all its metaphysical aspects.[7]

In the milieu of the fair, nothing is stable and nothing is as it seems. Like a butterfly metamorphosed from the grub, the fair has come into being from unlikely elements; what was raw and brown has been transformed into a make-believe world inhabited by mountebanks and deceivers of all types. It is an unreal entity

7. The imagery of *Fifine* is extraordinarily variegated. Because the speaker continually seeks for the proper imagery to embody his thoughts— "Thought hankers after speech" (xc)—and because his thoughts are protean, the imagery is also protean. In my opinion Mrs. Watkins misrepresents the poem when she ascribes fixed meanings to the various images ("The 'Abstruser Themes,' " p. 426).

obviously made only for the moment but yet apparently permanent. It is an enchanted creation containing structures that seem to belong more to air than to earth.

Fully aware of the unreality of all elements of the fair, Don Juan nevertheless soon yields to its enchantments. His heart leaps up when he sees above the airy structure the flapping pennon seemingly struggling to be free (v), and he yearns also to be free, not only of his marital bonds but also of the world's annoy.

> My heart makes just the same
> Passionate stretch, fires up for lawlessness, lays claim
> To share the life they lead: losels, who have and use
> The hour what way they will,—applaud them or abuse
> Society, whereof myself am at the beck,
> Whose call obey, and stoop to burden stiffest neck!   [vi]

Just as the amphibian swam out to sea to escape worldly noise and dust, so does the monologist trippingly and skippingly soar into metaphysical speculation to forget his earthly cares.

Don Juan wishes to become like the losels of the fair because he envies their freedom, their unwillingness to be bound. Unconstrained by society and its usages, they do not engage in social pretense: they are what they appear to be. Creators of illusion, they do not claim that what they fabricate is real. What makes these people, whose only "law" is "lawlessness" (xiii), so appealing is their absolute truthfulness. Yet despite their disdain of organized society, these truants must nevertheless enter into it from time to time in order to earn a livelihood, just as a bird has "made furtively our place / Pay tax and toll, then borne the booty to enrich / Her paradise i' the waste" (ix). Voluntary exiles from society, they still must depend in part upon the world of men for their existence.

In this manner the speaker leads into the theme adumbrated in the Prologue. Juan is aware of the contradictory forces in his nature: seeking escape into lawlessness, he simultaneously comprehends the necessity of law; cognizant of the infinite potentialities of the soul, he still realizes it to be limited by its finite situation. Nevertheless, there come times when the wish for freedom of soul predominates over rationality. Juan yearns, at least in fancy, to relax the bonds restraining him so as to seek new experiences.

With section xv Don Juan, in his consideration of "lawlessness," begins to focus on Fifine, who has only "loveliness for law / And self-sustainment made morality" (xvi). Judged immoral by the world, she none the less has an inner moral code. Yet he no sooner praises her than he withdraws his praise. "Loveliness" is not "law" enough. Hence, by using a device of "fancy-stuff and mere / Illusion," by manipulating illusion, he arrives at proper conclusions—judgment of "those the false, by you and me the true" (xxvi). In like fashion he moves forward in self-articulation by manipulating words.

Joining speculations on appearance and reality with his central concern of constancy, the speaker in xxvii recalls a legend about Helen, according to which Helen never left home, Jove sending her phantom to Troy to test which men would yield to her fatal beauty and which would spurn her; which, in other words, would "make half the world sublime, / And half absurd, for just a phantom all the time." Thus, by using the phantom wife and phantom mistress, Juan is able to evaluate his situation.[8]

In fact, says Don Juan, the body itself is only an illusion, a faulty sheath for the soul. The pity is that since souls cannot in this world exist independently, they must be housed in unsubstantial bodies, which hide far more than they reveal. The perceptive person, however, can see that "bodies show . . . minds, / That, through the outward sign, the inward grace allures, / And sparks from heaven transpierce earth's coarsest covertures" (xxviii). Each creature has its own excellence, could men but perceive it. Only he of "quick sense" can apprehend the truth of the creature (xxix): just as it requires the sun to strike a piece of glass on a dunghill to show that glass shines as bright as diamonds (xxx), so only the quick sense of Don Juan can perceive

8. It seems that Don Juan uses Elvire and Fifine in pretty much the same way that Hohenstiel-Schwangau employs the Head Servant and Sagacity.

the worth of Fifine. It is, he claims, her utter truthfulness that fascinates him: "So absolutely good is truth, truth never hurts / The teller, whose worst crime gets somehow grace, avowed" (xxxii).

With section xxxv the Don introduces the subject of art to exemplify his desire for freedom and novelty and to explore further this desire's relation to the world of illusions. Occasionally preferring to relish a Doré picture book, he momentarily forsakes his Raphael, though if a fire broke out he would of course rush, even at risk of life, to save the Raphael. In the human realm Elvire is his prized artifact, but created, as it were, by himself. She is his "new-created shape, without or touch or taint, / Inviolate of life and worldliness and sin" (xxxviii). The beauty and wonder of this gracious lady reside not so much in herself as "in the sense / And soul of me, the judge of Art." Art is, he goes on to say, his "evidence / That thing was, is, might be; but no more thing itself, / Than flame is fuel" (xli). For art touches and illuminates the essence of things, that unique but elusive quality that all phenomena possess behind a veil of semblances.

Art is, in effect, a kind of love. In every human, beneath the flesh there is a soul, more or less imprisoned by the body. Attempting to free and perfect itself, the soul seeks a complement, "goes striving to combine / With what shall right the wrong, . . . supplement unloveliness by love" (xliv). Art likewise searches in the parts to find the whole. In other words, art and love alike enlighten and activate the soul of things. So understood, art is what Plato said it is: the love of loving and rage for knowing, seeing, and feeling the absolute truth of things for truth's sake, not for any good it may bring the perceiver. Hence, Elvire is more beautiful to her loving husband's eyes than to the eyes of others, and hence, she is not her husband's Raphael, a perfect masterpiece, but his Michelangelo, an incomplete work that he struggles to perfect.

Like an artist the lover has only the covering of truth to work with: in a sense he must manipulate imperfectly formed matter. He must not allow himself to be limited by the tangible. What the physical eye of both artist and lover sees is mere appearance, an imperfect image half concealing and half revealing the soul within. Each must be free to pass beyond exterior semblances and hindrances to catch the quintessence of the object regarded. In this manner Don Juan discerns the beauty of his wife, who to ordinary eyes is only a "tall thin personage, with paled eyes, pensive face." "See yourself in my soul!" he admonishes (LIII).

At this point the speaker moves from discussion of the body's world to the realm of the soul. The seat and center of value, the soul, as he had previously suggested, activates the physical world and informs it with meaning, matter being but "stuff for transmuting,—null / And void until man's breath evoke the beautiful" (LV). Each soul makes a world for itself from its encounters with matter, and consequently the material world is a vale of soulmaking. When raw matter is thus transformed by the soul, the creation remains forever an achievement of soul, a permanent gain and advancement for it. Because the soul can create beauty and truth from roughness, because it can remove all achievement to the safe realm of the imagination where it will be protected from wrong, because it is arduous to perfect and help perfect, because, in sum, it can discern pattern in complete chaos—because it can do these things, the soul redeems an imperfect world, although, to speak truly, its actualization can be only in the flesh.

The sharing of the treasures gained by the soul is the meaning of love; at least, says Don Juan, this is what "to love" will mean hereafter, when the desire to share will have become the power to share. Love will come in aid of truth, one's grasp of truth being shared with the beloved. Regarded in this light, love marks an "eternal progress" toward truth, is characterized by the desire for perfection. Disregarding his previous consideration of "law," Don Juan formulates "love's law": "Each soul lives, longs and works / For itself, by itself, because a lodestar lurks, / An other than itself." Whatever this soul be—"or it, or he, or she" or "God, man, or both together mixed"—it is guessed at through the veil of flesh by parts which prove the whole, "Elvire, by me" (LIX). At last he seems to have arrived at a satisfactory statement of what law is.

But as before (XXXIII), Juan is unable to leave off at the point where his argument is most compelling, for no matter how high he soars in his metaphysical flights he always returns to earth or, to use the metaphor of the Prologue, the swimmer returns to land: as soon as he reaches the pinnacle of loving praise for Elvire, he reverts almost immediately to Fifine. At this point we begin to understand further the use Juan is making of these two ladies. They are representative of the opposing thrusts within him and, by implication, every man: the yearning for constancy ("law") and spiritual perfection on the one hand, the need for change ("lawlessness") and sensual satisfaction on the other.

Juan is thoroughly cognizant of what he is doing. He fancies Elvire saying: all this talk about soul is deceptive, because before you get to Fifine's soul you must penetrate her flesh. And his reply is that he will further try to explain, although to do so he must employ the unreliable medium of words just as (in section LV) the soul is forced to express itself with inadequate material. He must consequently range far afield, like the flag flapping far and wide; he must again resort to metaphysics and "lawlessness." The evening landscape offers an example of how one must proceed: one can divine what the landscape is like in certain places though one cannot actually see it—that is, one can guess at the whole by examining the parts, or, to put it another way, one may rise into truth out of the falseness of things (LXIII).

To explain what he means by rising into the true out of the false, the Don offers as example his morning swim in the bay. A swimmer breathes only by submitting to the limitations of the water—that is, to "law"; if he attempts to rise too far out of the water, he nearly drowns: "Fruitless strife / To slip the sea and hold the heaven." Comparably, the soul cannot live apart from the body; hence the spirit's life is betwixt "false, whence it would break, and true, where it would bide" (LXV). The human being would reside in "an element too gross / To live in," did not the soul inhale the air of truth above and thus capture just enough of truth to give the illusion that some day the obstructing medium will be transcended and the swimmer fly. At the moment of aspiration, when the soul would leave the body, just as the swimmer would rise into the air, the body ceases to support her and she begins to sink deeper into falsehood. Yet each soar upward and each resulting plunge beneath the water causes the soul more intensely to dislike the briny taste of falsehood. "And yet our business with the sea / Is not with air, but just o' the water, watery": we must endure the false, hoping that "our head reach truth, while hands explore / The false below" (LXV). So he begins "to understand the law whereby each limb / May bear to keep immersed" (LXVI). To howl at the sea, as Byron's Childe Harold did, is childish indeed (LXVII).

In this magnificant passage in which Don Juan, like Carlyle's Teufelsdröckh, closes his Byron, Browning again takes issue, as he had in *Sordello* years earlier, with Romantic metaphysics, which sought for the ideal untethered to the real. Few passages of poetry deal so brilliantly with man's dual nature. Although he yearns for the sky, man is of the earth, earthy—or "o' the water, watery"—and there is nothing he can do, or should do, about it save accept it.

Don Juan argues that by using the false wisely the soul can in fact come close to the true; indeed, the sea's waters, illusive matter, can be made nought by the fire of the soul. In such manner does Juan rise into the air above, and in such does he seize Elvire by catching at Fifine. This can be demonstrated by the very fact that consideration of Fifine has led to thinking on life's meaning, from the palpably real to the metaphysical.

Again the argument returns to the sexual level and its point of departure—Fifine. Elvire and Fifine, says Don Juan, convince him of the reality of himself: "I am, anyhow, a truth, though all else seem / And be not." A woman's love gives a man a sense of being, assists him to remain fixed amidst the flux of seeming, causes his soul to become disengaged from "the shows of things" and so makes him believe his soul is a fact. If Fifine can do this, how much more can Elvire (LXXX).

But is not one woman, the wife, sufficient for the purpose? Or, to translate the question into metaphysical terms, cannot one devote oneself directly and exclusively to the ideal—to the development of soul without consideration of the body? Life, Juan replies, is a series of tests: "Our life is lent . . . for this experiment / Of proving . . . that we ourselves are true!" (LXXXII). Accordingly, on the sea of life we accept difficult courses to steer in order to test our seamanship; hence we occasionally journey in small boats in preference to large ships. And when aboard a feeble craft we arrive at our destination, we prove that life is not a dream: the "false" proves to be "true." Suddenly, there is a shift in the Don's use of words (and Browning's real thought comes into focus with unexpected force): "Earth is not all one lie, this truth attests me true" (LXXXIII). Hence, the Don continues, if I use the ship Elvire there is even sailing, but with the boat Fifine I am forced to try my seamanship—in short to prove myself (and the phenomenal world) true.

Yes, says Don Juan, we live as if in a dream where all is false and fleeting. Life means learning to abhor the exterior falseness and to love the true essence. The charm of both the fair and Fifine is that in frankly professing falsity they are so completely true: "The histrionic truth is in the natural lie" (LXXXV), which means that Elvire becomes the danger on the voyage of life. The "true" is as much a lie as the "lie" is the truth.

Aware that discussion of marital fidelity has led him into "abstruser themes" (LXXXVII), the Don half apologizes for what has proved a philosophical disquisition. It was a dream he had that morning which impelled him to speak at such length, the kind of waking dream that he is frequently subject to. It was a dream about constancy and change and about appearance and reality. Being in a speculative frame of mind as a result of his noonday swim (spoken of in the Prologue), and thinking on the metamorphosis of the fair from grub to butterfly, and being overcome with fancies he could not articulate, he sat down to play Schumann's *Carnaval*. As he played, the fair expanded to the Carnival at Venice and the Carnival into the world: "With music, most of all the arts, . . . change is there / The law" (XCII). In this reverie each musical theme caused him to realize that truth is always the same, change coming in the seasoning or sauce, not truth but its expression being evanescent.

In sections xcv through cxxv, Don Juan, while playing Schumann, also plays a variation on his central theme by reflecting on how men's apprehension of truth is always changing. Domes of learning, seats of science, halls of philosophy—all rise and fall; all earthly institutions are transient, all standards relativistic: "Truth builds upon the sands, / Though stationed on a rock: and so her work decays, / And so she builds afresh, with like result" (cxiii). "Die Wahrheit immer wird, nie ist": it is the very nature of existence that truth does not and cannot stand nakedly revealed. Throughout history all mythologies have taught that they alone are true and permanent, yet each has yielded to other expressions of truth. Only at the end of time will the vesture of truth become permanent, only then will there be "the great clearing-up" (lxxxvi).

From his dream Don Juan also learns that much of a man's apprehension of truth is determined by his angle of vision. He points out, for example, that when he descended from the tower overlooking St. Mark's Square he discovered that what, from high up, had seemed defective in man was, on a lower level, to be discerned as purposeful: he "attained / To truth by what men seemed, not said: . . . one glance / Was worth whole histories of noisy utterance" (c). Browning, through Don Juan, makes a telling reversal of a commonplace: acting on his firmly grounded descendentalism, he insists that it is not the distant but the close perception—the thrust into the world, not out of it—that reveals purposefulness.

This perception of the significance of point of view leads the speaker to a further understanding of the descendental thrust in man's nature. Because he finds that what from afar seems hard and repellent is on closer view a necessity, he apprehends that "one must abate / One's scorn of the soul's case, distinct from the soul's self" (cii). Secondly, because he gains in human sympathy from his discovery of the importance of point of view, he learns from his dream that "the proper goal for wisdom was the ground / And not the sky" (cviii). Thirdly, he learns that the discovery that "there was just / Enough and not too much of hate, love, greed and lust" is "the lesson of a life" (cviii). Finally, Don Juan sums up the lessons of his dream in which Venice became the world, "its Carnival—the state of mankind, masquerade in life-long permanence" (cviii). To understand the world we must "bid a frank farewell to what—we think—should be, / And, with as good a grace, welcome what is" (cix). With the possible exception of the final lines of Wordsworth's "Elegiac Stanzas on Peele Castle," which it echoes, this passage is perhaps the most succinct statement in English verse of the descendental principle.

Eventually, in his dream the diverse buildings of the square in Venice blend into a common shape, multiformity yielding to unity. The new shape is the Druid monument where Juan and Elvire now stand. The origin and function of the monument are unknown, and erudition is as helpless as folklore to explain either. Tradition says that earth's earliest inhabitants built this edifice to remind men that earth was made by Somebody and did not make itself; that, while earth and its people change, the Somebody stays; that man should make the most of life, "live most like what he was meant / Become," since he lives in presence of this Some-body (cxxiii). Thus, even in folk tradition is manifest the intuitive awareness of the transcendental part of man.

At the same time, the descendental thrust of his nature is also evident. Consider, says Don Juan, the great stone pillar lying in the grass. Once it stood upright, and the women danced about it. The Church, in the person of the Curé, preached against the phallic worship, tried to show that its pagan meaning was no longer valid. Yet, in spite of all the Church taught, the people still enacted their rites, until at last the Church ordered that the stone be leveled. Even to this day, however, the people still remember the stone and its significance, seeing in it

> No fresh and frothy draught, but liquor on the lees,
> Strong, savage, and sincere: first bleedings from a vine
> Whereof the product now do Curés so refine
> To insipidity, that, when heart sinks, we strive
> And strike from the old stone the old restorative.

So there, laid flat, the pillar rests, "bides / Its time to rise again" (cxxiii). No matter how much a man may try to suppress his biological (and descendental) nature, it is always there waiting to exert its claims.

Returning to his dream, Don Juan tells how the monument sums up all aspects of his reverie. It betokens this central fact of existence: "All's change, but permanence as well" (cxxiv). Each soul works through this change, which is falsehood, to find the permanent, which is truth. The soul penetrates the shows of sense to find a complementary soul, which is the lodestar, the "other than itself" referred to in section LIX—"God, man, or both together mixed." If the soul will only look up, love, not hate, it will find the latest presentment of truth; and this continually new embodiment of truth under different guises tempts the soul farther upward. In each instance the soul is likely to believe it has finally arrived at the ultimate truth, but eventually, after successive failures, it learns that "truth is forced / To manifest itself through falsehood." Recognition of this fact causes the soul to abhor the false and prize the true, which is obtainable through the false. So, says the Don, "we understand the value of a lie": having served its purpose, it disappears, leaving instead of the singer the song, instead of the historic personage the Zeitgeist. So far does this other, this ideal of love, this "God, man, or both together mixed" lead us (cxxiv).

As with the other movements of his monologue (xxxiii and LIX), Juan cannot leave his argument on the highest level because always, at his back, he hears the call of Fifine. What, asks Don Juan, did Aeschylus mean by the locution "God, man, or mixture," which I have borrowed from his *Prometheus Bound?* Did he mean what I mean? Did he mean that Prometheus learned the Ultimate Truth by lifting the veil from the nymphs, just as I learn of the soul through the body of Fifine?

But enough of the dream, says Don Juan; dreaming does indeed disappoint. The higher man's pride lifts him in dream, the farther he falls. What seems fresh and strange in flights of fancy soon wears to trite and tame. The Druid monument long ago said all it had to say, and to dwell upon it in dream is simply to embroider upon the commonplace. "We end where we began," says the husband to his wife, referring explicitly to their walk but, on another level, also to his argument (cxxvii). He commenced his monologue with Fifine and, in spite of all he could do to philosophize sexual urge into creative oversoul, he ends with Fifine. Man is flesh after all, perhaps more flesh than spirit, certainly more animal than God. The truth is, the soul is always at the mercy of the flesh.

Half in dejection, Don Juan admits the error of his previous discourse. In his defense of the evolutionary nature of the soul each lie was presented as redounding to the praise of man because man was shown as gaining victory over it, conquering the false and base. As previously demonstrated, the false did not imply "submission to the reign / Of other quite as real a nature, that saw fit / To have its way with man, not man his way with it." But now comes a new understanding: man rises only to fall, "promotion proves as well / Defeat," "acknowledgment and acquiesence quell / Their contrary in man" (cxxviii). At the last, we admit that in this life sense does indeed conquer soul.

Finally, says the speaker, we arrive at the truth, but now this truth is no cause for pride. Only sense can be proud because, as biological evolution proves, reality responds to physical needs as it does not to spiritual aspiration: "Soul finds no triumph, here, to register like Sense / With whom 'tis ask and have" (cxxviii). Man is, therefore, not the lord of nature but its servant: he merely receives, he does not demand.

Here ends the quest begun in the first section. From the fair the wanderer returns home with "the sad surmise that keeping house were best," with the understanding that it is better not to go questing after all. For "love ends where love began. / Such ending looks like law" (cxxxix). America is here or nowhere. This is the "law" that he announced at the beginning of the poem he was seeking. Although the natural man feels lordlier free than bound, the only real freedom comes in remaining housebound: "Each step aside just proves divergency in vain." The disquisition on "abstruser themes" of the previous 128 sections was ill-begun. The subject should have been "From the given

point evolve the infinite"; not "Spend thyself in space, endeavor-
ing to . . ./ Fix into one Elvire a Fair-ful of Fifines" (cxxix).
No, says the Don, a man should act on the given, accept what he
has. Otherwise he will merely chase ghosts and phantoms, follow
wandering fires through quagmires.[9]
    Reverting to the marine imagery of the Prologue, Juan allows
that, though man is indeed an amphibian, he is better off as a
landlubber than as a swimmer. Fifine is a mere foam-flake, while
Elvire is a whole sea which could contain many foam-flakes. Although he left her calm profundity, now wiser, he realizes he has
had "enough of foam and roar": "Land-locked, we live and die
henceforth" (cxxix). He shall speak hereafter in different imagery: "Discard that simile / O' the fickle element! Elvire is land
not sea— / The solid land, the safe!" She is the land which the
amphibian of the Prologue finds pleasant to return to after a long
swim.

> All these word-bubbles came
> O' the sea, and bite like salt. The unlucky bath's to blame.
>   . . . no more the bay
> I beat, nor bask beneath the blue!

Instead of swimming and being "o' the water, watery," he will
confine himself to the "honest civic house" where there are "no
fancies to delude" and "of the earth be earthy." The nearest he
will approach the sea will be some token, shell or seaweed branch,
of former associations with it. So housed, he will wonder why on
earth he was ever tempted "forth to swim." Furthermore, his residence will be not a "tower apart" but a house in town (cxxxi).
    Forswearing the "passion and thought" of the Prologue and the
"passionate stretch" and desire for "lawlessness" of the early part
of the monologue (vi), Don Juan prepares to settle down into a

---

9. Compare this passage from Carlyle, in which the man who eschews
the real in seeking for the ideal "must wander on God's verdant earth, like
the Unblest on burning deserts; passionately dig wells, and draw up only
the dry quicksand; believe that he is seeking Truth, yet only wrestle among
endless Sophisms, doing desperate battle as with spectre-hosts; and die
and make no sign!" ("Characteristics," in *Works*, ed. H. D. Traill [London,
1897–1901], XXVIII, 32).

life of domesticity as a model bourgeois husband. Yet he does so
without taking into account who he is. For in spite of his best
resolutions he is, after all, Don Juan—the man who always sub-
mits "to the reign / Of other quite as real a nature, that saw fit /
To have its way with man, not man his way with it" (cxxviii).
This is exemplified in the last section by his stealing off to a tryst
with Fifine.

> I go, and in a trice
> Return; five minutes past, expect me! If in vain—
> Why, slip from flesh and blood, and play the ghost again!

In the end, the quondam quester cannot be domesticated. "Sense"
(in the figure of Fifine) has the final victory over "soul" (Elvire),
just as "soul" (the desire for complete freedom) triumphs over
"sense" (quotidian reality). The monologue ends with marvelous
ambiguities: who is the ghost—both Elvire and Fifine? And who
is flesh and blood—again both? This restoration of tension in the
end underscores the metaphysical complexity of the poem.

In the Epilogue ("The Householder") the former amphibian
has indeed become a householder, and he is no happier in the
house than we had reason to suspect he would be.[10] Grown aged,
he has experienced a loss of potency, "sense," which previously
kept him undomiciled. Too old for swimming, he can do nothing
but sit wearily in his house waiting for death. Householding is so
boring!

> time has dragged, days, nights!
> All the neighbor-talk with man and maid—such men!
> All the fuss and trouble of street-sounds, window-sights:
> All the worry of flapping door and echoing roof.

Quite unexpectedly his wife returns during a kind of waking

10. Many critics claim that the speaker in the Epilogue is Browning. For
example, DeVane in his *Handbook,* p. 369. As I shall try to show, the
speaker here is not the poet but the speaker in the Prologue and main
monologue, the speaker I have been calling Don Juan. He is even linked
through imagery with the speaker of the main body of the poem, wherein
"householding" is frequently used to suggest permanence.

dream, the ghost becomes flesh and blood again. He tells her all he has suffered, not only from the boredom of householding but also from "all the fancies." Doubtless one of them was the "fancy which turned a fear" in the Prologue, where the speaker was concerned to know whether the lady looked down on him with sympathy and pity from above. "If you knew but how I dwelt down here!" he says to her. Whereupon she replies: "And was I so better off up there?" The implication of her question is clear: the answer is in the negative. Can heaven do without earth any more easily than earth without heaven?

At last, the speaker has his answer to the question posed in the last stanza of the Prologue. Yes, the lady does still follow from another sphere his earthy pilgrimage, his "swimming," and as she is mindful she is also forgiving. It does not matter that the swimmer-become-householder is Don Juan, nor that the claims of the flesh occasionally (or perhaps frequently) predominate over the will. What alone counts is love, which having been must ever be. Love not only transcends the flesh, it even triumphs over death. In the epitaph which she helps to compose, the wife, echoing the last three lines of the epigraph from Molière in which Donna Elvira says that nothing can separate her from Don Juan save death, ends with "Love is all, and Death is nought!" The heavenly soul is mindful of the amphibian, Elvire forgives Don Juan, the erring husband is soon to be reunited with his departed wife, the fair has vanished, the comedy is finished. In the end, "amor vincit omnia."

Ultimately, love is the law that affirms the reality of the self. With Browning it is not a case of "cogito, ergo sum" but rather "amo, ergo sum." Love, the one constant in a world of change,

> Assists me to remain self-centred, fixed amid
> All on the move. Believe in me, at once you bid
> Myself believe that, since one soul has disengaged
> Mine from the shows of things, so much is fact: I waged
> No foolish warfare, then, with shades, myself a shade,
> Here in the world. . . .   [LXXX]

Although somewhat mockingly, Juan had fancied Elvire saying
that time and its changes serve to increase love:

> love defied
> Chance, the wind, change, the rain: love, strenuous all the
>   more
> For storm, struck deeper root and choicer fruitage bore,
> Despite the rocking world.   [xxxiii]

He learns that the words are true. Love is the one reality amidst
earth's myriad falsities, and to abandon constancy in love is to
leave oneself in a void with no certainty.

Yet such is Don Juan (and mankind in general)—"one who
loves and grasps and spoils and speculates," one who keeps "open
house" (lxxxix)—that he cannot always act on this truth. Although his better self attests to its validity, his lesser self prompts
him to ignore it. "Soul" and "law," consequently, often succumb
to "sense" and "lawlessness."

His protean nature prevents man from attaining that to which
he aspires. Because he is flesh he cannot reach "those heights, at
very brink / Of heaven, whereto one least of lifts would lead"
(cxxvi). Indeed, it is "not for every Gawain to gaze upon the
Grail!" (iv). But still the Grail beckons "through the fleeting"
and urges man on to "reach at length 'God, man, or both together mixed' " (cxxiv), the ultimate fixed point where the contradictory thrusts are finally resolved. A man gains this state, however, only when he ceases to be man. For as the progression of the
poem from Prologue to Epilogue suggests, permanence comes
only when the swimmer is metamorphosed into a butterfly, when
"sense" totally yields to "soul," when the amphibian is transformed into a householder. In the meantime man is merely (and
happily) "Don Juan."

4 ⇜ Red Cotton Night-Cap Country

One of the most compelling qualities of Browning's later poetry is its persuasive force, stemming from the poet's vigorous, insistent drive to argue each perception to a conclusion, impatiently and frequently with scorn for the timidity and slowness of others. Each of his poems is, as it were, a record of a quest, a distance traveled and a goal reached. A great deal of the energy of his work derives from his pleasure in the process of arriving at a conclusion, from, that is, his enjoyment of his own talents, his sophistries as well as his sincere passions. Finally, however, it is the formal enclosure of this process, the containment of seemingly uncontrollable energy within artistic bounds, that provides the main appeal of his later work. Nowhere, I believe, can this generalization about Browning's poetry be more aptly applied than to *Fifine at the Fair* and to the poem that followed, *Red Cotton Night-Cap Country or Turf and Towers,* published in May 1873.

Regarding *Fifine,* the poet's friend Alfred Domett records: "Browning tells me he has just finished a poem, 'the most metaphysical and boldest' he has written since Sordello, and was very doubtful as to its reception by the public."[1] He was right in doubting its reception, for it was generally misunderstood and deprecated. Several months after its publication Browning wrote two passages in Greek, from Aeschylus and Aristophanes, on the manuscript. DeVane translates (*Handbook,* p. 370) the Aeschylean passage: "And reading this doubtful word he has dark night

---

1. *The Diary of Alfred Domett, 1872–1885,* ed. E. A. Horsman (London: Oxford Press, 1953), p. 5; hereafter cited as Domett, *Diary.*

before his eyes, and he is nothing clearer by day." To this Browning added in English: "—if any of my critics had Greek enough in him to make the application!" The second quotation is dated 5 November 1872: "To what words are you turned, for a barbarian nature would not receive them. For bearing new words to the Scaeans you would spend them in vain."

The point to be noted is that Browning did not doubt his own powers or the value of his work; rather, he was contemptuous of those who could not or would not understand the work. Furthermore, he was unwilling to accommodate those friends and critics who asked that he make his poetry more accessible. He insisted that what proceeds from a genuine inspiration is justified by it.

He was disinclined to depart from the bold and metaphysical vein exploited in *Fifine*. During a summer holiday in Normandy, he later wrote, "I heard" the story of a man in the neighborhood who had "destroyed himself from remorse at having behaved unfilially to his mother. In a subsequent visit . . . I [learned] . . . some other particulars, and they at once struck me as likely to have been occasioned by religious considerations as well as passionate woman-love,—and I concluded that there was no intention of committing suicide; and I said at once that I would myself treat the subject *just so*" (Hood, *Letters,* p. 309). Here was a tale after Browning's own heart, involving love, sex, religion, and social conformity intermixed to the extent that they focused on a central question of self-identity; in other words, the story touched on the chief topics of *Fifine at the Fair.*

In *Fifine* Browning had probed by means of the interior method of the dramatic monologue, his speaker trying to find within himself the answer that would reconcile the polar thrusts of personality. Perhaps now he would subject the problem of selfhood to an exterior method, a narrative proceeding by a spiraling motion downward from the surface to the heart of the matter. In such a narrative the narrator, as in Conrad's novels, would become the focusing figure, the maker of the fiction and the molder of its meaning. Some subjects, the poet apparently felt, simply will not yield to a direct approach and consequently must be caressed or pulled or crushed before revealing their significance.

> Along with every act—and speech is act—
> There go, a multitude impalpable
> To ordinary human faculty,
> The thoughts which give the act significance.
> Who is a poet needs must apprehend
> Alike both speech and thoughts which prompt to speak.
>
> [IV. 24–9]

Red Cotton Night-Cap Country begins in a deceptively unassuming fashion: so casual is the manner of exposition, one initially believes that he is reading a loosely constructed descriptive idyll. The first thousand lines or so seem, like the strollers themselves, to ramble on about the Norman countryside. The fact is, however, that the speaker is busily and ingeniously establishing the themes that will inform his narrative.

The manner in which the story will develop is suggested in the beginning lines by a series of diverse images, which also give metaphorical support to the poet-narrator's underlying philosophical beliefs. Things are not necessarily what they look to be, he says. The creative soul can, nevertheless, pierce through the false appearances of the phenomenal world to arrive at the truth hidden behind them, can at least gain intimations of the truth. This idea is first implied in the speaker's descripton of walking through a field of wild-mustard flowers on his way to the sea:

> Of that, my naked sole makes lawful prize,
> Bruising the acrid aromatics out,
> Till, what they preface, good salt savors sting . . .   [I. 29–31]

And then the idea is expounded in more forthright terms: the countryside the strolling pair now view is totally unexceptional, yet the speaker likes it

> just because
> Nothing is prominently likable
> To vulgar eye without a soul behind,
> Which, breaking surface, brings before the ball

> Of sight, a beauty buried everywhere.
> If we have souls, know how to see and use,
> One place performs, like any other place,
> The proper service every place on earth
> Was framed to furnish man with: serves alike
> To give him note that, through the place he sees,
> A place is signified he never saw,
> But, if he lack not soul, may learn to know.   [I. 53–64]

This is, of course, an echo of Don Juan's contention that the soul, appropriately oriented and employed, can penetrate the falseness and see the truth of things.

In developing this idea, the speaker touches on the Carlylean philosophy of worn-out clothes.[2] He alludes to a notice on a barn which "repeats / For truth what two years' passage made a lie" and to signs proclaiming the Emperor's confidence in a war that has already been lost. What is needed is removal of these vestiges from the past: "Rain and wind must rub the rags away" (I. 129–37). Quite beguilingly, then, does the narrator establish the primary motifs of the poem.

Structurally, *Red Cotton Night-Cap Country* is divided into four parts and a coda. It is perhaps helpful to think of it as modeled on the sonata form. Beginning with a slow introduction, the first movement, with its interplay between "white" and "red" leading to the story, is allegro, rapidly and intricately setting forth the major themes. The second movement, telling the love story, is andante, lyrical and melodic. The third, developing the conflict between "turf" and "tower," is scherzo vivace in character, speedily and relentlessly leading to the tragedy. The fourth movement, which reviews, elaborates on, and comments on the story previously told, is a triumphal climax, resolving the aspiration and struggle of the earlier parts, "white" at last proved "red." Lastly, the coda, alluding to the initial point of departure in the speaker's conversation, reaffirms the tonic.

In Part I the narrator considers the appellation "White Cotton

2. See Charlotte Crawford Watkins, "Browning's 'Red Cotton Night-Cap Country' and Carlyle," *Victorian Studies,* 7 (1964), 359–74, for a study of some Carlylean echoes in the poem.

Night-Cap Country," which his friend applies to the section of France the two are visiting for the summer. The nightcap is a fitting head covering for those in this lazy, untroubled land, for it symbolizes not only the idleness of the inhabitants but also their insulation from the modern world. Suspicious of the light, the people cover their heads and retreat into the darkness. So, though the use of nightcaps, like dying religious faith, "may be growing obsolete, / Still, in the main, the institution stays" (233–4).

As the narrator ponders further the use and meaning of night-caps, he asks, is this land properly *white* cotton night-cap country? Behind the seemingly innocent drowsiness of the inhabitants might there not lie some evil or some horror? Might not the land also be called red cotton night-cap country? Aroused by his own suggestion, he seeks with fervor to prove that the color red is the more appropriate epithet. "You put me on my mettle," he says to his companion, who reasonably accuses him of being argumenta-tive; "Suppose we have it out / Here in the fields, decide the question so." And without awaiting her reply, he urges, "Quick to the quest, then—forward, the firm foot" (381–3, 399).

The walk, as in *Fifine at the Fair*, thus becomes a quest, an exploration into history, human psychology, and phenomenal ex-istence. Although the speaker puts words into the mouth of his companion, essentially his is, like Don Juan's, a dialogue with himself, an accompanied sonata (to use an analogy previously offered) designed primarily for one instrument: it is a disquisi-tion undertaken not only from a perverse wish to argue but also from a desire to penetrate appearances and explain why things appear as they do.

As they begin their stroll, the two rise to an elevated place and survey the whole countryside with its many churches and spires. The narrator's eye lights on the spire of the famous shrine La Ravissante: "There now is something like a Night-cap spire" (433). Only recently the church had received gifts of gold crowns for its Virgin and Child, the Virgin's topped with an extremely precious stone. A week earlier a festive celebration of the event had drawn people from miles around. The narrator had, however, "struck to [his] devotions at high-tide" and disdained to join the crowd. Yet why should he be contemptuous of the multitude's belief in miracles? For, though "sceptical in every inch of me," suddenly, "even for me is miracle vouchsafed." In thinking of the shrine and the name of the donor of the Virgin's jeweled crown, he receives an illumination, a possible answer as to why this should be *Red* Cotton Night-Cap Country. "Did I deserve that . . . a shaft should shine, / Bear me along . . . till, lo, the Red is reached, / And yonder lies in luminosity!" (532–47). The rest of the poem is an amplification of this flashing moment when the poet penetrates to the heart of the story and perceives all the surrounding circumstances in relation to that center.

As they continue their walk, the strollers see in the distance the edifice Clairvaux, which had been the residence and architectural plaything of the jeweler Miranda, who died two years previously. Originally the building had been a priory, but since "nothing lasts below" (621) it had been taken over by the state at the time of the Revolution and later sold to private owners. Miranda had utterly transformed it, and, upon closer inspection, the narrator finds it entirely different from what it seemed to be from a distance:

> Those *lucarnes* which I called conventual, late,
> Those are the outlets in the *mansarde*-roof; . . .
> And now the tower a-top, I took for clock's
> Or bell's abode, turns out a quaint device,
> Pillared and temple-treated Belvedere—
> Pavilion safe within its railed-about
> Sublimity of area. . . .   [671–81]

The point is that Clairvaux, a religious edifice now secularized, is decorated to *appear* as what it originally had been. And in still another way Clairvaux is also deceptive: renovated and made regal, it represents the owner's attempt to carry Paris, the city from which he escaped, to the country. Regarding this establishment the narrator says: "A sense that something is amiss, / Something is out of sorts in the display, / Affects us, past denial, everywhere" (710–12). What is right for Paris is perhaps wrong for Normandy. The narrator has by now thrown us into a kind *paysage moralisé* with ominous shadows.

The owners of the place were a "happy husband and as happy wife." The man was both generous and devout, the wife was likewise. Where then lies the "red"? Going on to describe the wife whom he had seen the day before, the speaker tantalizingly enumerates only "white" facts about the pair who lived at Clairvaux. Finally, at the end of Part I, he reveals the "red" in his story: Miranda had met a tragic death two years earlier, "and not one grace / Outspread before you but is registered / In that sinistrous coil these last two years / Were occupied in winding smooth again" (1023–6). At last the narrator is ready to prove by example that things are not what they seem.

The story of Léonce Miranda recounted in the poem's second movement is a tale of a divided life. From his father he inherited passionate Castilian blood and from his mother a French spirit, critical and cold. It was an unfortunate mixture, making "a battle in the brain, / Ending as faith or doubt gets uppermost" (II. 125–6). Trained in strict religious principles, he gave full assent to Christianity as embodied in the Roman Catholic Church: he believed in miracles and an earthly life of pietistic purity. This is the side of his nature symbolized in the poem by "towers." Yet this part was not long to predominate. At the age of twenty-two the young man, stimulated by his French blood, found that "there spread a standing-space / Flowery and comfortable" (II. 210– 11); in short, he discovered the "turf" of the poem's subtitle. Should he then forsake the towers for the turf? Believing that his life should properly be lived among the towers, he nevertheless is unwilling to forgo the all too earthy turf. So at this point Miranda is seduced by the spirit of Molière's pusillanimous Sganarelle to accept a compromise. He decides to remain on the turf but to "keep in sight / The battlement, one bold leap lands you by." The voice of Sganarelle urges, somewhat in the manner of Sagacity in *Hohenstiel-Schwangau:*

"Resolve not desperately 'Wall or turf,
Choose this, choose that, but no alternative!'

No! Earth left once were left for good and all:
'With Heaven you may accommodate yourself.' "

[II. 238–43]

Heeding this advice, Miranda joins the spirit of La Ravissante with the spirit of the boulevard, thereby planting the seed of his downfall. He gives blind assent to the tower, never stopping to inquire whether the tower is partially damaged or whether, in fact, it is merely a ruin still standing as a monument from some former age. Moreover, he does not listen to the "voice / Not to be disregarded," which said: "Man worked here / Once on a time; here needs again to work; / Ruins obstruct, which man must remedy" (II. 22–5). Instead, he simply accepts the tower for what it seemed to be or for what it might once have been.

Settled on compromise, he works hard in his jewelry business and is a model of what pious bourgeois parents wish their child to be, but on holidays he seeks occasional pleasure with women: nothing serious, nothing indiscreet, only "sport: / Sport transitive—such earth's amusements are" (II. 362–3). Thus "realistic" and "illusion-proof," he sees one night at a playhouse a woman who captivates him and makes him "for life, for death, for heaven, for hell, her own" (II. 421). Ceasing to be "realistic," he gives up his "sport" and devotes his energy to gaining her love. For, says the narrator, " 'Tis the nature of the soul / To seek a show of durability, / Nor, changing, plainly be the slave of change" (II. 338–40).

More than once, the speaker guarantees that "this love was true," on the lady's part as well as her lover's. Clara is a beautiful flower grown in inferior soil. Reared in poverty, exposed to sordidness and humiliation, married to an unsuccessful tailor, she nevertheless retains her youthful innocence. And though, because of her divorce, she can never wed Miranda, she is to him very like a wife.

Superficially regarded, Miranda's alliance with Clara is unlikely. A son of the Church, he chooses to live with her in defiance of the Church's teaching. A dutiful child, he elects a way of life which his pious parents cannot approve of. A believer in the transiency of all things terrestrial, he opts for an earthly love which he fears is opposed to his love of God. In brief, he seems in every case to choose the turf in preference to the tower. Yet in actuality he refuses to make any choice at all: he will both have his cake and eat it. Moreover, both Church and parent join with his own "Saint Sganarelle" to countenance, somewhat grudgingly and halfheartedly to be sure, his relationship with Clara.

Avoiding the social ostracism of Paris, the couple retires to Normandy. Miranda knows, deep within himself, that his every act is "provisionary" but tries to blot out from his conscious mind just how temporary is all of man's earthly existence. The world offered its advice:

> "Entrench yourself,
> Monsieur Léonce Miranda, on this turf,
> About this flower, so firmly that, as tent
> Rises on every side around you both,
> The question shall become,—Which arrogates
> Stability, this tent or those far towers?
> May not the temporary structure suit
> The stable circuit, co-exist in peace?—
> Always until the proper time, no fear!
> 'Lay flat your tent!' is easier said than done."   [II. 935–44]

This counsel he receives favorably, and so repairs to Normandy to make his pavilion on the turf. Clairvaux becomes the Earthly Paradise, its owners crying out: "Permanency,—life and death / Here, here, not elsewhere, change is all we dread!" (II. 975–6). But Miranda and his lady do not accept the necessarily provisional nature of their Eden, deluding themselves that they are proprietors, not tenants for a term.

Unlike the truly perceptive, the pair did not want to understand that all material building only harbors man, who was indeed meant to build, but "with quite a difference, / Some time, in that far land we dream about, / Where every man is his own architect" (II. 990–92). The building Léonce and Clara undertake is mere mimetic reconstruction, their impulse being to live in Normandy the life of Paris.

The imitative nature of their building, both literal and figurative, is exemplified in Léonce's taste in art. Sufficiently discerning to recognize that genuine artistic endeavor requires of the artist enormous expenditure of physical and spiritual energy to combat outmoded forms, Miranda did not care to be creative. In dilettante fashion he played at art and life, blotting out of his mind the fact that sooner or later his pavilion would collapse: "Wrong to the towers, which, pillowed on the turf, / He thus shut eyes to" (II. 1112–13).

For five years Léonce and Clara lived the "Paradisiac dream" recounted in the lyrical second movement, and self-entrenched, kept the world far off. In the frenetic third movement, the world intrudes and the sleepers wake when Léonce's mother summons him to Paris, berating him for his extravagant and sinful life. The return is disorienting. When confronted by "Madame-mother" and "Monsieur Curé This" and "Sister That," everything in short that represents the towers, he is forced to acknowledge that his life with Clara at Clairvaux had been in clear violation of what he was reared to accept as good and true. " 'Clairvaux Restored:' what means this Belvedere?" the mother asks. "This Tower, stuck like a fool's-cap on the roof— / Do you intend to soar to heaven from thence? / Tower, truly! Better had you planted turf" (III. 64–7).

The anxiety occasioned by his return to Paris resulted not so much from a conviction of sinfulness as from an unwillingness to choose either the tower or the turf. If, says the narrator, he had been called upon to make a decision in favor of one or the other, then he might have done so and lived happily. But he was told to keep both halves, doing detriment to neither but prizing each opposite in turn. Believing that he has wronged both, Léonce plunges into the Seine, seeking thereby to avoid the problem of choice. He is rescued, however, and returns to Clairvaux.

No sooner does he recover than he is recalled to Paris to find his mother dead. Made to feel responsible for her death, he decides to give up Clara and name his heirs. And so, in an instant, the pavilion built for permanency collapses:

> down fell at once
> The tawdry tent, pictorial, musical,
> Poetical, besprent with hearts and darts;
> Its cobweb-work, betinselled stitchery,
> Lay dust about our sleeper on the turf,
> And showed the outer towers distinct and dread. [III. 269–74]

But before the final arrangements are completed, he reads over Clara's love letters and in a paroxysm of guilt burns both the letters and his hands so that he may be purified. But the result is once again the same: in time he returns to Clara and Clairvaux.

The contrapuntal effect of the architectural imagery is beautifully worked out. Having vacillated between tower and turf, Miranda now admits the validity of each: "Don't tell me that my earthly love is sham, / My heavenly fear a clever counterfeit! / Each may oppose each, yet be true alike!" (III. 678–80). He realizes that it had been a mistake to attempt to build, independent of the towers, a durable pavilion on the turf. He now must harmonize the two, uniting the opposites and holding both in perfect balance. As to how this is to be done he seeks, in this land of miracle, guidance of The Ravissante.

The narrator does not hesitate to point out Miranda's false move in looking to the reputedly miraculous for aid. In all recorded time, he claims, no miracle was ever wrought to help whoever wanted help. To resort to the miraculous for direction is, in effect, to ask that truth stand fully revealed. In the phenomenal world, however, the truth can never be completely disengaged from the false. To be sure, certain aspects of truth may be grasped, but the achievement results from occasional penetrations of truth's false covering. One must, therefore, deal with phenomena that lie at hand. Enunciating Browning's firmly held descendental principle, the narrator says: "When water's in the cup, and not the cloud, / Then is the proper time for chemic test" (III. 853–4). The world is a vale of soul-making, and one becomes a living soul, sharing some aspects of truth with the Divine, only through experience with the phenomenal.

To the narrator "our vaporous Ravissante" is water in the

cloud. He refuses to speculate about how "fable first precipitated faith," but he does say that the faith represented by the shrine belongs to the past. The monk, the nun, the parish priest—all, in fact, who go to La Ravissante "for the cure of soul-disease" do but "practise in the second state of things," bringing "no fresh distillery of faith" but only "dogma in the bottle, bright and old." For Browning, theirs is an outmoded faith, one inherited rather than proved on the pulses and therefore hardly worthy of the name. Miranda, however, "trusts them, and they surely trust themselves. / I ask no better"—which is to say that, if accepted, faith must be embraced wholeheartedly: "Apply the drug with courage!" (III. 861–76)'.

For two years Miranda deludes himself with the notion that by presenting gifts to God and to the poor he might stay in sin and yet stave off sin's punishment. Then Léonce one spring day climbs to the top of the Belvedere and, gazing at La Ravissante, begins, in Part IV, the magnificent meditation that ends with his death.

Stepping off the Belvedere, he believes he will be miraculously transported to La Ravissante. Instead, he lands on the turf. The world judges Miranda insane for putting his faith in the Virgin to the test. The narrator, however, considers him sane, because, given his premises, he has at last acted on what he believes:

> Put faith to proof, be cured or killed at once!
> . . . . .
>   In my estimate,
> Better lie prostrate on his turf at peace,
> Than, wistful, eye, from out the tent, the tower,
> Racked with a doubt. [IV. 356–62]

Or as Browning had said years earlier in "The Statue and the Bust": "Do your best . . . / If you choose to play!" Miranda finally settles his wavering between turf and tower.

In the opinion of the narrator, Léonce should be condemned only for having waited so long to choose. The wish to reach the tower was thoroughly vain, one worthy of the Middle Ages, perhaps, but not of the nineteenth century. A more enlightened man would have found love enough, which is the means by which

God is "participant" in time. In it lies that permanency the jeweler had been seeking. But Miranda never properly comprehended what it means to love. In the beginning he came close to realizing its full power because in his relationship with Clara he arrived at a profounder understanding of life than would have otherwise been possible. Only at the last, however, in his apostrophe to the Virgin, does he perceive that his was a "mock love, / That gives—while whispering 'Would I dared refuse!' " (iv. 210–11).

Clara, on the other hand, is more worthy of respect, although she too is not free from blame. Her fault was that she regarded love as an end in itself, not as a means to truth. No doubt she loved Miranda, no doubt she was to be preferred to the statue of the Virgin at La Ravissante. She was both the nurturing mother and the doting wife to Miranda. Yet, says the narrator, "I do not praise her love." For properly conceived, "Love bids touch truth, endure truth, and embrace / Truth, though, embracing truth, love crush itself." Like the grub that is to become a butterfly, Clara fed on her leaf, Miranda, and did not stop till she had consumed him. She did not urge, "Worship not me, but God," which is the expression of "love's grandeur" (iv. 861–7). So, though Clara is "the happier specimen," she still must be judged morally a failure. She simply accepted what was given. In no instance did she attempt to "aspire, break bounds" (iv. 764).

At the end of his story the narrator leaves his listener with no uncertainty as to the causes of the tragedy. First, the spirit of compromise—that is, an unwillingness to commit oneself fully—infected the personality and ended by poisoning all of Miranda's relationships. He was encouraged in his indecision by parents, mistress, and representatives of the Church, but he was no less wrong not to choose and thenceforth to act. Thus, what the world sees as his madness was, correctly viewed, the moment of his triumph. Perhaps the choice was a poor one, but at any rate it was consonant with his belief. Secondly, Miranda did not use what intelligence had been granted him. He simply accepted an inherited faith, its superstitions as well as its doctrines and dogmas. If he had put his mind to work, he would have seen that the religious faith signified by La Ravissante belongs to history and should remain buried with the past. The attempt to "bring the early ages back again" was the vainest kind of activity. Thirdly, neither Léonce nor Clara ever comprehended the meaning of love. For them it was a means by which "self-entrenched / They kept the world off." Seeking for constancy amidst the flux of life, they built a pavilion on the turf which had the "show of durability" but which they mistook for permanency itself, forgetting that "soon or late will drop / Pavilion, soon or late you needs must march." Love for them, in other words, was the end-in-itself instead of the means by which the soul conquers the false on its journey toward perfection. In the last analysis, all the "white" facts of life proved the "red" of Miranda's undoing.

At the end of the quest that began with the walk in the fields the speaker has attained his goal: ingeniously, he has shown that things are not always what they appear. He has proved that it is not enough to regard an object or an incident as "normal, typical, in cleric phrase / *Quod semel, semper, et ubique*" (I. 336–7). Everything has its own special truth. A nightcap is not just a nightcap any more than a fiddle is just a fiddle. A man must "recognize / Distinctions,"examine thoroughly the nightcap, and, if needs be, "rub to threads what rag / Shall flutter snowily in sight" (I. 256, 411–12).

This is, of course, the business of the creative imagination, especially as exercised in poetry. The imagination deals with the multitudinousness of phenomena by piercing through the false covering of reality to see the thing-in-itself, reducing multiplicity to unity, and turning thought and action into language. In the coda Browning, identifying himself as narrator, reveals that such indeed has been the aim of his poem. Moreover, he suggests that *Red Cotton Night-Cap Country* is ultimately a poem about poetry and what it means to be a poet.

Speaking in his own voice, the poet explains that the endeavor of making the poem out of his few sordid facts has meant a step forward in self-articulation and, thus, a triumph of personality over seemingly meaningless data. The moment of insight which, he says in the postscript addressed to his walking companion, came "months ago and miles away"—"that moment's flashing" has been "amplified" and "impalpability reduced to speech": "Such ought to be whatever dares precede, / Play ruddy herald-star to your white blaze / About to bring us day."

The overcoming of the false outer appearance of things and the subsequent advance toward ultimate Truth is the meaning of poetry. Just as, in the beginning, the narrator spoke of making "lawful prize" of the wild mustard flower from which he had forced "the acrid aromatics out," so his extraction of meaning from the Miranda story is also a personal victory. Referring in Part I to Clara, the narrator asks:

> Yet is there not conceivably a face,
> A set of wax-like features, blank at first,
> Which, as you bendingly grow warm above,
> Begins to take impressment from your breath?
> Which, as your will itself were plastic here
> Nor needed exercise of handicraft,
> From formless moulds itself to correspond
> With all you think and feel and are—in fine
> Grows a new revelation of yourself,
> Who know now for the first time what you want?   [I. 850–59]

Indeed the poem itself becomes for its maker a new revelation of himself, for in penetrating to the truth of another's personality he adds a new dimension of truth to his own and thus gains an understanding of the self otherwise unrealized.

Yet because the poet's apprehension of truth is always and necessarily in advance of any accepted formulation of truth, he finds himself set apart from his fellows. The "life-exercise" of poetry means, then, that the poet assumes an almost intolerable burden:

> such exercise begins too soon,
> Concludes too late, demands life whole and sole,
> Artistry being battle with the age
> It lives in!
>   . . . . .

To be the very breath that moves the age,
Means not, to have breath drive you bubble-like
Before it—but yourself to blow: that's strain;
Strain's worry through the life-time, till there's peace;
We know where peace expects the artist-soul.

It is precisely because he recognized the "strain" of art that Miranda did not wish to be a creative artist, choosing instead "the quiet life and easy death" of "Art's seigneur, not Art's serving man" (II. 1049–75).

The artist-soul, on the other hand, refuses to work with other men's formulae. In art as in religion, nothing is so damning in Browning's eyes as acceptance of inherited beliefs and practices. To work in traditional modes is to submit to the world with all its falseness. Being an artist means breaking rules and bounds; being an artist means attempting the impossible. What matter whether the result is, in the world's opinion, a success? "Success is naught, endeavor's all." Art's value lies in its revelation of truth hitherto undisclosed. Whether the world judge it incomplete and unpolished, if it gains a grasp on the truth then "there the incomplete, / More than completion" (IV. 766–79) should stand respected.

Undoubtedly, Browning was speaking out of his own experience when he referred to the burden of loneliness and misunderstanding to which the modern poet is subject.[3] Mindful of the kind of criticism leveled against him, Browning nevertheless refused to heed the demands of his critics, who would prefer "work complete, inferiorly proposed, / To incompletion, though it aim aright" (IV. 762–3). No, a poet is ever attempting a task impossible to finish: submitting life itself to the control of langauge.

3. After publication of the unfavorable reviews of *Red Cotton Night-Cap Country* Browning wrote to Annie Thackeray, to whom the poem is dedicated: "Indeed the only sort of pain that any sort of criticism could give me would be by the reflection of any particle it managed to give *you*. I dare say that, by long use, I don't feel or attempt to feel criticisms of this kind, as most people might. Remember that everybody this thirty years has given me his kick and gone his way . . ." (Annie Thackeray Ritchie, *Records of Tennyson, Ruskin, Browning* [New York: Harper's, 1892], p. 181).

Who is a poet needs must apprehend
Alike both speech and thoughts which prompt to speak.
Part these, and thought withdraws to poetry:
Speech is reported in the newspaper. [iv. 28–31]

The triumph of the artist lies in his endeavor to "break through Art and rise to poetry." If he succeeds, "Then, Michelagnolo against the world!" (iv. 780).

To ascribe either lack of geniality or bitterness to *Red Cotton Night-Cap Country*, as critics so frequently do,[4] is to catch the wrong tone. No bitterness is reflected in the observations on the loneliness of the artist. On the contrary, the narrator maintains that more than a compensatory joy is to be derived from the artistic exercise. Furthermore, there is nothing harsh about the narrator's reflections on religion as practiced by Miranda. Although written soon after the first Vatican Council and under the shadow of the ultramontanism of Pius IX, *Red Cotton Night-Cap Country* expresses Browning's belief that even the superstitious faith embraced by Léonce, benighted though it be, is preferable to doctrinaire materialism, which affirms the body while denying the soul. The only sardonic note in the entire poem is to be found in the narrator's description of the anticlerical doctor with his "new *Religio Medici*," which refuses to admit the existence of spirit (iii. 491–510). Far from being acerb, *Red Cotton Night-Cap Country* is gay in tone. Friendly, playful, even self-mocking—"ready to hear the rest? How good you are!" (iv. 1) —it disguises a profundity of ideas under a surface of conversational banter.

Earlier, I suggested that it might be helpful to think of the poem in terms of a musical structure. The closest analogue would be a

4. For example, Mrs. Orr calls it a "manifestation of an ungenial mood of Mr. Browning's mind" (*Life*, p. 286). G. K. Chesterton agreed that it reflects "one of the bitter moods of Browning" (*Robert Browning*, p. 124). John M. Hitner, "Browning's Grotesque Period," 1–13, refers to it as "another morbid newspaper story, dealing with mental disease and abnormal sex, culminating in suicide" (p. 5). Arthur Symons's *An Introduction to the Study of Browning*, rev. ed. (London: Cassell, 1906), pp. 161–3, is a notable exception in praising the poem and in detecting its humor.

work by Berlioz, a *sonate fantastique* (if he had written such), cast basically in a classical pattern but distorted to the point where the structure is barely recognizable. Hillis Miller describes *Red Cotton Night-Cap Country* as "a huge, awkward monstrosity, with its parts blown all out of size. It has a wild, disordered, undulating vitality, like the buildings of the Spanish architect Gaudí."[5] In any case, the manner in which the tale is recounted —the constant expansion to periphery and contraction to center, the blending of casual humor and philosophical observation—is emblematic of Browning's belief that the universal is to be found in the particular, the ideal in the real. Even in the distasteful and seemingly unpromising story of Léonce Miranda the poet beheld the illuminating "flash" which enabled him to "imbibe / Some foretaste of effulgence" (iv. 990–91). It is a mark of Browning's genius that he could make out of this material, which basically is that of a naturalistic novel,[6] an intriguing and ultimately delightful philosophical poem.

5. *The Disappearance of God,* p. 132.

6. For a consideration of Browning's use of novelistic techniques see Hugh Sykes Davies, *Browning and the Modern Novel* (Hull: University of Hull Publications, 1962). Drew, *The Poetry of Browning,* pp. 321–31, has interesting and kind remarks about Browning's narrative technique. Roy E. Gridley, *Browning* (London: Routledge & Kegan Paul, 1972), makes interesting comparisons between Browning and the French realists, especially Balzac and Flaubert.

5 ᔍ Aristophanes' Apology

Red Cotton Night-Cap Country was generally disliked, receiving from the reviewers more damning notices than even *Fifine at the Fair.* Browning's only success in the seventies to this point had been *Balaustion's Adventure,* which alone went into a second printing. Reflecting on the reception of his works after *The Ring and the Book,* the poet must have felt attracted toward another poem similar to *Balaustion.* Perhaps he could even write a sequel to the Greek poem which had proved so popular; perhaps he would drop the innovative narrative technique of *Night-Cap Country* and return to the dramatic monologue. Thoughts like these may well have passed through his mind as he considered a new undertaking.

Browning composed his first four long poems after *The Ring and the Book* with almost incredible speed, the hastiness occasionally being reflected in the lack of polish of the verse. *Balaustion* was written in one month, *Hohenstiel-Schwangau* in two months, *Fifine* in five, and *Red Cotton Night-Cap Country* in just under two. His next work, however, was to take considerably longer: he was in the process of writing or preparing himself to write *Aristophanes' Apology* for about a year and a half. The transcript from Euripides that forms part of the poem was finished in June 1873. In August of that year, when Browning was in France on his annual holiday, he communicated to a friend that he was deeply involved in a study of Greek books, especially Aristophanes (Hood, *Letters,* p. 158). Presumably he was turning the poem over in his mind during the following year, because he indicated on the manuscript that the matter surrounding the Euripidean play was begun in mid-August and completed in November 1874. The poem was published in April 1875. It is not surprising that the poet took more time to write *Aristophanes' Apology*. It is the third longest of his works (after *The Ring and the Book* and *Sordello*) and certainly the most erudite. In his attempt to re-create life in Athens at the time of the death of Euripides, he ransacked the scholarship on fifth-century Greece so that, as he was to say some years later, "the allusions require a knowledge of the Scholia, besides acquaintance with the 'Comicorum Graecorum Fragmenta,' Athenaeus, Alciphron, and so forth" (Hood, *Letters*, p. 208).

Because the poem in both length and learning is so formidable, it has, with the exception of the lyric "Thamuris Marching," been almost universally misprized and neglected. While a study of the sources of *Aristophanes' Apology* is interesting and informative, I cannot agree with the scholars who claim that "the best approach to genuine understanding of the poem is through a study of the sources of Browning's information."[1] Instead, I believe, to quote the anonymous reviewer of *Balaustion's Adventure* in the *Examiner* for 12 August 1871, that "the story has so filtered through Mr. Browning's mind that it is a thoroughly original poem, and as such it claims to be read and mastered before classical criticism is allowed to play."

Let me begin by stating what, in my opinion, the poem is not. It is not, as Swinburne called it, a "libel on Aristophanes" nor, as DeVane believed, "an erudite, garrulous piece of special pleading for Euripides against his mocker Aristophanes."[2] Browning him-

1. Frederick Tisdel, "Browning's *Aristophanes' Apology,*" *University of Missouri Studies*, 2, No. 4 (1927), 1. Two other studies of Browning's classical sources may be found in the *Harvard Studies in Classical Philology*: Carl N. Jackson, "Classical Elements in Browning's 'Aristophanes' Apology,' " 20 (1909), 15–73; T. L. Hood, "Browning's Ancient Classical Sources," 33 (1922), 79-180.

2. *Letters of Swinburne*, ed. Cecil Y. Lang, III, 40; DeVane, "Browning and the Spirit of Greece" in *Nineteenth Century Studies*, p. 184. Browning told Carlyle in reference to the poem: "I felt in a manner bound to

self stated: "Indeed, I am no enemy of that Aristophanes—all on fire with invention,—and such music! I am confident that Euripides bore his fun and parodying good humoredly enough . . ." (Hood, *Letters*, p. 193). Nor is the work a mere glorification of the character of the narrator, Balaustion: we must not accept uncritically everything she says about the two dramatists and about herself.[3] Though Euripides might bear no enmity toward the comic dramatist, still, says Browning, "a friend of Euripides, —above all, a woman friend,—feels no such need of magnanimity" (Hood, *Letters*, p. 193).

I believe it is most fruitful to regard *Aristophanes' Apology* formally as a further attempt by Browning to experiment with and overcome the limitations of the dramatic monologue and thematically as an expression of his philosophy that human beings must accept the antinomies of existence without strict adherence to one pole of a dialectic. The form of the poem is extremely complex, but the work is so designed that the form is reflective of the theme. To quote Roma King on Browning's earlier monologues: "The unity is a tension produced by the interplay of opposing intellectual and moral forces"; the *Apology* is a dramatization of what David Shaw calls the poet's "dialectical temper."[4] Early in the poem Balaustion says, without necessarily accepting her own statement, that "progress means contention" (141). Accordingly, the poem progresses by statement and counterstatement, being divided into three main parts—Aristophanes' apology, Balaustion's admonishment of him, and a translation of Euripides' *Herakles*—with a prologue and a conclusion. As I see

---

write it, so many blunders about Aristophanes afloat, even among the so-called learned" (William Allingham, *A Diary*, ed. H. Allingham and D. Radford [London: Macmillan, 1907], p. 240).

3. I feel that this point should be made to counter the critical efforts to identify Balaustion with Elizabeth Barrett Browning. See, for example, Andrew Marshall, "Balaustion and Mrs. Browning," *Cornhill Magazine*, 51 (1921), 586–93, and J. H. Friend, "Euripides Browningized," 179–86.

4. King, *The Bow and the Lyre: The Art of Robert Browning* (Ann Arbor: University of Michigan Press, 1957), p. 140; Shaw, *The Dialectical Temper: The Rhetorical Art of Robert Browning* (Ithaca: Cornell University Press, 1968).

it, the translation is not a mere flexion of Browning's classical muscles but an organic part of the work whose full title is *Aristophanes' Apology; Including a Transcript from Euripides: Being the Last Adventure of Balaustion.*

At first glance, the form is reminiscent of that of *Balaustion's Adventure:* a combination of three dramatic modes—monologue, dialogue, and fully realized drama—resulting in a multilevel technique first essayed in *The Ring and the Book.* As we have noted, Browning learned earlier in his career that both monologue and dialogue suffer from the limitation of the speakers' personalities. Seeking to overcome this limitation and to arrive at a more nearly objective mode, he included a play in *Balaustion's Adventure.* But even there the hoped-for objectivity of the *Alkestis* was diminished by Balaustion's commentary on and her version of the play. Browning must have reasoned that one way to circumvent the subjectivity of his monologist was to provide within the monologue a full-fledged drama, the most objective of literary forms, unedited and without commentary. The special pleading of the two characters in the dialogue, the "contention" of which Balaustion speaks, would thus perhaps be resolved by a play which is not bound by an immediate audience—in this case, Balaustion and Aristophanes and, maybe, Euthukles—and which presumably did not owe its origin to any strategic purpose. To include a complete play might then be the real "progress," the objectification and resolution of diverse points of view.

If I am correct in my guess about Browning's intention, we can then understand the reason for the nature of the translation of the *Herakles.* It is extremely literal, what Browning called in his preface to his translation of the *Agamemnon* of Aeschylus "a mere strict bald version of thing by thing," giving only "the action of the piece"; and to most lovers of poetry it is barely readable. It is not that Browning was incapable of making beautiful translations,[5] but that with the *Herakles* he wished to be as neu-

---

5. Carlyle, not quick to praise, called the rendering of the *Alkestis* in *Balaustion's Adventure* the "very best translation I ever read." Later, when Browning called on Carlyle on his eighty-third birthday, Carlyle said, "I

tral and objective in style as possible. Within the design of the poem the *Herakles* would be the "pure" statement, distinct from the biased utterances of Aristophanes and Balaustion.

What we have then in *Aristophanes' Apology* is a complicated work in three different parts and three different modes. It is important to note, however, that the subsuming formal locus of the poem is Balaustion's monologue, in spite of the fact that she is by no means the main character. It is she who tells us all, and consequently the poem is ultimately hers. The poem exists because she decided to speak. And why does she speak? To distance and objectify a personal dilemma; that is, to alleviate present suffering—the collapse of Athens before Spartan invaders and her own retreat to Rhodes—by talking about it:

> That fate and fall, once bedded in our brain,
> Roots itself past upwrenching; but coaxed forth,
> Encouraged out to practise fork and fang,—
> Possibly, satiate with prompt sustenance,
> It may pine off far likelier than left swell
> In peace by our pretension to ignore,
> Or pricked to threefold fury, should our stamp
> Bruise and not brain the pest.   [151-8]

So "wanting strength," she will "use craft, / Advance upon the foe [she] cannot fly, / Nor feign a snake is dormant though it gnaw" (148-50). But simply to relate what happened and to dwell on her own involvement in the events will offer no relief. What is needed is a "middle course." Out of the experience she will devise a play: "What hinders that we treat this tragic theme / As the Three taught when either woke some woe" (158-60). The fall of Athens will be the tragedy that will "re-enact itself, this voyage through" (168). She and her husband will be the chorus.

Balaustion is thus the poet-maker and the commentator-chorus. Her narrative is necessarily to be her story, with her as an actor

---

still exhorted him to give us, as the best thing possible, a Greek Theatre, done like that from Euripides in *Balaustion*" (quoted in William Allingham, *A Diary*, pp. 240, 260).

in the piece. She will not only mold the narrative but also project her own character into the drama, with a prologue that she will "style" from her own adventure (184–5). Immediately we realize that little objectivity can be gained this way. For she can only delude herself that she will be able to transcend the limitations of her own personality. In effect, the Balaustion of the poem is really two characters—her present self and her re-creation of her past self. As her present self she is subject to the same vacillation between hope and despair as other people and shares with them all the earthly desires that characterize the human condition (1–3, 39–46). In her re-created self, on the other hand, she is depicted only as one who constantly stands as the representative of hope and idealistic thought, the advocate of soul who recoils from "fleshly durance dim and low" (42). It is this imagined self that can declare upon first hearing of Euripides' death: "Thank Zeus for the great news and good!" It is the present real self, however, that suffers intensely the loss of a beloved poet who had become her friend: "No Euripides / Will teach the chorus, nor shall we be tinged / By any such grand sunset of his soul" (214–16)! What we have in her monologue, therefore, is two narrative perspectives: the Balaustion who talks to her husband and the Balaustion who tells Euthukles, in an unfinished sentence: "I somehow speak to unseen auditors. / Not *you*, but—" (242–3). Or, to put it another way, what we find in her narrative is a disjunction between her present and past voices.

Like nearly all of Browning's monologists, Balaustion speaks out of a compelling need of personality. She says plainly that she speaks only to escape "not sorrow but despair, / Not memory but the present and its pang" (2–3). Yet we wonder whether there might not be an additional reason: a need, so often felt by other characters in Browning, for self-justification. As earlier remarked, she presents herself in her story as wholly the advocate of idealistic thought, ever shunning "body" in favor of "soul." And in her representation of herself she strikes us as too soulful and, possibly, too self-righteous. We detect at least a hint of truth in Aristophanes' characterization of those like Balaustion who dream of themselves as the "sole selected few / Fume-fed with self-superiority" (2681–2). In fact, we are led to wonder just how much of "body" she suppresses.

Balaustion's prudery is readily discernible. What distresses her as much as the fall of Athens is the licentiousness which she believes caused and accompanied it (95–102), and what troubles her most about Aristophanes is not his satire but his frank celebration of man's animal nature. Perceiving her extreme repugnance to talk of sexual matters, the comic poet gently mocks at this element in her character (2020–24) and suggests that she is but the "merest female child," whom he will try not to offend (773–7). The Athenians chide her for her refusal to attend Aristophanes' comedies and wonder that she is "wife and ignorant so long" (415). She prizes Euripides' *Hippolytus* mainly because its presentation of Phaidra is of "the chaste" one who died distraught rather than "loose one limb / Love-wards, at lambency of honeyed tongue, / Or torture of the scales which scraped her snow" (420–26). In brief, there is in her nature some deep loathing of the physical.

Browning allows us to catch sight of this aspect of her in order to suggest a certain deficiency in her makeup. He would have us see that his monologist seeks to obviate a very basic part of human nature and, further, that she herself half understands that her denial of the body is not totally praiseworthy. Her monologue is, therefore, in part an effort to convince herself of the rightness of her ideals and of the idealism that she believed Euripides taught and that she fain would live by. While Euripides was alive and Athens stood, she needed no reassurance. But now unable to support her belief in the reality of the ideal because of the present loss of the great ideals in her life—namely, of Euripides and Athens, whose demise and downfall she equates and collapses into one moment in time—she is "wanting strength," for in her present position she feels the need for her customary props. Originally, as we learn in *Balaustion's Adventure,* her attachment to Euripides was wholly altruistic. But now, in *Aristophanes' Apology,* it is more personal, more necessary for self-sustainment.

Through Euripides she won her husband, her home, her friends; through him she achieved all that Athens symbolized for her. Thus a loss of her beloved dramatist is a deeply personal loss, and any threat to Euripides and his ideals as she understood them is a threat to herself. Therefore she speaks not to Euthukles but to "unseen auditors," and seeks to combat Aristophanes, whose diatribes against Euripides she conceives as assaults upon herself and her ideals. In the Conclusion to the poem she makes explicit her identification of herself, her husband, her home, and Euripides: "Saved was Athenai through Euripides, / Through Euthukles, through—more than ever—me, / Balaustion, me who, Wild-pomegranate-flower, / Felt my fruit triumph, and fade proudly so" (522–5). Her utterance is, then, limited by her strategic purpose, which is a justification of her own philosophy and ultimately of herself.

If Balaustion's constant plea is for "disembodied soul" flying "distinct above / Man's wickedness and folly" (39–46), it is because she espouses only one aspect of man's nature, the transcendental, and denigrates the other. She stands, in other words, for one pole of a dialectic and as such represents but a limited truth. The other pole, the descendental, is figured in Aristophanes, who defends "body" as vehemently as Balaustion advocates "soul."

Aristophanes, though more interesting a character than Balaustion, is just as doctrinaire as she. Like her, he insists there is but one way to understand life, although, as we shall later see, his "apology" is more limited in its vision than the man himself is. Euripides is regarded as an opponent by Aristophanes, not because he dislikes the tragic dramatist but because Euripides taught that there is no single way in which to apprehend truth. Euripides questioned everything, to the point that he left "no longer one plain positive / Enunciation incontestable / Of what is good, right, decent here on earth" (2221–3).

As in Balaustion's viewpoint there is a disjunction between past and present, so in Aristophanes' there is a fear that the values of the past cannot be crystallized; somewhat like Balaustion, he despairs that change means the end of his most cherished values.

No Rhodian but a native Athenian, he loved a small, self-contained Athens whose citizens believed themselves "undoubted lords of earth." Athens was enough; the present was all-sufficient. Why then should a man wish to consider anything above or beyond this happy moment in time when all was easy and beautiful? Euripides and his friends, however, have quite perversely changed all this (1971-2019), introducing "restless change, / Deterioration" (2024-5). If, as Euripides claimed, "There are no gods," then "man has no master, owns, by consequence, / No right, no wrong, except to please or plague / His nature" (2140-43). That is why in his plays Aristophanes' whole aim has been to flog with the club of comedy those fellows who would change the customs of Athens (1850-54). As for his own teaching, he has insisted upon respect for kings and gods (2480-85) and has urged the populace to "accept the old, / Contest the strange" (2649-50).

Using the same arguments (and frequently the same words) as Prince Hohenstiel-Schwangau, Aristophanes claims that his object has been "sustainment of humanity" (1887). To be sure, he admits, the doctrines of Euripides and his coterie are not totally without validity. But they are not such as will nourish the populace. They preach "purity" (1882), asking men to "unworld the world" (1952). Indeed, the whole thrust of "modernism" has been to exalt spirit at the expense of sense. And what can a common lout know of spirit? No, Euripides has offered ethereal vapors to men who want and need rich red wine. Hence his plays are factitious because they render a vision of a world "where what's false is fact," where ugliness is transformed into beauty, where life itself is disguised as immortality. "No, this were unreality" (2157-60, 2166).

Aristophanes, on the other hand, knows that "men are, were, ever will be fools" (1649): "I paint men as they are" (2199). His plays consequently have been an antidote to the "poison-drama of Euripides" because they recall "our commonalty" to "primaeval virtue, antique faith," which flourished before these so-called days of enlightenment (1061-6). And "once true man in right place, / Our commonalty soon content themselves / With doing just what they are born to do, / Eat, drink, make merry, mind their own affairs / And leave state-business to the larger brain" (2449–53).

Throughout his conversation with Balaustion we see that he is not so much berating Euripides as attempting to justify himself. If his plays have been vulgar, it is because men are vulgar and incapable of understanding refinement. If they expound the virtues of the status quo, it is because the populace is resistant to change. Man, as Aristophanes sees him, is basically an animal, a creature of sense: "Eat and drink, / And drink and eat, what else is good in life?" (1089–90). To try to show him as something else is to elevate him to a station he cannot comprehend and certainly cannot sustain.

Aristophanes personally can conceive of a new kind of comedy, but one lifetime is not sufficient to "penetrate encrusted prejudice, / Pierce ignorance three generations thick" (843–4). In fact, he did once attempt a comedy in good taste, containing absolutely nothing base, but it did not win acceptance. So he has kept to the old ways: "Purity? / No more of that next month, Athenai mine / Contrive new cut of robe who will—I patch . . ." (1140–42). A time will doubtless come when a new kind of comedy is possible—"when laws allow" and "had I but two lives"—but as things stand he must simply carry on in a vein started by other men, which means that he will spend his life planing the knobs and adding shining studs to the club of comedy (837–50). Besides, a new art demands of the artist seclusion and loneliness: "No such thin fare feeds flesh and blood like mine" (934). In the end, therefore, Aristophanes places himself squarely at the pole of sense opposite the pole of spirit occupied by Balaustion.

Neither Balaustion nor Aristophanes is fully at ease with the extreme position taken. Browning would have us see that, in the words of his Rabbi Ben Ezra, "All good things / Are ours, nor soul helps flesh more, now, than flesh helps soul!" Body and soul need each other. That is why Aristophanes seeks out Balaustion (see lines 763–72, 1521–9), and why she recalls, a year later, his visit to her. In the midst of despair body and soul meet to find comfort. The whole discussion of the differences between comedy and tragedy is evidence of their awareness of incompleteness. Aristophanes says that comedy, dwelling on all the ugliness and absurdity of life, suggests by contrast the perfection man might attain (1762 ff.); and he also admits, though fleetingly, that tragedy presents a vision of truth which might be grasped. Both comedy and tragedy have the same end in view, even if they approach it by different means. Therefore, "both be praised" (1465). He and Euripides do not differ in their aims, only in their methods (2550–67). The comic poet and the tragic poet both serve "complex Poetry," which operates "for body as for soul." The man who dares disjoin these, by ignoring either body or soul, "maims the else perfect manhood" (1471–80). As for Aristophanes himself, he will defend, at least at this moment, "man's double nature" (1494).

Prior to his nocturnal visit, Balaustion had deemed Aristophanes among the basest of humanity, the great enemy and defamer of her "soulful" Euripides. She is surprised to find him both "impudent and majestic" (617), "like some meteor-brilliance, fire and filth, / Or say, his own Amphitheos, deity / And dung" (226–8):

> What I had disbelieved most, proved most true.
> There was a mind here, mind a-wantoning
> At ease of undisputed mastery
> Over the body's brood, those appetites.   [620–23]

At this moment of confrontation each stands stripped of disguises and attitudes. "You see myself?" asks Aristophanes.

> "Balaustion's fixed regard
> Can strip the proper Aristophanes
> Of what our sophists, in their jargon, style
> His accidents? My soul sped forth but now
> To meet your hostile survey,—soul unseen,
> Yet veritably cinct for soul-defence
> With satyr sportive quips, cranks, boss and spike,
> Just as my visible body paced the street,

Environed by a boon companionship
Your apparition also puts to flight.
Well, what care I if, unaccoutred twice,
I front my foe—no comicality
Round soul, and body-guard in banishment?
Thank your eyes' searching, undisguised I stand." [763–76]

As for Balaustion, she appears as but the "merest female child" (804): "I who, a woman, claim no quality" (2739). Bare of externals, each can recognize the worth of the other. Yet the longer they talk, the more they resume their customary attitudes. Aware of the need that body has for soul and flesh for spirit, they nevertheless retreat to their opposite poles, because apparently each can orient himself by only one position. Their dialogue ends up as two monologues, an expostulation and a reply. What is needed is some way to join the two in more nearly perfect counterpoint. And this is precisely the purpose of the *Herakles*. For Euripides himself is not the antagonist that Aristophanes fancied him, nor is he quite the disembodied spirit whom Balaustion pictured. He is, in this poem at any rate, the one who, speaking to both soul and sense, creates the kind of drama reflective of a true understanding of human nature.

Euripides recognized that Athens was in a period of transition —from a mythifying past to a more secular future—and it was his task to help ease the pangs of this change. From the beginning he "shrank not to teach, / If gods be strong and wicked, man, though weak, / May prove their match by willing to be good" (428–30). Then in his *Elektra* he first "dared bring the grandeur of the Tragic Two / Down to the level of our common life, / Close to the beating of our common heart" (Concl., 481–3). He showed that the old gods are dead but that a new kind of responsibility had been placed on men: mankind has to rely upon itself. Instead of the old gods there is "Necessity," which signifies "Duty enjoined you, fact in figment's place, / Throned on no mountain, native to the mind" (2147–9).

During this trying period in history art too must undergo change. The old categories of tragedy and comedy are not adequate to the new age. Euripides envisioned a new type of drama in which comedy and tragedy meet, one which "fain would paint, manlike, actual human life, / Make veritable men think, say and do" (1312–13). He himself had attempted such a new mode but had not perfected it, this task awaiting "the novel man / Born to that next success myself forsee" (1321–2). "Never needs the Art stand still," he told Aristophanes (1304). An artist must always be remolding the old; otherwise, art becomes stale and retrogressive (1321 ff).

The *Herakles,* his last work presented to Athens, embodies all these ideas. In the *Alkestis,* which played such a vital role in Balaustion's first adventure, Herakles was represented as an heroic redeemer. In this play, which forms part of Balaustion's last adventure, Herakles is stripped of his heroic and godlike nature to stand revealed as a fully human being. The whole point of the drama is to humanize Herakles so that he shares common ground with all other men, who are subject to necessity and do not have the heroic stature which hitherto has exempted Herakles from subjugation to necessity. For the first time he comes to know that compensatory virtue—love, *philia*—which makes necessity bearable and life endurable. The play shows that man, finding himself in tragic circumstances, can redeem himself by love. Indeed, the drama demonstrates that modern man is beyond tragedy and even provides him with a new mythology: a change from outmoded heroic strength to very human fortitude, courage, and endurance. This is the point Herakles iterates in his final lines: "Whoso rather would have wealth and strength / Than good friends, reasons foolishly therein!"

The drama stands in striking contrast to the views of both Aristophanes and Balaustion. The gods are dethroned, a hero is stripped of his power, the gentle virtue of love is trumphant— everything that Aristophanes professes to despise is to be found in it. As for Balaustion, this is not the "cheerful weary Herakles / Striding away from the huge gratitude, . . . / Bound on the next new labor 'height o'er height / Ever surmounting,—destiny's decree' " (511–15), the Herakles whom she would follow. The play shows that Balaustion's belief in the essential spiritual nature of man is a distortion of man's true nature. The *Herakles* demonstrates that in the best of men are seeds of animalistic behavior, that to be human is also to be weak. Euripides here insists that the human condition is a dialectic between strength and weakness, hope and despair, good and evil. As Theseus says, "None of mortals boasts a fate unmixed" (1414).

At the end of the reading of the play Aristophanes penetrates to the perception that he and his plays have been defective to the extent that they have misrepresented the human condition. "Much may be said for stripping wisdom bare" (Concl., 16), he says, referring doubtlessly to his encounter with Balaustion as well as to the reading of the play. "The ripe man ought to be as old as young— / As young as old. I too have youth at need" (Concl., 14–15). He should have been less resistant to change, more willing to experiment with his art. Yet the insight is fleeting, for almost immediately he claims, illustrating by the game of kottabos, that Eurpides was fixed to see only the lofty and good, while he, Aristophanes, glimpses successively the low and wrong as well as the high and right. "Man's made of both," he says (Concl., 54), forgetting, of course, that the second part of the dialectic he has almost completely suppressed. Nevertheless, he is now willing to admit the dual nature of man, which previously he had tended to deny, and within his heart he knows that he has failed where Euripides has more nearly succeeded:

> There's no failure breaks the heart,
> Whate'er be man's endeavor in this world,
> Like the rash poet's when he—nowise fails
> By poetizing badly,—Zeus or makes
> Or mars a man, so—at it, merrily!
> But when,—made man,—much like myself,—equipt
> For such and such achievement,—rash he turns
> Out of the straight path, bent on snatch of feat
> From—who's the appointed fellow born thereto,—
> Crows take him!—in your Kassiterides?
> Half-doing his work, leaving mine untouched,
> That were the failure. [Concl., 67–78]

In the figure of Aristophanes, Browning again turns to one of his favorite speculations, a question he had pondered in considering Hohenstiel-Schwangau, Don Juan, and Miranda—namely, why men fail to live up to their best capacities and potentialities. The answer suggested here is similar to that formerly offered: men fail when they do not admit the dual thrusts of their natures and recognize only one pole of the dialectic tension.

With Balaustion it is not so much a case of success or failure. As she herself says, she can "claim no quality" (2739), lacking the creative quality of the artist. From the *Herakles,* however, she learns that the body has as much claim to consideration as the soul. Aristophanes has his genius and deserves recognition. No longer is it a question of "the antagonist Euripides," who contended with the comic dramatist (3464), but rather of "Euripides and Aristophanes," each of whom sows a seed and "seed bears crop, scarce within our little lives" (Concl., 280–82). Her reconciliation with Aristophanes is, nevertheless, only momentary. She ends her story by condemning the licentiousness of Aristophanes' next play, *The Frogs,* and ascribing the fall of Athens to the deleterious effects of comedy. At the end Euripides and Aristophanes remain for her poles apart. As she nears Rhodes, her vision remains a transcendental one: the wind and waves sing out that Euripides lives. Yet the poem does not end as it began, for language has relieved the despair she had experienced at the beginning. The "middle course," of which she spoke in the beginning, has had the desired effect, having allowed her to rise above despair to greet the morn of her new life in Rhodes with hope: "Life detests black cold" (Concl., 601).

It should be readily apparent that in once again writing about fifth-century Athens Browning was also dealing once more with the analogous cultural situation of the nineteenth century. At a time when an established civilization was waning the poet offered, to those who would make the application, a message of hope. Though the old gods might be dead or dying, there was no reason to despair. Though customs may change, chaos is not the only alternative. Though the conventional literary categories might no longer prove adequate, new ones would arise. All this is summed up in the final lines, when Balaustion joyfully sings: "There are no gods, no gods! / Glory to God—who saves Euripides!"

The poem also has a personal application. In dealing with the unsympathetic critics of Euripides, Browning was attacking those reviewers who did not comprehend what he was attempting to do.[6] And in the long consideration of a new type of drama that would combine the best qualities of comedy and tragedy he was partially explaining and defending his own experiments in mode and form.

With *Aristophanes' Apology,* Browning stretched the dramatic monologue almost to its breaking point. The poem makes a tremendous demand on the reader, requiring him to bear in mind two long monologues and a complete play—5,711 lines in all— and to remember that they are set within the confines of one dramatic monologue. It is no wonder that most contemporary reviewers could make neither heads nor tails out of it or that to most readers even today it remains hopelessly confusing.

Browning was attempting exactly what Balaustion (3435–45), Euripides (1302–5), and Aristophanes (1468–94) speculate on in their discussions of a new type of drama and what he himself had posited as a possibility in the *Essay on Shelley,* where he considered how the "objective" and "subjective" might be combined to produce a "perfect shield [of] . . . gold and . . . silver" (xii. 285). He was aiming at what Aristophanes speaks of in the Conclusion, when he alludes to the future poet who, "by mechanics past my guess," will take in both high and low, right and wrong, and, by implication, man's transcendental and descendental impulses, "every side at once, / And not successively" (57–9). Here Browning has essayed to give an overview of man and life in general, not sequentially but simultaneously. It was a bold experiment, with the exception of *The Ring and the Book* perhaps the most daring that he ever made with the dramatic mono-

6. For an interesting account of the quarrel Browning carried on with his critics in the poem, see Donald Smalley, "A Parleying with Aristophanes," *PMLA,* 55 (1940), 823–38.

logue. That he could go no farther is indicated by the fact that he never returned to it again as the mode for a long poem.

It is easier to admire *Aristophanes' Apology* than to like it. The demands it makes on the reader's knowledge are enormous,[7] and its gigantic, complex structure requires keeping in mind a vast amount of incident and constantly recalling to oneself that it is the narrative of one person. No wonder Carlyle was led to say that, though he liked it much, he wondered why Browning "could not tell it all in a plain straightforward statement."[8] The impression one has of the work is that it is a mélange of huge bits and pieces. The diction, furthermore, is tiresome, especially in the use of a great number of compound epithets that attempt to approximate Greek.[9] Even the admirable depiction of the characters of Balaustion and Aristophanes is not sufficient to redeem the poem from a charge of tediousness. Most readers will doubtless agree with Park Honan's witty remark (slightly revised) that the *Apology* resembles "a masque staged by two muttering Greek professors in the airless corridor of a large library."[10]

The one portion of the *Apology* that stands out as a masterpiece is the lyric "Thamuris Marching," sung by Aristophanes in the Conclusion (104–80). It is a triumphal march in which the poet encounters earth's beauties and imposes himself on them, thereby conferring on them heightened beauty and meaning. Nowhere else in Browning's later work is the poetic imagination

---

7. Browning's friend Alfred Domett remarked to the poet upon the large demands that the poem makes of its readers and said he believed "no one even classical scholars, unless they were in the daily habit of reading Aristophanes . . . would be able to understand all the numerous allusions in it without referring over and over again to his Comedies; and that Browning thus wilfully restricted the number of his readers to comparatively few. He would not hear of 'explanatory notes'. . . . Browning said it could not be helped, but he was not likely to try anything of the sort again" (Domett, *Diary*, pp. 149–50).

8. Quoted by Domett in *Diary*, p. 161.

9. The following passage is a fair sample:

> Orchard-grafted tree,
> Not wilding, race-horse-sired, not rouncey-born,
> Aristocrat, no sausage-selling snob! [2440–42]

10. Irvine and Honan, *The Book, the Ring, & the Poet*, p. 475.

so highly exalted (although Aristophanes in singing it wishes to
suggest that Euripides' aspiration as a poet was, like Thamuris's,
presumptuous) :[11]

> Was there a ravaged tree? it laughed compact
> With gold, a leaf-ball crisp, high-brandished now,
> Tempting to onset frost which late attacked.
>
> Was there a wizened shrub, a starveling bough,
> A fleecy thistle filched from by the wind,
> A weed, Pan's trampling hoof would disallow?
>
> Each, with a glory and a rapture twined
> About it, joined the rush of air and light
> And force: the world was of one joyous mind. . . .
>
> Such earth's community of purpose, such
> The ease of earth's fulfilled imaginings,—
>
> So did the near and far appear to touch
> In the moment's transport . . .   [131–47]

The lyric is in Browning's bravura style,[12] musical in spite of an
occasional harshness, sound supporting sense and sense heighten-
ing sound. In effect, the poem shows us music, raising it to song,
in which form and content are one:

> It reached him, music; but his own outburst
> Of victory concluded the account,
> And that grew song which was mere music erst.   [173–5]

11. George M. Ridenour, "Browning's Music Poems: Fancy and Fact,"
PMLA, 78 (1963), 369–77, studies "Thamuris Marching" in relation to
the other music poems of Browning's later career.
12. For a treatment of Browning's bravura style see Park Honan, "The
Iron String in the Victorian Lyre: Browning's Lyric Versification,"
Browning's Mind and Art, ed. Clarence Tracy (Edinburgh and London:
Oliver and Boyd, 1968), pp. 82–99.

6 § The Inn Album

With *The Inn Album*, published in November 1875, only six months after the appearance of *Aristophanes' Apology*, Browning takes up a recent historical moment and turns it into a narrative, as he had in *Red Cotton Night-Cap Country*. The story, based on a scandal of the mid-thirties, is told here, however, by an omniscient narrator who is not involved in the narrative itself. Various critics have classified the poem as a kind of drama or as a novel in verse.[1] While Browning uses some techniques of drama and prose fiction, the form is, nevertheless, unique. It may best be characterized as a dramatic poem composed of a series of monologues joined by narrative passages.

The poem demands of the reader an effort similar to that required by the dramatic monologue—namely, to come to terms with the characters by a sympathetic understanding of them. Here the suspension of judgment is more difficult than is needed to read one dramatic monologue. In *The Inn Album* the monologues are continually interrupted by either the narrator or other actors in the story, preventing us from ever penetrating to a

1. Swinburne called it Browning's "new sensation novel" (quoted in DeVane, *Handbook*, p. 390). DeVane himself thought of it as a kind of drama, citing Browning's friend Domett to the effect that the poet "had intended originally to write a tragedy upon the subject, but hearing Tennyson was engaged upon one (*Queen Mary*) gave up the idea" (p. 385). John Meigs Hitner, in his *Browning's Analysis of a Murder: A Case for THE INN ALBUM* (Marquette: Northern Michigan University Press, 1969), labels the poem "a curious . . . hybrid cross between the novel and drama" (p. ix). Philip Drew sees it as a morality play, like *Comus* (*The Poetry of Browning*, p. 355).

character's individual viewpoint long enough to allow him to compel assent to his own moral perspective. The perspective is constantly altered so that an individual point of view is established not within it own confines, but exists within the broader confines of the entire poem. The problem, then, is how to arrive at something approaching the truth of the situation presented.

The narrator himself is not of much help. Indeed, his very presence and purpose are to discourage us from making spot judgments. His stance is most nearly that of one who raises the curtain and, at the end, says, "Let the curtain fall," in the manner of the narrator of *Vanity Fair*. Yet his characters are not puppets like those of Thackeray's narrator. Though he is detached from them, he is, at the same time, sympathetic to them, not unlike one of George Eliot's narrators. He is in the work not so much to guide the reader as to divert him—which is to say, his manner of coming between us and the characters forces us to postpone judgment; or, to put it another way, he exists to destroy the dramatic illusion of his art and so keep us from identifying with one of the characters at the expense of understanding them all. *The Inn Album* is not a work in which some characters are right and others are wrong, although most readers apparently understand the poem in precisely this way. The characters are not unnamed in order to represent various aspects of good and evil in the manner of a morality play, but each, on the contrary, is a different type of Everyman, possessing within himself both good and bad. The poem allows us to witness, mainly in the young man, who may properly be seen as the chief character, a growth in human understanding. Its point is not that there is "truth" in any one character but that there are truths in them all, even in the blackguard betrayer, and that from interaction of one with the others a kind of general truth may arise.

Because the poem is about self-discovery, it is structured on a series of recognition scenes, each of the eight parts beginning or ending with a new situation or perception. The story is fraught with coincidence, to an extent unacceptable even in second-rate melodrama. But the reader accepts this because the interest lies in character rather than situation. As in a piece of detective fiction, suspense keeps the story moving, serving the same function as the intrusions of the narrator—to remind the reader that his putative judgments are based on partial information. Moreover, suspense serves to suggest the manner in which we acquire knowledge of ourselves, of others, and of human nature in general—not by a sudden flash of total illumination but in a fragmentary, surprising way. Browning here, more than in the earlier dramatic monologues, would have us see that we know ourselves not in isolation but in relation.

The basic theme of the poem is again the discrepancy between appearance and reality. To the reader as well as to the actors in the piece, *The Inn Album* shows that things are most often not what they seem. This theme results in a number of highly ironic situations, the main one being that the appointed teachers are the least competent to teach. The action of the poem, consequently, centers on the human ontological burden.

Both the young man and the girl, fearing their own inexperience and inability to judge, seek help in making their evaluations. For the girl it is merely a question of whether or not to marry the young man. Feeling herself incompetent to decide, she asks the help of an older friend whom she believes to be happily married and to "hold / Inside [herself] secrets written" (III. 207–8). The woman's authority is confirmed for the girl by her beauty: "Such beauty does prove something, everything" (III. 230). In other words, the appearance warrants authenticity.

The young man has placed himself in the hands of an older man, a nobleman, to be molded by the elder as he pleases. Disappointed in love, the youth had retreated to Dalmatia, where he lived secluded to devote himself to useful knowledge and, being rich, to follow Ruskin's philanthropic example. From his retreat he was rescued by the nobleman, whom the young man finds "the best head going," although possessing an unsavory reputation. Others may value Gladstone, Carlyle, Tennyson; he himself will place his faith in the nobleman (II. 35–7). Now, "after one year's tutelage" (I. 331), he has become a cynical man of the world "all through" his mentor (I. 271-4), even to the extent of allowing himself to be persuaded into a loveless marriage with his cousin. As yet, however, he is not thoroughly depraved, the narrator calling him "the good strong fellow, rough perhaps" (I. 110). He is not entirely at ease in the worldly role assumed under the guidance of his tutor—"I do nothing but receive and spend" (I. 441)—and from the beginning we suspect that he will seek to escape his dependency on the lord. Throughout the rest of the poem we see him struggling to cast off his bonds and to rely more fully on himself.

He is first led to ask of his mentor, "You, who teach me, why not have learned, yourself?" (II. 68). Why is the lord not a rich or great or happy man? Then he commences to wonder how he came to like the man so much whom he "ought not court at all" (II. 404-5). Surely there are others "able and willing to teach all you know" (II. 410). Little by little, as he questions his reliance on the older man, he comes to wonder "who is who and what / Is what" (V. 17-18), knowledge that he gains only "by strange chance" (V. 99). Finally—through the circumstances surrounding the appearance on the scene of the lady he loved and of his learning about the lady's former alliance with the lord—his previously held illusions about the lord, and about the lady as well, crumble; and he must act on his new perceptions because "there's no unknowing what one knows" (V. 288). Henceforth he will trust intuition and right feeling. He will not need to be told how to act and how to feel. Whereas formerly he was emotionally dependent, first on the lady and then on the lord—"made him my love" (VII. 175)—he will now rely on himself, not caring "what I am, what I am not, in the eye / Of the world" (VII. 142-3). Having come to a better understanding of himself, he will renounce the loveless marriage proposed to his cousin.

Where the girl and the youth profess innocence and ignorance, the lord and lady claim experience and knowledge. He is the master ever in need of a pupil: "The polisher needs precious stone no less / Than precious stone needs polisher" (I. 405-6). No mere debaucher of youth, he relishes the molding of personality, teaching his pupils that life is tolerable only so long as it is not taken seriously. The only real mistake, he insinuates, is to form attachments, not to see life as a game. His main misfortune, he says, was in allowing his heart to become involved in a love affair, and then being rejected. In the young man he finds an apt pupil until the cousin's friend arrives, when all his teaching is exposed as cynical and, ultimately, false. Wisdom cannot be acquired, as he maintains, simply by following directions to "strip the tree / Of fruit desirable to make one wise" (vi. 196–7).

The lady, while appearing more reluctant to instruct (iii. 189–98), also is given to the magisterial role. To meet her aged husband's requirements she had sufficient knowledge, and through her work in his parish she gained the additional knowledge of the baseness and brutality of human kind that permits her special insights into character. Having arrived at the inn to advise the girl, she takes on the instruction of the youth, telling him to renounce his old mentor as "hero-sham" and to marry the girl. This is the "lesson I was sent,—if man discerned / Ever God's message,— just to teach" (v. 139–40).

In the last three parts of the poem she debates with the lord the meaning of ignorance and its deleterious effects, but can come to no fixed conclusion. "Ignorance is not innocence but sin" (v. 191)', she claims, but she would not wish to disturb the innocence of either the girl or her husband with knowledge of her past, even though her husband's innocence is wrong, "ignorance / Being, I hold, sin ever, small or great" (v. 221–2). Furthermore, she would wish that the youth had not known of her previous involvement with the nobleman: "Better would white ignorance / Beseem your brow" (vii. 8–9). As for herself, experience, bitter though it has been, has given her certain insights which she should have shared with others earlier. She should, in other words, have become a teacher sooner, assumed her "proper function" and so "sustained a soul," instead of "being just sustained" by someone else (vii. 56–8).

The action of the poem makes it plain that no soul can "sustain" (in the sense of teach) another. Even the best of those persons who would become instructors are too bounded by their own personalities to see sufficiently clearly for the edification of someone else. The lady, for instance, declares the youth worthy of marriage with his cousin, yet her judgment, as she herself learns, is obviously wrong. Moreover, even those persons who claim knowledge as the result of experience frequently misinterpret their own experience. The lady is a case in point.

She feels the action she has taken perfectly justified. A believer in absolutes, she did not accept the chance for love when it was offered. Originally, the lord was attracted to her beauty and, like Don Juan, would enter that beauty in his catalogue of conquests; in short, he trifled with her. Yet, when he learned that she was as beautiful in soul as in body, he confessed his previous dishonorable intentions, asked her forgiveness, and offered himself to her in marriage. For once he acted decently and responsibly toward someone else. But the young lady had her own strict ideas of right and wrong. Having believed him true and then having discovered the falseness in his nature, she could not recognize his human cry for love and help. He asked for redemption, but she turned a deaf ear. He had been false, she had been sullied, her life was over, only the grave remained.

Thus having once failed in love, she said farewell to all thoughts of love and beauty. She would wait to have them in heaven while on earth she buried herself in ugliness and, if not hate, indifference: "Better have failed in the high aim, as I, / Than vulgarly in the low aim succeed / As, God be thanked, I do not!" (IV. 449–51). She therefore gave herself, like Dorothea Brooke, to an old man whom she didn't love and whom she married out of a mistaken sense of duty. He was "cold and old" and wanted a helpmate: "No coarsest sample of the proper sex / But would have served his purpose equally / With God's own angel" (IV. 263, 271–3). For four years she buried herself with brutish people in an ugly village doing work for which she admittedly has no vocation. Her life has been a living death.

Having once discovered falseness in human existence, she has turned her thoughts from earth to heaven. Everything she sees seems to call her to leave sordid earth for the purity of the sky. The elm glimpsed through the window of the inn seems to say, *"Leave earth, there's nothing better till next step / Heavenward!"* (III. 68–9). Though beautiful, she could easily exchange her loveliness for the strength to find repose in death (III. 90–95). The lady is, in brief, "world-weary" and desires only sleep (IV. 365–8). Her sole animating emotion remains the hatred of her former lover, who deluded her by his "seeming" (v. 108).

One of the basic metaphors of the poem is that of the Garden of Eden. No one employs it more frequently than the lady. She thinks of herself as Eve whose paradise is lost (v. 156–60). The nobleman is the "tempter" (IV. 225), the "Adversary" (IV. 669), a "reptile" (v. 153), who for her is both "hell" and "Death" (IV. 30, 34). Commentators on the poem have understood her rhetoric to reflect the fundamental truth of the situation. It is necessary to recall, however, that the rhetoric is her own and not the narrator's and that her utterances are no more reliable than anyone else's. The narrator tells us explicitly in reference to her characterization of the lord as a serpent that "he neither gasps nor hisses" (IV. 40). To be sure, when he later turns malignant, the narrator does call him the Adversary (VI. 2), but this occurs when he is beyond redemption. It may well be that he is changed into Satan by the unforgiving nature of the lady.

It is worthwhile to note that the lord also refers to the myth of the Garden. He considers the lady his evil genius, relentlessly pursuing him (IV. 41–63), a "woman-fiend" who finds in their meeting her triumph, his despair (IV. 70), a lamia who has haunted and enchanted him (IV. 72–83, 111–19). He thinks of her in this way for the same reason that she thus characterizes him. Their relationship was the one glimpse of perfection that each attained: their love could have been Paradise; having lost it, each loathes the instrument responsible. For once in his life the lord was willing to affirm the value of something independent of self, being in fact willing to give himself to another; and when he was rejected he found himself defenseless in failure, "so, hate alike / Failure and who caused failure" (II. 138–9). Here was what he needed to save himself from his own baseness, but he did not at first recognize his salvation, "mistaking man's main prize / For intermediate boy's diversion" (II. 320–21). Too late he laid bare his soul, and ever since he has been convinced that this was "life's prize grasped at, gained, and then let go" (II. 349); a great sense of failure has haunted him constantly thereafter. So he has hated her to keep from hating himself: "Or her or else / Malicious Providence I have to hate" (II. 303–4). Formerly, he was certainly a poor creature but since his failure in love he has become a knave—all through this woman who has made damned both soul and body.

In light of his actions in the concluding parts of the poem, it is not entirely clear what we should make of his protestations to the lady, in Part IV, after the initial mutual recriminations. No doubt Satan can speak with honeyed tongue, yet his cries for help have the ring of sincerity. For he asks her to forgive:

> "God forgives:
> Forgive you, delegate of God, brought near
> As never priests could bring him to this soul
> That prays you both—forgive me! I abase—
> Know myself mad and monstrous utterly
> In all I did that moment; but as God
> Gives me this knowledge—heart to feel and tongue
> To testify—so be you gracious too!
> Judge no man by the solitary work
> Of—well, they do say and I can believe—
> The devil in him: his, the moment,—mine
> The life—your life!"   [IV. 525–36]

Then he begs her to bend down and accept the low, not remain aloof from the pleas of those less loftily placed. "Accept, redeem me!" he cries (IV. 556). "Call me yours—/Yours and the world's —yours and the world's and God's!" (IV. 608–10). Throughout, the lady "looks the large deliberate look" and at the end laughs scornfully in rejecting his plea.

It would, of course, be wrong in the eyes of the world for her to leave her husband and run away with her former lover. Yet with her husband she is mismatched and miserable. We are meant to understand not that she should elope with the nobleman but that her passivity in this event is characteristic of her entire life and makes both salvation and damnation impossible for her, a position Browning holds throughout his poetry, most notably perhaps in "The Statue and the Bust." Moreover, the lord's charge to the lady resounds with echoes of other Browning poems in which soul is asked to blend with soul:

> Why did your nobleness look up to me,
> Not down on the ignoble thing confessed?
> Was it your part to stoop, or lift the low?
> Wherefore did God exalt you? Who would teach
> The brute man's tameness and intelligence
> Must never drop the dominating eye:
> Wink—and what wonder if the mad fit break,
> Followed by stripes and fasting? Sound and sane,
> My life, chastised now, couches at your foot.
> Accept, redeem me!   [IV. 547–56]

The point to be made here is that we cannot judge the lord out of context—out of the context of the specific poem or out of that of Browning's previous work. It is important to keep an open ear and mind to catch the note of truth that the nobleman, who admittedly later becomes a villain, might utter.[2] The essential point is

2. The character of the lord may have been partly modeled on a character in Trollope's *Framley Parsonage,* which Browning greatly admired (see *Letters of the Brownings to George Barrett,* ed. Paul Landis and Ronald E. Freeman [Urbana: University of Illinois Press, 1958], pp. 247–8, and *Dearest Isa,* pp. 76–8). Indeed, the relationship between the lord and the youth is reminiscent of one in Trollope's novel. Nathaniel Sowerby, a man of fifty, is cast in the role of tempter and seducer of Mark Robarts, a young clergyman in his twenties, who is led into serious financial difficulties as a result of his friendship with Mr. Sowerby. In spite of Sowerby's evil ways, however, the narrator of *Framley Parsonage* retains a certain sympathy for the older man, much in the same fashion, I think, as the narrator of *The Inn Album* for the lord. In the penultimate chapter of the novel the narrator says:

Unfortunate Mr. Sowerby! I cannot take leave of him here without some feeling of regret, knowing that there was that within him which might, under better guidance, have produced better things. There are men, even of high birth, who seem as though they were born to be rogues; but Mr. Sowerby was, to my thinking, born to be a gentleman. That he had not been a gentle-

that both the lady and her lover, like Balaustion and Aristophanes in the poem immediately preceding this one, have aspects of truth and falsity in their speech and in their characters. The loss of their Eden may be the fault of both.

The attitude of each is that man is base and vile. She strongly indicates her contempt for mankind in her description of her life as a clergyman's wife, speaking of the parish as full of beasts (IV. 324–412). The nobleman is a knave as a result of seeing men as depraved hypocrites (VII. 230–39). This is the bitter knowledge that each fancies to have learned from experience. It is why, basically, she yearns for death and at the close of the poem kills herself. It is why at the beginning he is cynical and at the end villainous. She dies to escape earthly depravity; he lives, until killed by the youth, to act in concord with it. Their view of life means isolation from their fellow men and ultimately their death. The Tree of Knowledge is, indeed, for each the Tree of Death.

The characters in *The Inn Album* know their Milton well—there are allusions to *Paradise Lost* throughout—but they do not sufficiently understand him. They forget that *Paradise Regained* follows as sequel to *Paradise Lost;* they fail to remember that a scene of human compassion and loving endurance closes Milton's first epic. Limited as they are in so many ways, they are restricted in their understanding of art, not only Milton's but that of others as well. In fact, they look to art to provide them with role models almost as much as they look to other people—that is, they tend to place a certain dependency on art.

All of them are "arty" to a fault. The girl-cousin thinks life, like art, is to be learned by instruction. Just as she must practice Czerny to prepare herself to play Raff, perhaps also she should set aside her suitor so as to exercise at Trollope's novels (III. 161–7). And at the end of the poem she fancies the lady's verdict and the outcome of her situation in terms of German opera, which,

---

man—that he had bolted from his appointed course, going terribly on the wrong side of the posts—let us all acknowledge. . . . But, nevertheless, I claim a tear for Mr. Sowerby, and lament that he has failed to run his race discreetly.

tellingly, she quotes in Italian. The boy, having read his Milton, thinks that *felix culpa* is the pattern for every man (I. 432–3). He conceives of himself at the time of his first meeting with the nobleman in Dalmatia as Timon being coaxed down from his tower (I. 305–7). He describes himself in pursuit of the perfect woman as Sancho Panza dreaming he might be Pope (II. 428–33). Upon discovery of the lord's relationship with the lady he sees the elder man as Iago (v. 51–4); and believing the woman guilty of duplicity, he accuses her of being a fellow artist of the lord's, but greater than he because she knows that "art means just art's concealment" (v. 55–60). Yet, in spite of his tendency to understand himself and others in terms of art, he nevertheless values art very slightly. A racehorse, a Gainsborough, and a Correggio are mere possessions, of very nearly equal worth—all the equivalent of a betting debt (I. 354–5, 393); the piano is a "bore" (II. 45).

In similar fashion the lord sees others in terms of art: the beloved lady as a Greek statue (IV. 84–92), her account of her sad married life as a picture she has painted (IV. 317–19), her description of her suffering and endurance as a Byronic pose (IV. 230), the youth's despair in love as likewise Byronic. Yet he, like the youth, is only a dilletante in regard to art: for him, opera, picture exhibitions, china sales, horseracing are all mere (and equal) entertainment (I. 163–5). As for the lady, she views her life as a book entitled, not *Paradise Lost* as the girl suggests, but *Inferno* (III. 264), in spite of her frequent allusions to Eve, Adam, Satan, the Tree of Knowledge, and the Tree of Life. What she most regrets about her detested existence with her husband, which after all may be seen as a life of service, is the absence of music and pictures (IV. 342). Brutal harm, she feels, was thus done to her "who still / Could play both Bach and Brahms" (IV. 414–15).

Not one of the characters in the piece is truly serious about the art to which each pays lip service. For each it is either a passing amusement or something to be mined for stereotypes—that is, something to ease the individual burden of seeing life on its own terms. Browning prepares for this in his description of the inn. On the walls are reproductions of paintings that may have real meaning but are only decoration here, where there has been "fingered blunt the individual mark / And vulgarized things comfortably smooth" (I. 32–3). Landseer's pictures of a bloody stag and a couching deer face Millais' Huguenot and Holman Hunt's Christ, all in a meaningless jumble. In contrast to this dark and lifeless room, which epitomizes "vulgar flat smooth respectability" (I. 43), there is the light and life of the English landscape, which epitomizes art and civilized existence, the triumph of culture over wildness (I. 62–4). Few are they, however, who prize this beauty and absolute peace for what it is. Tourists who come to the inn on a hill dominating the surroundings are impressed only by its picturesque quality and try to make "art" of it with their drawings and watercolors.

Symbolizing the discrepancy between appearance and reality, the major theme, which subsumes those of art and dependency, is the inn album itself. Containing only doggerel as the poem begins, it hints at the meaning the book is to acquire. *"If a fellow can dine On rump-steaks and port wine, / He needs not despair Of dining well here."* In other words, the book contains the "facts" that can nourish a sympathetic reader. There is in it, as in the "Old Yellow Book" which provided the facts from which *The Ring and the Book* was fashioned, the sordid actuality that will yield art. No wonder that the lord, with his superficial view of art, prefers doggerel to "Browning" (I. 17). As the poem proceeds, written into the album are the nobleman's calculation of his gambling debt, his blackmail note to the lady, and her exoneration of the young man. Almost the entire story is contained within it, so that it does become "queer reading," as the youth had remarked earlier (I. 130). The "defacement" of it (I. 122) ironically becomes an enrichment of it, just as the line "Hail, calm aclivity, salubrious spot!" becomes an ironic joke, like the album itself a telling symbol of how truth and seeming are so frequently at variance. In a manner of speaking, the "defaced" album becomes "Browning."

The Inn Album is quite different from anything that Browning had previously attempted. In it he does not abandon his old con-

cerns—point of view and the nature of truth—but he does treat
them in a new way. Instead of beginning with a specific character
in a certain location, he lets "sight and speech / Happen" on
"neutral ground" (III. 271–2), a point called only the "Some-
thing-Arms," where four nameless characters are brought together. There is not one line of soliloquy, no special pleading,
allowed to go untested. It is not only character but also the interaction of character with character on which we are invited to
focus our interest, so that what we have finally is a poem that
combines the exterior method of drama with the interior method
of the dramatic monologue within a narrative framework. Ob-
serving the unities of time and place, and with only four characters to act out a very complex story, it is a technical tour de force
and in its own way a masterpiece. It has not enjoyed a wide read-
ership, probably because it engenders no close sympathy for any
one of the characters. There are victims but no hero, nor is there
truly any villain in the sense that an antagonist is set against a
protagonist—no Guido opposed to a Pompilia. To this extent *The
Inn Album* is a more realistic and even more naturalistic poem
than *The Ring and the Book*. Coming at the end of a series of six
long poems dealing with the nature of good and evil in human
personality, it embodies Browning's mature thought on the problem. By 1875 he was convinced that human nature is never black
or white, but rather a blend of the two in differing proportions;
and in *The Inn Album* he was making the point that if we view
life in terms of absolutes, we fail to see its amazing complexity
and, thus, its truth. Apparently satisfied that he had plumbed in
this direction as far as he could go, he turned to other subjects.
As DeVane says, Browning's delight "in writing sordid matters
out in long difficult poems . . . comes to a close with *The Inn
Album*" (*Handbook,* p. 391).

7 ❧ *Pacchiarotto and Other Poems* and *The Agamemnon of Aeschylus*

Browning's output during the years 1871–1875 was enormous —six long poems, totaling somewhere in the neighborhood of twenty thousand lines. Even Tennyson, who was experiencing a new outburst of creative energy at about the same time, did not match Browning's prodigious activity. Yet no sooner had Browning seen *The Inn Album* through the press than he began work on the poems that were to comprise his first volume of shorter pieces since *Dramatis Personae* in 1864. Beginning with "Bifurcation," dated 29 November 1875 in the manuscript, he worked steadily until mid-May 1876 in order to complete the poems to be published in *Pacchiarotto and How He Worked in Distemper: With Other Poems.*[1]

The long poems commencing with *Balaustion's Adventure* and ending with *The Inn Album* were an amazing feat. As I have previously intimated, I believe they are among Browning's greatest achievements. Yet, with the exception of *Balaustion,* they enjoyed little critical esteem, most of the reviewers attacking each successive one for its obscurity and confusion. "I have written a good deal of late years," Browning told his old friend John Forster, "and it could hardly be hoped that attempts in various and opposite directions should always equally hit the mark."[2] But

1. "Hervé Riel," "House," and "Shop" were composed earlier. The Prologue, "Natural Magic," and "Magical Nature" may have been written earlier, although they are undated in the manuscript.
2. *New Letters of Robert Browning,* ed. William Clyde DeVane and

to be blindly and stupidly assailed and even virulently ridiculed as he had been by Alfred Austin—this was more than he could endure.[3]

I had always intended, for the benefit of my successors [he wrote to Mrs. FitzGerald], to leave on record some memorial of my feeling for the authorities which have sate in judgment on me this long while—especially the "poets" who, dropping out of the ranks, condescended to hide behind a wall, throw a handful of mud at their so-called "rival": and then slink out and stand by his side as a "fellow-poet" just as if nothing had happened: and one man, who has been playing these tricks with me for I can't tell how long, seemed the most perfect specimen of the "little man" I ever met with or imagined [Austin]: I gave him [in *Pacchiarotto*] one fillip in return for fifty or more flea-bites. It seems, he *is* little—physically as well as morally & intellectually: but you may be sure that had he equalled Golia[t]h in stature such a creature would figure in my eyes as a pygmy.[4]

Paradoxically, just during these years when he felt rejected, Browning was increasingly bothered by persons wanting to pry into his private life. Periodically he learned of someone wishing to write a biography of his wife or publish her letters; frequently he received inquiries from unknown correspondents asking for personal information about himself, especially about his marriage. For decades he had assumed a dramatic mask because, among other reasons, he did not wish to reveal too much of himself in his poetry. Why, then, should anyone believe that he would declare in prose what he had refused to relate in verse? The attempts to learn more about him were a cause of embarrassment and suffering. To Isa Blagden he wrote concerning an unauthorized publication of some of his wife's letters: "But what I suffer in feeling

Kenneth Leslie Knickerbocker (London: John Murray, 1951), p. 230; hereafter cited as *New Letters*.

3. For a discussion of the reviews and Browning's reaction to them see Kenneth L. Knickerbocker, "Browning and his Critics," *Sewanee Review*, 43 (1935), 3–11.

4. *Learned Lady: Letters from Robert Browning to Mrs. Thomas Fitz-Gerald*, ed. Edward C. McAleer (Cambridge: Harvard University Press, 1966), p. 36; hereafter cited as *Learned Lady*.

the hands of these blackguards . . . —what I undergo with
their paws in my very bowels, you can guess & God knows!"
(*Dearest Isa*, p. 149). Browning was determined that the world
at large would never know the man who wrote the works which
they now seemed to despise. Therefore, in his life in London the
poet and the man seen by the public were, in Henry James's observation, "dissociated in him as they can rarely elsewhere have
been; . . . the wall that built out the idyll . . . of which memory and imagination were virtually composed for him stood there
behind him solidly enough, but subject to his privilege of living
almost equally on both sides of it. It contained an invisible door
through which, working the lock at will, he could swiftly pass and
of which he kept the golden key—carrying the same about with
him even in the pocket of his dinner-waistcoat, yet even in his
most splendid expansions showing it, happy man, to none."[5] How
a man like Rossetti could reveal his most intimate thoughts and
feelings in his verse, particularly in *The House of Life,* first published in part in 1870—this was nothing less than betrayal of a
beloved one and of the lover himself; and Browning was shocked
by it.[6] In his view, every person has a right to privacy, and he for
one would shut out the curious who wished to know more of the
man who wrote the poems.

The ill-treatment by reviewers and his determination to close
the door of his private life to the inquisitive public were foremost
in his mind when he sat down to write the poems that would
comprise the *Pacchiarotto* volume. He had been asked to show
the poet behind the poems? Well, he would satisfy that demand
and speak in his own voice to tell, first, the critics that he was indifferent to their views of his poetry and, second, the curious who
wanted to know more about him personally that he was not going
to tell them anything more than could be gleaned from his work

5. *William Wetmore Story and his Friends* (Boston: Houghton, Mifflin,
1903), II, 89.
6. DeVane's speculation that the title of the poem "House" in this volume is an allusion to Rossetti's sonnet sequence *The House of Life* is
doubtless valid (*Handbook,* p. 400).

itself. Not without irony did Browning drop his dramatic mask and speak to those who needed to be spoken to.

While *Pacchiarotto* is a forceful assault on the poet's critics and curiosity-seekers, it is also a defense of his art and an adumbration of his views on man as an ethical being. The poems are, in a word, about a man's house and the life he lives therein, and they declare that no one can build a home for another person, that each individual must do this task for himself. Moreover, the house, like the pavilion in *Red Cotton Night-Cap Country,* is depicted as a temporary structure, a resting place on the journey leading to a final home.

The unifying theme is announced in the Prologue. Reminiscent of the Prologue to *Fifine at the Fair,* the introductory poem notes that man is surrounded by a wall separating his earthly existence from the life of the spirit, "the house, no eye can probe." In his visible house he is a "prison-bird," enclosed by "wood, brick, stone, this ring / Of the rueful neighbors," and his song, unlike the perfect lyric to be divined, is that of a bird "with a ruddy strife / At breast, and a lip whence storm-notes start." All the poems that follow are related to existence in this house and speculation on an unseen home.

The title poem is the one which, naturally enough, was most commented on by the reviewers and which later critics have likewise little valued. "Of Pacchiarotto, and How He Worked in Distemper" is, in my opinion, a lively and amusing affair full of rollicking good humor. Written in Hudibrastics, it tells of an artist who wished to remake the world according to his conception of what it should be and how he came to change his mind about repatterning man and his ways. Attempting to make men into angels, Pacchiarotto deals with "fancy," not "fact" (55), both in his life and art, and is relieved of his illusions when forced to spend two days in a tomb with a rotting corpse—his transcendental aspirations thus modified only by a strong descendental thrust. Seeking refuge, he flees to a monastery where he is thoroughly chastened and his ideas clarified by the abbot. This much of the poem is based on "fact," that is, the part found in Browning's sources in Vasari and Baldinucci; now having established fact, the author is free to give rein to fancy: "I reserve fancy / For Fancy's more proper employment" (345–6).

The fanciful part of the poem is the abbot's admonition to Pacchiarotto, which is strikingly Carlylean and Kierkegaardian in both language and ethical content. *"Earth is earth and not heaven, and ne'er will be,"* he says. "Man's work is to labor and leaven— / As best he may—earth here with heaven" (367–9). A man must work, however, "as if" he were furthering earth toward heaven but "not dream of succeeding" (371–2): "Though round goes the mill, we must still post / On and on as if moving the mill-post" (381–2). Earth is resistant to moral redemption, but this does not relieve an individual of the responsibility for attempting its improvement. The good lasts a while, a person's work may have some temporary effect, but in the end its influence is fleeting. In sum, a man works for work's sake, works in fact for his own development. Personal salvation is all that one can hope for: one makes a house for himself in preparation for a later home.

As for the poet's own house, he must constantly ward off those who would invade it. In "Pacchiarotto" the critics pretend to come to help with the housekeeping, but they bring "more filth into my house / Than ever you found there" (476–7). Here he has sung, but his singing, which they claim they wish to hear, they have consistently misunderstood and berated. So, for once, instead of those "harsh analytics" (457) they object to, he will whistle a tune that faulty ears may easily apprehend, its message being to keep away from his door. And, he says in the Epilogue to the volume, to them who find the wine he serves lacking in sweetness and mellowness, he will offer nettle broth.

As for those who would peep inside the house to learn more about its inhabitant, he has only scorn. He will not, he says in "House," allow anyone to enter and see the man at home:

> Outside should suffice for evidence:
> And whoso desires to penetrate

Deeper, must dive by the spirit-sense—
No optics like yours, at any rate!

While his work is doubtless reflective of the man who built it, it still is not his whole life. Like Shakespeare's, his poetry is "blank of such a record," and to all who wish to glimpse a view of the man he will bar his portal ("At the 'Mermaid' ").

Whether observers of the edifice like it or not, he is indifferent, at least he so pretends. He cares to please no one except the "Landlord" to whom he pays "rent" for his "freehold" ("Pacchiarotto"). Like the speaker in "Pisgah Sights.II," he is deaf to men's praise or blame, being interested only to win the approval of the "Mightiness yonder."

The figures in the volume held up for admiration are those who live quietly and enjoy the task of housekeeping, although never forgetting that their houses are but temporary abodes. Shakespeare, the speaker in "At the 'Mermaid'," turns a deaf ear to those critics who complain about his house and wish it altered. Unlike Pacchiarotto, who took "reform" for his motto, Shakespeare would encourage no "revolt," not being disposed to provoke "song-sedition" or "a schism in verse."[7] He is happy in what he does and preserves a cheerful outlook, adopting an "as if" philosophy and finding "earth not grey but rosy, / Heaven not grim but fair of hue." The speakers in these poems realize that life cannot be changed; in it there is both rough and smooth, so "rough-smooth let globe be, / Mixed—man's existence!" ("Pisgah-Sights.I"). And they know that the greatest wisdom is acquired not by instruction but through experience and so "would teach no one" ("Pisgah-Sights.II").

On the other hand, the persons who fail to find happiness are those who, unmindful of their housekeeping, view life as a case of either/or. They are set against such individuals as Hervé Riel,

---

7. Shakespeare's disclaimer of any desire to be "next poet" probably reflects Browning's own touchiness about being compared with Tennyson. See Chapter 8, on "La Saisiaz," for further remarks on Browning's attitude toward Tennyson.

who, combining love and duty, can "save the squadron, honor France, love his wife." The lovers in "Bifurcation," for example, are torn between love and duty and so live incompletely. The speaker of "A Forgiveness" had been glad to have love and duty combined: "Work freely done should balance happiness / Fully enjoyed; and, since beneath my roof / Housed she who made home heaven, in heaven's behoof / I went forth every day, and all day long / Worked for the world." But the wife became jealous of her husband's attention to his work and pretended to love another so as to provoke her husband to forgo the claims of duty. The result is the unhappiness of both and eventually her death. The pair in "St. Martin's Summer" are divided on the question as to whether for their life together they should erect a "mansion" or a "bower" and end by building nothing at all.

In Browning's world householding is no easy matter, requiring as it does a certain dexterity, open-mindedness, and tolerance of frustration. To maintain a freehold a man must tread warily a delicate balance between the antinomies of existence which, should one become predominant, threaten to destroy him. His vision must always be set on that other home where truth abides. Yet he cannot afford to lose sight of the physical world, the seat of falsehood that nevertheless provides the soil for the pathway to truth. Behind the thing there is spirit, the body but a covering for the soul. A flower, while not a jewel, none the less has a jewel inside if only correctly perceived ("Magical Nature"). The barreness we often think we encounter may suddenly be transformed into richness. How? "All I can say is—I saw it! . . . / All I can sing is—I feel it!" The insight comes quickly in an instant of almost blinding illumination, a lyrical moment, as it were; and it no sooner occurs than its reality is cast into doubt, "A fairy tale"? Perhaps. "Only—I saw it! . . . / Only—I feel it!" Somehow its reality is true ("Natural Magic"), a glimpse of that distant home partially and imperfectly perceived.

Browning maintains that the present has meaning and quality only in the context of eternity. Many of his contemporaries, he implies, never catch even a glimmer of their eternal home because they are too blind to have desire to see. They have allowed themselves to be weighted down by material concerns, have focused on the present thing to the exclusion of that in the distance which can be but dimly viewed. For them there is only the bodily appearance, no soul at all, no house but a shop. Certainly a man must tend to everyday concerns, yet

> Because a man has shop to mind
> In time and place, since flesh must live,
> Needs spirit lack all life behind,
> All stray thoughts, fancies fugitive,
> All loves except what trade can give?   ["Shop"]

Sadly, there are those who insist that "shop" is the only reality, convinced as they are by the arguments of the world that earthly existence is the only one ("Fears and Scruples"), just as, on the other hand, there are those, like the unreformed Pacchiarotto, for instance, who hold that "home" is the sole reality.

"Hold on, hope hard in the subtle thing / That's spirit," the speaker in the Prologue advises. Yet at times the hope is almost impossible to sustain. Nowhere is this more clearly set forth than in "Numpholeptos," in which the Absolute is figured as a nymph who imposes impossible tasks on her lover in his quest to reach her. Dwelling in the white light of purity and coldness, the nymph demands that the lover gather all the experience of the seven colors into which her white light resolves and come back to her unstained by the rays of light he must follow. The lover does as she requests, but every time, though he "break through bounds" (98), he returns to find not her love but her "calm," "the old statuesque regard, / The sad petrific smile" (131–3). At last he rebels against the intolerable burden placed on him, but the rebellion is short-lived, proving only "the true slave's querulous outbreak" (148); and he goes on in the hope that this "crimson-quest" may one day "deepen to a sunrise, not decay / To that cold sad sweet smile" (150–52). Eventually, perhaps, the body and the spirit, the descendental and the transcendental, may come together in glorious union.

As we have noted in our examination of earlier poems, Browning viewed love and art as the dual means by which aspects of the Absolute may be chiefly discerned, and he frequently talked about one in terms of the other. *Pacchiarotto and Other Poems* is no exception in proposing this view. "Numpholeptos" is as much about an impossible task required of the artist as about that imposed on the lover. The true artist and lover alike assume an "as if" philosophy, employing their talents in "forging and filing and finishing" such work as is "worth such Author's evolvement" ("Of Pacchiarotto," 549, 438). Neither the artist nor the lover ever achieves perfection; still he must try. In his endeavor he becomes a pilgrim whose quest is important not for what is attained but for the seeking itself. That is why "Numpholeptos," like the poems specifically devoted to art, is more about questing than about the object of the quest. And, in addition to their attacks on his style, it is the critics' inability to discern that Browning's work is frequently more about process than product that so infuriated him and caused him to rail against them.

Such obtuseness in artistic matters is the major theme of "Filippo Baldinucci on the Privilege of Burial." Ostensibly about anti-Semitic prejudice, the poem tells of how Christian art is forced on some Florentine Jews. Here, as in "Of Pacchiarotto," Browning takes the first of his poem (stanzas i–xxvi) from an Italian source, "fact," and then concludes with a sequel of his own invention, "fancy." The poet argues that the Christians in the story see only the narrowest aspect of art, responding solely to its immediate meaning within a rigidly confined context, while the young Jew at the end takes a wider view. The young Florentine is not abashed to have a painting of the Virgin in his home because "a philosophic mood . . . / Has altogether changed [his] views / Concerning Art" (379–82). Henceforth, he will bear in mind that a picture must "be judged / Just as a picture" (436–7). Browning's point is that a work of art must not be viewed in a limited context of traditional "meaning" and "instruction" but should be valued for itself. His own work, he evidently felt, had been depreciated because his critics were unable to take it on its own terms and insisted on judging it in the light of what they thought poetry should be. And it is this very impercipience that he addresses himself to (more good-naturedly, I think, than most commentators usually allow) in "Of Pacchiarotto" and the Epilogue.

What concerns him most in the Epilogue is judgment and justice, which in art as in other phases of life are often initially faulty but eventually corrected. His poetic footnote to Shelley, "Cenciaja," reminds us of the miscarriage, and eventual vindication, of justice. Likewise his poetry, so misprized now, will, he hopes, finally be found praiseworthy. At present his work is like new wine, a "stiff drink," and must be allowed to age before it can develop the requisite mellowness to be savored for body and bouquet alike. Yet those who cry out for such vintage are they who, in spite of their protestations, hardly value wine, leaving the perfect casks of Shakespeare and Milton (to which they pay lip service) largely untapped. Perhaps they shouldn't be offered wine at all but nettle broth. Still, the poet will persevere in gathering the grapes ("Man's thoughts, loves, hates") from his vineyard and make his vintage, even though it may not gain the approval that he hopes will come later. In brief, he will mind the shop and keep the house, guarding from the inquisitive the wine of memories (198–200) reserved for an intimate few.

Pacchiarotto begins and ends with an elaboration of the theme first mined in *Fifine at the Fair*—householding. It is not an ambitious volume. In my estimation, only "Numpholeptos" is worthy of inclusion in a selection of Browning's best work.[8] Some of the pieces are downright bad. The Epilogue, for example, is not logically consistent, at least not logically clear, because Browning does not make plain whether it is possible for wine to be both strong and sweet (as he seems to say in the beginning), or whether it can be first sweet and then become strong, or whether mellowness can be the result only of an aging process. In addition, the poet is not wholly in control of the tone, which runs from play-

8. Browning himself believed that "A Forgiveness" would fairly represent his narrative powers in a selection of his work. See Hood, *Letters*, pp. 235–6.

fulness to virulence. Moreover, the poems that insist on the dramatic and objective nature of Browning's work contradict, in their unfolding, the very stipulation they insist upon. "At the 'Mermaid'," "House," "Shop," and the Epilogue repudiate poetic self-delineation, yet in these very poems Browning sets forth his own poetic principles. Finally, to focus on the chief concern of this study, in none of the pieces is Browning formally innovative. *Pacchiarotto* is, therefore, for us, mainly of biographical interest. In Browning's career it marks a stopping point from which the poet could vent his anger at, and also have some fun with, his critics before going on to more serious matters. In the dominant metaphor of the volume, *Pacchiarotto* was but another task in the job of householding.

Browning's vendetta with Alfred Austin should have come to an end with *Pacchiarotto.* Unfortunately, it did not. Austin replied with a (probably untruthful) disclaimer of authorship of the reviews Browning had found offensive, and Browning retorted with a piece of doggerel, "To My Critics (Written Since My Late Publication)," in which he continued to heap scorn upon Austin's head in retort: "You say my large poems are only a spate / Of dirty brown water, a hullabaloo!" The *Examiner,* in which Austin's and Browning's items appeared, issued its own judgment that Browning had acted indecorously in his personal attack upon the critics.[9] Here the affair ended, at least in print. But it seems to have had its effect upon the poet. We find him at the end of

9. The text of these three items is reproduced in Hood, *Letters,* pp. 359–63. Griffin and Minchin question the authenticity of the stanzas of invective signed "R—— B——" because the verses "are such shocking doggerel that it is hard to believe that Browning wrote them. Can the Editor of the *Examiner* have been taken in?" (W. Hall Griffin and Harry C. Minchin, *The Life of Robert Browning* [London: Methuen, 1938], p. 261 n.; hereafter cited as Griffin and Minchin). DeVane thinks so (*Handbook,* p. 560). I personally think not. Browning did not deny authorship after publication of the poem and of the article summing up the controversy. Also, the stanzas touch on just those sore spots where Browning was most sensitive—his privacy and the depreciation of his long poems.

1876 passing "a dispiriting Christmas time" with "no jollity of any kind" (*Learned Lady,* p. 39).

Perhaps also causing his low spirits was his lack of employment. After *The Inn Album* Browning's robust vitality appears temporarily to have been spent. To be sure, he had composed the pieces included in *Pacchiarotto*; but for more than a decade he had devoted his energies to long poems of extraordinary complexity, and now shorter forms no longer seemed to engage his fullest creative powers. "Aspire, break bounds!" Browning had admonished in his own voice in *Red Cotton Night-Cap Country*: "I say, / Endeavor to be good, and better still, / And best!" (IV. 764–6). In *Pacchiarotto* he had broken no bounds at all; he was continuing to work in the modes he had previousely perfected. He needed some new scheme on which to exercise his ingenuity. Yet evidently his genius for imaginative innovation was dormant and he could conceive of no plan for a new work. It may have been, then, a feeling of stagnation, in addition to irritation with his critics, that left him dispirited in late 1876.

It was, I think, with a sense of keeping occupied that Browning undertook to translate the *Agamemnon* of Aeschylus. Carlyle had, after the publication of *Aristophanes' Apology*, suggested that he "ought to translate the whole of the Greek tragedians— that's your vocation" (Griffin and Minchin, p. 256). But the idea of undertaking such a task probably was decided as the result of a visit to Balliol College, Oxford, in mid-January 1877. There he had a "pleasant meeting with Jowett" and "dear Mat Arnold" among others (*Learned Lady,* pp. 40–41). Benjamin Jowett, the Master of Balliol, was at the time the most distinguished Hellenist in England, and Matthew Arnold was well known for his advocacy of Greek culture. Browning had been nettled when reviewers of *Aristophanes' Apology* "reported the poem to be 'the transcript of the talk of the Master of Balliol' " (Hood, *Letters,* p. 171). Earlier, in "Cleon," he had taken issue with Arnold's insistence, in the preface to his *Poems* of 1853, that Greek literature, both in style and subject matter, stand as the model for aspiring young poets.[10] So it may well be that his meeting with Jowett and Arnold in early 1877 decided him on a translation of Aeschylus's drama to prove, first, that he was capable of such an undertaking without help from Jowett or anyone else[11] and, second, that Greek literature is inadequate as a model for contemporary poets.[12] There is, of course, no way of knowing what Browning had in mind, but this surmise appears to be not unlikely. In any event, he seems to have been engaged on his translation during the late winter and early spring of 1877. The volume itself was published in October as *The Agamemnon of Aeschylus* "Transcribed by Robert Browning."

The version is indeed more nearly a transcription than a translation, Browning having here, even more than in the *Herakles* included in *Aristophanes' Apology,* sought to be as literal as possible—"to furnish," he says in the preface, "the very turn of each phrase in as Greek a fashion as English will bear." The result is almost unreadable, as this passage chosen at random will indicate:

> But when he underwent necessity's
> Yoke-trace,—from soul blowing unhallowed change

10. See A. W. Crawford, "Browning's *Cleon,*" *Journal of English and Germanic Philology,* 26 (1927), 485–90.

11. Domett records Browning's pride in his scholarship. The poet told him that, "while engaged on the translation, he met 'one of the first Greek scholars in England, who asked him if what he heard was true, that he was translating the *Agamemnon?*' Browning answering in the affirmative, the other said, 'And you understand it? for I have known it these twenty (?) years and *I* can't' " (*Diary,* p. 209). The *Agamemnon* is, of course, the most difficult of all Greek plays to deal with in a scholarly way. Browning himself says in the preface that "the text is sadly corrupt, probably interpolated, and certainly mutilated" and that he has borne in mind the recent scholarship devoted to the play.

12. Mrs. Orr says, in reference to the translation: "Mr. Browning's deep feeling for the humanities of Greek literature, and his almost passionate love for the language, contrasted strongly with his refusal to regard even the first of Greek writers as models of literary style. The pretentions raised for them on this ground were inconceivable to him; and his translation of the *Agamemnon* . . . was partly made, I am convinced, for the pleasure of exposing these claims, and of rebuking them. His preface to the transcript gives evidence of this. The glee with which he pointed to it when it first appeared was no less significant" (*Life,* p. 294).

Unclean, abominable,—thence—another man—
The audacious mind of him began
Its wildest range.
For this it is gives mortals hardihood—
Some vice-devising miserable mood
Of madness, and first woe of all the brood.
The sacrificer of his daughter-strange!—
He dared become, to expedite
Woman-avenging warfare,—anchors weighed
With such prelusive rite!   [232–43]

Far more interesting is the preface, in which the poet explains
what he was about in offering as his version of Aeschylus's play
"a mere strict bald version of thing by thing." To those of Matthew Arnold's persuasion he says: "Learning Greek teaches
Greek, and nothing else: certainly not common sense, if that
have failed to precede the teaching." And quoting from Arnold
himself he goes on, evidently with tongue in cheek, to claim:

Fortunately, the poorest translation, provided only it be faithful,—
though it reproduce all the artistic confusion of tenses, moods, and
persons, with which the original teems,—will not only suffice to display what an eloquent friend maintains to be the all-in-all of
poetry—"the action of the piece"—but may help to illustrate his
assurance that "the Greeks are the highest models of expression, the
unapproached masters of the grand style: their expression is so
excellent because it is so admirably kept in its right degree of
prominence, because it is so simple and so well subordinated, because it draws its force directly from the pregnancy of the matter
which it conveys . . . not a word wasted, not a sentiment capri-
ciously thrown in, stroke on stroke!" So may all happen!

"So may all happen!" He wanted to prove to Arnold that even
the work said to be the greatest of Greek dramas would not stand
up as the highest model of expression when rendered without the
coloring of the poetic imagination. Perhaps his transcription was
"a somewhat toilsome and perhaps fruitless adventure," but he
had had his fun in showing up the pretensions raised for the
Greek writers as models of literary style and, incidentally, had
fired another volley in the battle with his critics, this time against

those who claimed that "Mr. Browning in his English" could never hope to emulate the "matchlessly musical" expression of the Greeks. Finally, the task of translating had provided occupation during a period of poetic aridity.

8 §❧ La Saisiaz: The Two Poets of Croisic

For the late summer of 1877 Browning, accompanied by his sister and their friend Miss Anne Egerton Smith, rented a chalet, "La Saisiaz," near Geneva. It was a lovely spot under Mont Salève, treasured for "its solitude and seclusion, with its trees and shrubs and flowers, and above all its live mountain stream which supplies three fountains, and two delightful baths, a marvel of delicate delight framed in with trees . . . —and then what wonderful views from the chalet on every side!" (*Learned Lady,* pp. 44–5). It was, without exaggeration, the setting for a pastoral idyll. On 14 September, the day on which Browning and Miss Smith were to ascend to the peak of Salève for a full view of the Jura and Mont Blanc, Miss Smith was discovered dead on her bedroom floor.

Browning's acquaintance with her had begun in Florence, flourished in London as they went to musical events together, and, beginning in 1874, was capped by summer holidays abroad when Miss Smith joined the poet and his sister. They were very close friends, and her death, following an evening in which she seemed in the best of spirits, was a terrible shock. Moreover, it came soon after the death of another friend, Virginia Marsh, whom the poet "knew particularly, and parted with hardly a fortnight ago, leaving her affectionate and happy as ever" (*Learned Lady,* p. 45). The suddenness of the demise of two friends and the resulting sense of loss set the poet to reflecting upon death and immortality in general and, probably, upon his own death specifically.

In 1877 Browning was sixty-five. Doubtless when he thought of his age and of (in all likelihood) the few years remaining to him, he also thought of his work, its reception over the years, and his fame at present and in ages to come. We have already noted in *Pacchiarotto* that he felt unappreciated and looked to the future as the time when his "wine" would be recognized for both its body and bouquet (Epilogue); and, speaking through the mask of Shakespeare, he claimed he would wait for his worth to be recognized, "wait— / Waive the present time: some new age . . . / But let fools anticipate" ("At the 'Mermaid' "). During the seventies Browning experienced some bitterness because his long poems of that period were not widely accepted, and this undervaluation of his work caused him, bit by bit, to change his notions about the purpose of poetry in general and of his own in particular. Though with the writing of *Sordello* he renounced the Promethean urge to embody in his poetry the divine fire that would save mankind, he nevertheless continued, throughout the fifties at least, to conceive of himself as a *vates* charged to enlighten the world. No matter how much the poet may suffer from the crowd's lack of appreciation, "never dares the man put off the prophet" ("One Word More"). During the sixties he became ever more willing to drop the bardic mantle, leave the "British Public, ye who love me not," mired in their own stupidity, and devote his art, "wherein man nowise speaks to men, / Only to mankind!" (*The Ring and the Book,* I. 405, XII. 854–5). In the mid-seventies he began to look upon art primarily as the means of the artist's development, dealing with "no problem for weak wits to solve meant, / But one worth such Author's evolvement." Men cannot be taught; they have to be left the fools they are. Henceforth he would be "stript . . . of that costume / Of sage" ("Of Pacchiarotto"). Yet no poet can be totally indifferent to either his audience or its appreciation of his work. Fame, that last infirmity of noble mind, was as important a consideration to Browning as to his fellow artists. Not unnaturally then did the death of Miss Smith evoke ruminations on his own life and his present and future fame. When he set to putting his thoughts about his friend's death into verse, the poem that was to memorialize her became a work as much about the author as about the ostensible subject of his poem.

When poets turn to elegy, their thoughts apparently also turn to other poets who have written memorial poems. For the problem of how to commemorate—that is, how personal and how philosophical to be—is a difficult one, and for aid they recall the manner in which their predecessors have gone about it. The pastoral elegy must surely be the form that first occurs to them. Even Tennyson, when he wished to write a deliberately modern elegy, turned to the pastoral mode as a substructure for *In Memoriam*. No wonder, then, that Browning, who adored Milton and Shelley probably more than any other English poets, should think of "Lycidas" and "Adonais." Yet for him as for Tennyson a formal elegy in the pastoral mode was unthinkable. "Why should any man / Remodel models?" Tennyson had asked in "The Epic." And Browning, as we noted in the previous chapter, refused to regard even the greatest of Greek writers as literary models. He agreed with his wife that "we want new forms . . . as well as thoughts." "Why," the future Mrs. Browning had wondered, "should we go back to the antique moulds . . . ?"[1] Nevertheless, the pastoral elegy might provide a general pattern for a poem lamenting the death of a friend.

Furthermore, Milton was very much in Browning's mind in the seventies. In the workroom of his home in Warwick Crescent he kept a lock of Milton's hair in a glass-topped cabinet near his desk (Hood, *Letters*, p. 347) and a portrait of him hanging on the wall (*New Letters*, p. 252). In March 1877 he was a guest at Trinity College, Cambridge, and was shown Milton's manuscripts (*Learned Lady*, p. 43). And we recall that in *The Inn Album* of two years earlier there are many allusions to *Paradise Lost*. It would not be surprising, therefore, that "Lycidas," with its celebrated digression on fame, should come to the poet's mind

1. *The Letters of Robert Browning and Elizabeth Barrett Browning, 1845–1846,* ed. Elvan Kintner (Cambridge: Harvard University Press, 1969), I, 43; hereafter cited as *Letters of RB and EBB*.

as he was preparing a poem on death. I do not mean to suggest that "Lycidas" was the model for the poem to be entitled "La Saisiaz," but I do think it possible that Milton provided the precedent for extending a poem that was ostensibly an elegy into a consideration of the poet's own fame.

In form, "La Saisiaz" is somewhat like *Red Cotton Night-Cap Country*: it is a re-enactment, in the poet's study in London, of an experience which occurred elsewhere several weeks previously. It is a narrative consisting of a prologue, a long monologue, and a coda. The poem, made somewhat objective by being made distant in time, relates the discovery of his friend, dead on the morning when they were to climb Salève, his walking up it alone, his thoughts on immortality and fame, and his descent from the mountain.

The opening section, spoken from atop Salève, is largely descriptive, almost in an idyllic vein. As in *Red Cotton Night-Cap Country* Browning begins with natural description as a prelude to his narrative, using natural details to suggest the movement of the poem. The solitary ascent of Salève is a symbolic act: the mounting to a prominence from which the speaker can view the world and, here cut off from it, review his own thoughts on God, nature, and the world of men. The chief contrast is that between the beauty and plenitude of the landscape and his own desolation. In such a situation the abyss between the height on which he stands and the village of Collonges where Miss Smith is buried suggests the separation between the living and the dead. "Yes, there you dwell now." Yet somehow he is "no less certain you are here, not there" (22, 25). Momentarily, she lives on as the good and charming person he knew in the flesh; but soon he is led to exclaim: "Here I stand: but you—where?" (139). In fact, she is not really here at all. Does that mean she has completely ceased to be? Asking such a question forces him to consider another: "Does the soul survive the body? Is there God's self, no or yes?" (144). The next four hundred lines are devoted to finding an answer.

If there is to be an answer it must come from within: "I will ask and have an answer,—with no favor, with no fear,— / From myself" (208–9).[2] Moreover, whatever it be, affirmative or negative, he will accept it "so the answer were but truth" (146). "How much, how little, do I inwardly believe / True that controverted doctrine?" he asks, reformulating the question that he most wishes to have answered.

> Is it fact to which I cleave,
> Is it fancy I but cherish, when I take upon my lips
> Phrase the solemn Tuscan fashioned, and declare the soul's
>   eclipse
> Not the soul's extinction? take his "I believe and I declare—
> Certain am I—from this life I pass into a better, there
> Where that lady lives of whom enamoured was my soul"—
>   where this
> Other lady, my companion dear and true, she also is?
>   [209–16]

Here he puts the doctrine not in general or abstract terms but in the words of Dante, the passage he had recorded in his wife's Testament after her death (Hood, *Letters,* p. 172). The question now is, will he ever meet Miss Smith (and, by implication, his wife) again?

He must begin with two presuppositions:

> that the thing itself which questions, answers,—is, it knows;
> As it also knows the thing perceived outside itself,—a force
> Actual ere its own beginning, operative through its course,

2. In 1877 a series of articles by various authors on "The Soul and Future Life" appeared in the *Nineteenth Century.* Browning and Miss Smith avidly followed the debate (162–4). DeVane proposes that "La Saisiaz" is Browning's contribution to the discussion and that hence his arguments, like those of most of the contributors, deliberately leave aside the question of Christian revelation (*Handbook,* p. 422). Roma King wisely notes that this explanation for the absence of divine revelation is not wholly satisfactory: "Browning himself, significantly, makes no such allowances. Indeed, both the substance and the tone of the poem undercut such speculation. Browning's obvious sincerity and his sense of urgency, his emphatic rejection of 'fence-play,' suggest that he is using all the resources available to him. Unlike Bishop Blougram, he has held nothing to fall back upon if present ground gives way beneath him" ("The Necessary Surmise," in *Romantic and Victorian,* p. 354).

> Unaffected by its end,—that this thing likewise needs must be;
> Call this—God, then, call that—soul, and both—the only
> facts for me. [218–22]

Like most modern thinkers, he begins with the reality of the self and, going beyond it, the independence of the not-self. These are not facts in any scientific sense because they are unprovable. But, the speaker says, "that they o'erpass my power of proving, proves them such: / Fact it is I know not something which is fact as much" (223–4). They are, in other words, "existential" facts accepted as true because known in the heart and proved on the pulse. Everything else follows from them; everything else is a construction of the mind—"fancy" and "surmise" and "conjecture," "not knowledge." The traditional arguments that God's goodness, wisdom, and power, as well as man's need, are reasons for belief in an afterlife are all faced with counterarguments which make them untenable (225–48). At the end a man is forced to fall back on the "half-escape: / 'We believe.' " As Walter Pater had said some four years previously in the Conclusion to *The Renaissance,* all we can be certain of is our self-consciousness and our own experience. Or as Browning puts it, "My own experience—that is knowledge"; "this is sure, the rest —surmise" (250–64). And one man's experience is not that of another.

Time after time, the speaker makes the point that no man can teach others either how to live or what to believe. This is the very lesson that the young man in *The Inn Album* had to learn, and it is what Pacchiarotto apprehended from his misguided scheme to reform the world. Yet the uniqueness of personality and personal experience does not imply that truth is relative. If a neighbor is color-blind and calls grass red and the speaker maintains that it is green, "were we two the earth's sole tenants, with no third for referee, / How should I distinguish?" Once again experience must help a man decide, the earth being a giant teaching machine from which to learn what is beautiful, right, and good (274–85). The problem thus set every individual is:

> "From thine apprehended scheme of things, deduce

Praise or blame of its contriver, shown a niggard or profuse
In each good or evil issue! nor miscalculate alike
Counting one the other in the final balance, which to strike,
Soul was born and life allotted: ay, the show of things
    unfurled
For thy summing-up and judgment,—thine, not other
    mortal's world!" [287–92]

The speaker's own experience has taught him that wisdom, goodness, and power cannot be reconciled with the ignorance, evil, and failure he finds wherever he looks. If this life is all, then one must conclude that it is more sorrowful than happy. The only way in which the miseries of earthly existence can be seen as meaningful—that is, permitted by a wise, benevolent, and all-powerful Deity—is to understand them as prelude to something better: "Only grant a second life, I acquiesce / In this present life as failure, count misfortune's worst assaults / Triumph, not defeat, assured that loss so much the more exalts / Gain about to be" (358–60).

He recognizes that such a view is but surmise, and he will accept, as he stated earlier, only fact. What then may "fact's self" reveal? Just as God must stand as referee " 'twixt man and me" (278), so will his soul be umpire between the surmises of Fancy and the conclusions of Reason in their debate on the question of immortality. In other words, Browning reverts to interior dialogue such as characterized *Prince Hohenstiel-Schwangau,* dividing himself into two persons to do battle with each other. For purposes of discussion Fancy and Reason agree to the postulates that there is life after death, that suicide is forbidden, that life is the testing ground for a future life, and that the moral law must be discernible but not imposed on man so as to preclude freedom of choice. F. E. L. Priestley sums up the debate: "All these postulates or 'surmises', granted as 'facts', make human life intelligible; they represent, in short, what Browning finds a coherent explanation, based on his own experience and guided by his reason and fancy, of the meaning of life. Each item is necessary to the explanation; apart from the first two 'facts' the rest depend on each other."[3] Thus, through an interior dialogue Browning has his speaker discover within himself the "truth" of his views about life. Yet this careful exposition is but "superstructure." Both Fancy and Reason are forced to conclude that an afterlife is not provable from first premises. Break through the superstructure and

> all is empty air—no sward
> Firm like my first fact to stand on "God there is, and soul
>   there is,"
> And soul's earthly life-allotment: wherein, by hypothesis,
> Soul is bound to pass probation, prove its powers, and exercise
> Sense and thought on fact, and then, from fact educing fit
>   surmise,
> Ask itself, and of itself have solely answer, "Does the scope
> Earth affords of fact to judge by warrant future fear or hope?"
>
> [518-24]

There can be no certainty on the matter. What stance must then one adopt? To hope and to act as if the "surmise" were "fact." The consideration of the question is brought to a close with a ringing declaration of hope which echoes the end of Shelley's *Prometheus Unbound:*

> So, I hope—no more than hope, but hope—no less than
>   hope, because
> I can fathom, by no plumb-line sunk in life's apparent laws,
> How I may in any instance fix where change should meetly
>   fall
> Nor involve, by one revisal, abrogation of them all
> —Which again involves as utter change in life thus law-
>   released,
> Whence the good of goodness vanished when the ill of evil
>   ceased.
> Whereas, life and laws apparent re-instated,—all we know,
> All we know not,—o'er our heaven again cloud closes, until,
>   lo—
> Hope the arrowy, just as constant, comes to pierce its gloom,
>   compelled

3. "A Reading of *La Saisiaz*," *University of Toronto Quarterly*, 25 (1955), 47–59; reprinted in *Robert Browning: A Collection of Critical Essays,* ed. Philip Drew (London: Methuen, 1966), pp. 242–56. The quotation here is from p. 251.

By a power and by a purpose which, if no one else beheld,
I behold in life, so—hope!   [535–45]

This is the "sad summing-up of all to say" (545), and the speaker becomes irritable when there is not more to be affirmed. I have usually referred to the "I" in the poem as "the speaker" and not as "Browning"—and I think the poet himself would want it that way. It is, after all, a monologue in which the speaker is not named. Yet the final lines so clearly reveal the poet himself to be the monologist that we need not be overly cautious in ascribing the thoughts expressed to the author. As we know, Browning's method throughout his career to this point had been largely dramatic—objective and impersonal; rarely had he even appeared to speak in his own voice. The demands of elegy, however, led him to speak *in propria persona*. And here when he was dropping the mask to reveal the man, he found that he lacked the confidence to rise to an elegiacal peroration and utter in assured tones that all is well here and hereafter. He was fact-bound and could not offer any vision that did not have a factual basis. So he could only say, as it were, "Here are the facts as I know them. Whatever else I long for is surmise. I only hope it is true." He could not proclaim a message of certainty to all men, nor was he prepared to utter a message of despair. Here he was, ready to speak; and so far as elegy is concerned, he had nothing to say. To tell the truth was simply to say "I don't know."

Other poets, however, had been ready and willing to speak out at the drop of a hat, and they had been listened to when they declaimed and prophesied. And, frankly, he was more than a little petulant that they had had the assurance to do so. Alexander Pope could write his *Essay on Man*, but Robert Browning could not even truthfully write an elegy giving assurance that a beloved friend still lived on. Rousseau and Byron had boldly preached a gospel of despair. And they had been listened to. *"Athanasius contra mundum"* indeed! Why should Athanasius or Pope or Rousseau or Byron be heeded? Simply because men are so made that "such magnetic virtue darts / From each head their fancy haloes to their unresisting hearts!" (546–8). Whatever the message, men are prepared to accept it if "the famous bard believed" (572)'. As for Browning himself, "here I stand" (549) with no message and no fame. That is why he is contemptuous of Pope's sublime self-confidence (355–6) and why he sneers at Rousseau and Byron. To paraphrase Goethe's observation about Byron, when they philosophized they were as children. Yet men believed what they said. While Robert Browning was a deeper thinker than any of them, and no one heeded him at all.

The poet's self-pity accounts for the marked change of tone right in the middle of line 545, resulting in a passage (545–604) that is scornful, sardonic, mocking, self-pitying, and playful. Since men will listen only to the famous, then let him for the moment have the requisite fame—and the brilliance and the power and the wit—to lift the blazing torch of influence over them so that they may receive his message and say:

> "He there with the brand flamboyant, broad o'er night's
>   forlorn abyss,
> Crowned by prose and verse; and wielding, with Wit's bauble,
>   Learning's rod . . .
> Well? Why, he at least believed in Soul, was very sure of
>   God." [602–4]

In the end he can say no more than he was able to say in the beginning: "God, . . . soul, . . . the only facts for me" (222).

So with this restatement of the "summing-up of all to say," which now is finally and fully accepted as a fact and thus is no longer "sad" as in line 545, Browning leaves off and concludes with a coda. These are not his present thoughts, he says. The "poor smile," the "pallid smile" is long extinct here in London in November. The chain of thoughts he weaved near Geneva were "flawless till it reached [her] grave," apparently meaning that faced with death all thought is powerless. Yet the chain was not too fragile for him to bring it back to England and work it to un-ravel any tangle. With a kind of Tennysonian reticence, which retreats in face of open statement, Browning implies that the words in the poem reveal only his partial thoughts on the subject. "Life is stocked with germs of torpid life; but may I never wake /

Those of mine whose resurrection could not be without earth-
quake!" The memories of the past, specifically of his wife, whose
death is linked earlier in the poem with Miss Smith's, are too
awesome to bring forth, for the one thing he does not wish to
question is the permanence of his love. To go any further into the
problem of life after death, to examine the quality of his hope, is
too fearful a matter. Let then the sad yet sweet memory be all
that is revived. "Least part this: then what the whole?" If the
poem represents only part of his possible speculations on life and
death, then how much greater must be those unexpressed. He has
said all that he is capable of saying metaphysically. And having
rested his argument on experience ("fact"), he is unwilling to
offer for public consumption his most overwhelming argument
("fancy") for immortality—namely, his love for Elizabeth Barrett Browning and his confidence that it transcends death itself.

The Prologue gives voice to the sentiment of the last lines of the
coda. It is the "fancy" that accompanies the "fact." Ostensibly
the lyric utterance of a soul disembodied by death, it sings:
"Good, to forgive; / Best, to forget!" The soul is now free to wander happily untroubled by the annoyances of mortal existence;
cares for fame and doubts about survival may now be abandoned.
Undoubtedly written after the main part of the poem, the Prologue represents Browning himself temporarily released from the
somber mood displayed in "La Saisiaz."

Since the time of its publication practically everyone who has
studied the poem has remarked that Browning took for "La
Saisiaz" the measure Tennyson had made famous in "Locksley
Hall." Many have found it unsuitable: "The skimming lilt of the
long eight-stressed line with its facile couplet rhymes, so serious
in effect in Tennyson, seems here, in Browning, too light, at first
hearing, for the grave theme."[4] I do not entirely agree with this
judgment because the line is not inappropriate to the meditative,
exploratory, and at the same time deeply lyrical, emotional quality of the subject itself. But I can well imagine that Browning

4. Porter and Clarke, Introduction to Vol. XI of *Complete Works*, p. xiii.

chose this measure because he had, at the back of his mind and perhaps subconsciously, a wish to make an oblique comment on Tennyson's poetic theory and practice.

Browning's friendship with the Tennysons was sincere.[5] But I think it not unlikely that he was occasionally jealous of his contemporary's greater fame. If this is true, then it might be that a verse form closely identified with Tennyson should suggest itself when the poet undertook to write a poem not only about fame but also about the death of a beloved friend, *In Memoriam* of course coming to mind as the chief example of a modern elegy. There are a number of correspondences between "La Saisiaz" and *In Memoriam,* but there are far more differences. Unlike Tennyson, Browning could not offer a "vision," could not pronounce that all would be well, could not confidently say that his lost friend was richly throned in another world. Unlike Tennyson, he refused to don the bardic mantle and become the prophet and sage. And as we have seen, he was annoyed that he could not speak out to his generation or become its spokesman, irked that he had not gained the fame that a man like Tennyson enjoyed. The unpopularity of his early years still rankled, and the neglect of his long poems of the seventies revived much of the bitterness of former times. Not unnaturally then did he cast his determinedly antivisionary poem in the same form as one of the visionary poems of his more famous colleague.

The other poem in the 1878 volume, "The Two Poets of Croisic," was begun on 10 November 1877, immediately after completion of "La Saisiaz" the preceding day. It is a companion poem in every sense; indeed it is a sequel, a fact previously overlooked.[6] It begins (leaving aside for the moment the Prologue,

5. Although he admired much of Tennyson's verse, he did disagree with the Laureate as to how certain poetic materials should be handled. See, for example, his comments on "Enoch Arden" in *Wedgwood Letters,* pp. 75–7, and his remarks on "The Holy Grail" in *Dearest Isa,* pp. 328–9.

6. William E. Harrold, *The Variance and the Unity: A Study of the Complementary Poems of Robert Browning* (Athens: Ohio University Press, 1973), makes no mention of the connection between the two poems.

which was probably written later): " 'Fame!' Yes, I said it and you read it," clearly referring to "La Saisiaz" and its long digression on fame. "First," it continues, "praise the good log-fire! Winter howls without," meaning, perhaps, "Don't bother to praise the poem; praise the fire instead on this cold day in 'London's mid-November.' " The tone is light and at first glance only slightly ironic, but the reflections on fame, if not bitter, reveal Browning's hurt that he had not been more highly acclaimed and his hope that some day his true worth would be recognized. The form of the poem is less tortuous than its companion, being a straightforward monologue advancing by the logic of associations.

"The Two Poets of Croisic" opens with two persons seated before a fire made of ship-wood. The narrator recalls the game he played as a child, when sparks from the fire were given names and their fate tied to the life of the sparks, and he suggests that this evening they make the sparks symbolic of those souls who perished in mid-career. In search of such, his mind drifts with the ship-wood to the coast of Brittany and the town of Croisic, a poor village that has little to recommend it—Browning proceeding here by his usual method of indirection, locating an unpromising subject, circling round it in the manner of *Red Cotton Night-Cap Country,* and then forcing it to reveal its story locked inside: "For point me out the place / Wherever man has made himself a home, / And there I find the story of our race / In little, just at Croisic as at Rome" (xviii).[7] He thinks of two poets of

7. Before the major theme is introduced for full consideration the speaker glances at a secondary theme—immortality, to which fame is of course related—which also serves to link "Two Poets" with "La Saisiaz." Immortality is introduced indirectly, by allusion to Druid ruins in Brittany and the Druid worship, which continues (as we learned in *Fifine at the Fair*) to the present day. The Druids believed in the immortality of the soul, and, the speaker implies, this has been a matter of religious concern throughout the ages:

> Druids their temple, Christians have their dome:
> So with mankind; and Croisic, I'll engage,
> With Rome yields sort for sort, in age for age.

> No doubt, men vastly differ: and we need
> Some strange exceptional benevolence

the town who may be represented by the ephemeral sparks. Each in his day achieved a certain fame, but each is now forgotten, even by the town in which they lived.

The first is René Gentilhomme, page and versifier in the retinue of the Prince of Condé. One day as he was composing an ode, a bolt of lightning struck a bust of the Prince and shattered the crown atop. René took this to mean that the Prince would not become King of France. Feeling himself inspired, he wrote a poetical prophecy foretelling the birth of a new king. When indeed the dauphin was born the next year, René was made Royal Poet and proclaimed "bard and seer" (xLVI). The irony is that his fame proved short-lived and soon he and his poetry lapsed into oblivion. What interests Browning most about him is not his fleeting fame but that he believed himself the recipient of divine revelation.

Here Browning gets to the main subject of his poem, which is the vatic poet. It will be remembered that in "La Saisiaz" the speaker turned most peevish when he began to consider those writers who had assumed the prophetic role and his own inability or unwillingness to do so. At this point in "The Two Poets of Croisic" Browning refers to the acclaim received by René, now called "poet without peer": "He's the master: they must clank / Their chains of song, confessed his slaves; for why? / They poetize, while he can prophesy!" (xLVI). This echoes the last lines of "La Saisiaz," in which the poet speaks of his own poem as a chain. What is it like, the speaker wonders, to have direct communication from the Divine? It would mean, he realizes, the end to ordinary life, common phenomena becoming mere mists in face of the greater reality. Perhaps the oblivion into which René fell may not have been entirely unsought. It was right that he wrote no more poetry and retired to a secluded life. For the man who has experienced revelation has little interest in other men, in

Of nature's sunshine to develop seed
    So well, in the less-favored clime, that thence
We may discern how shrub means tree indeed
    Though dwarfed till scarcely shrub in evidence. [xIx–xx]

either their praise or their blame. Divine illumination means death to life, so it is better that we live without it, learning in the end what ultimately we should know. There are around us sufficient glimpses of the beyond which better suit our human needs. No, to be a true seer and bard one must cease to be a poet entirely: "After prophecy, the rhyming-trick / Is poor employment" (LXVI).

As one firmly committed to the descendental principle, Browning himself had to prefer verse writing—what in *The Ring and the Book* he had said was "the one way possible / Of speaking truth," to mouths like his at least (XII. 839–40), and what in the parleying "With Bernard de Mandeville" he was later to describe as a focusing artifice (304–5). He had to prefer art to direct illumination. "An absolute vision is not for this world," he said in the *Essay on Shelley*, "but we are permitted a continual approximation to it . . ." (XII. 288). As well as did Kierkegaard, Browning knew that the concept of an absolute God is beyond human comprehension and, indeed, that such a notion, were it miraculously received, would be utterly useless to everyone, including the recipient.

The second poet of Croisic to be conjured from the flames is Paul Desforges Maillard. He wrote worthless verses which, rightly, no one published. His sister, however, hit on the trick of copying them and signing her name: fame, she perceived, depending on wile more than on merit. Immediately, they received praise from all the leading literary lights of the day, including Voltaire and Rousseau. Eventually, Paul, refusing to efface himself any longer, revealed the ruse. The great men of letters in Paris turned their backs on him, and without their sponsorship he was not able to achieve fame.

The story of the two forgotten poets famous in their day leads the speaker to conclude that fame is dependent upon externals. How then may the worth of poets be weighed? To determine who is the better or best bard—"bards none gainsay / As good, observe! no matter for the rest"—he proposes a simple test, namely, "Which one led a happy life?" (CLV). This manner of evaluation is not so simpleminded as it is often made out to be. Browning's question means, which poet has best observed life and, facing its sorrows, not been undone by it? A bard is said to feel and see deeply. But what do "feel" and "see" mean? It is easy to yell and shriek and wail about the sorry state of the world, as so-called bards do because they supposedly feel and see more deeply than other men (CLV–VI). Oh, the world is bad enough and in most lives there is more sorrow than joy. As the speaker in "La Saisiaz" admitted: "Howsoever came my fate, / Sorrow did and joy did nowise,—life well weighed,—preponderate" (333–4). Yet the true poet looks at life head-on and does not flinch, sees it for what it is and accepts it; he endures and emerges a "strong since joyful man who stood distinct / Above slave-sorrows to his chariot linked" (CLVI). In Yeats's words he knows "that Hamlet and Lear are gay; / Gaiety transfiguring all that dread" ("Lapis Lazuli"). Finally, it is not a question of the poet's optimism but of his gladness of vision.

"Bards" may proclaim to their heart's content. But the better poet will always have a certain reticence in face of the important problems. "Who knows most, doubts most; entertaining hope, / Means recognizing fear." To be sure, he has insights into the world beyond the senses, but he keeps his focus on men and women, dealing with the infinite in the finite. It is an "offence" to look at the stars and forget the ground: "Stars abound / O'er head, but then—what flowers make glad the ground!" (CLVIII). The poet who finally gains the prize is he who will

> Yoke Hatred, Crime, Remorse,
> Despair: but ever mid the whirling fear,
> Let, through the tumult, break the poet's face
> Radiant, assured his wild slaves win the race!   [CLIX]

"Therefore I say . . . ," the speaker mutters in an unfinished sentence, "No, shall not say, but think." To those who have read "La Saisiaz" and "The Two Poets of Croisic" carefully, the sentence may be easily completed as, "Therefore I say Robert Browning wins the prize over all self-styled 'bards'; he controls his passions and emotions, enslaves his sufferings and gains strength from them, and so in his art transmutes even evil into beauty." The poem, which is told in rather *Beppo*-like ottava rima,[8] ends with what, in effect, is a rousing declaration that Browning will cast aside forever all notions of the poet as seer. He here reinforces what he had said at the end of *Sordello,* when he admitted that poetry at best will remain an inadequate agency, which can only partially express a total poetic vision, and thus had renounced as vain any desire to become a bard. The difference perhaps is that after a lifetime of experience he now takes his resolution with complete seriousness.

The Epilogue tells the story of a poet, a "bard," who entered a contest and was about to win the prize when one of the strings of his lyre broke. Marvelously, a cricket flew to the instrument and chirped in replacement of the lost string, and the poet was acclaimed winner. Thereafter, he did not spurn the lowly creature but had a statue made of himself and his partner, immortalizing her whom he had enthroned and him whom she had crowned. This cricket, then, for the love of music, represents the love sound that mends the broken harmonies of life. For the teller of the tale,

8. As eight-stressed trochaic couplets are most closely associated with Tennyson, so, in English, is ottava rima identified with Byron. Eventually the full story will be told of Browning's ambiguous attitude toward Byron. Here we have only to recall the fulminations against the Romantic poet in *Prince Hohenstiel-Schwangau* (517–55), *Fifine at the Fair* (LXVII), *Pacchiarotto and Other Poems* (especially "At the 'Mermaid'," 129–36, and the Epilogue, 158–60), and "La Saisiaz" to be reminded that Byron came to epitomize for Browning the Romantic "bard" who presumed to speak with divine authority or Promethean audacity. When Browning decided to compose a poem about bards, their fame, and the determination of poetic worth, he perhaps thought first of Byron as the chief representative of a modern "bard" and second of the poem in which Byron himself had written about weighing the merits of poets. So his mind turned to "The Vision of Judgment" and to its verse form—ottava rima. "The Two Poets of Croisic" would become Browning's "Vision of Judgment" and he would use the stanzaic form of Byron's poem to have his say about its author.

For Byron's formative influence on Browning, see Irvine and Honan, *The Book, the Ring, & the Poet,* pp. 13–16, 123–4. For Browning's later reaction to Byron, see Drew, *The Poetry of Browning,* pp. 46–9.

" 'Love' comes aptly in when gruff / Grows his singing." Whatever fame he achieves he will owe to love. The "live pretender" of whom Browning spoke in the last line of "Two Poets" will continue to sing for the sake of love and will be indifferent to present fame. As the Prologue relates, the world walled life about with disgrace "till God's own smile came out: / That was thy face," the face of the beloved. Elizabeth Barrett Browning, the embodiment of love for the poet, is thus the key to hope, not only for the future life, but for his poetic achievement in the present as well. Both "La Saisiaz" and "Two Poets" end with a common declaration.

9 § *Dramatic Idyls* and *Jocoseria*

For Browning the autumn of 1877 and the winter, spring, and summer of 1878 were marked by restlessness and despondency. The death of Miss Smith and the writing of "La Saisiaz" plunged him into a kind of depression that was not relieved by the hurried composition of "The Two Poets of Croisic." "In my own experience, this has been a trying year for me," the poet wrote to his friend Mrs. FitzGerald in August 1878. "I am increasingly lazy. . . . I confess to having been quite idle of late." For his late summer holiday he began to think of going to Italy, which he had not visited since his wife's death seventeen years earlier, because Italy was "the only part of the world I seem at present to fancy might stimulate me a little" (*Learned Lady,* pp. 54–5). He and his sister set off in August from London, spent five weeks in a mountain village in Switzerland to await the passing of the hot weather in the Lombard plain, then visited Verona, Asolo, and Venice for three weeks. The trip proved even more restorative than Browning had anticipated.

His return to Venice and Asolo "after above forty years absence"—"such things have begun & ended with me in the interval" (*Learned Lady,* p. 68)—revived his fallen spirits. Apparently the very thought of revisiting Italy roused him to begin a new series of poems, for we find him in Splügen writing two of the tales to be included in the *Dramatic Idyls* of 1879. Here he was fully enjoying the scenery and was also hard at work. "And to think that none of this was in my mind when I set out—very unwillingly—from London! All that reconciled my laziness to the step was the notion of seeing once again *Venice*—and perhaps Asolo" (*Learned Lady,* p. 61).

Part of Browning's depression and idleness was perhaps owing to a concern about his poetry. Despite "La Saisiaz" and "Two Poets" he seems to have continued to worry, as he had when he undertook the translation of the *Agamemnon,* that his poetic spring had simply run dry. His last two volumes of poems had been devoted mainly to a consideration of bards, their fame and their function in society. This was a vein that could not be constantly reworked. Furthermore, the idea of yet another long poem —most of his previous ones having had little critical success— evidently did not appeal to him. Over the past eight years he had exploited practically all the possibilities of the dramatic monologue, and he had no interest in returning to it. He had busied himself with translation and gained no satisfaction from that. How then was he to proceed? If he were to continue his exploration of perspective, hoping always to gain a more nearly total overview of an object or an experience, he had to hit on a new method. Moreover, he had to find subject matter other than poetic theory if he were to make headway.

Presumably the idea of a return to Asolo and Venice evoked memories of himself when he had visited those cities forty years earlier.[1] In 1838, when he made his first Italian journey, he was also in the midst of a fallow period: he could not find the right way to complete *Sordello.* He had got himself bogged down in a consideration of poetic practice and could see no way out. Suddenly, in Venice, it came to him that a poet need not focus on poetic visions but could treat mankind "dizened out as chiefs and bards" (*Sordello,* III. 721); so then and there he modified his poem to include consideration of suffering humanity.[2] Something

1. For years Browning had a recurrent dream in which he saw Asolo in the distance but was prevented from going there (William Allingham, *A Diary,* p. 248). When he finally returned to Asolo in 1878, the dream did not recur (Lilian Whiting, *The Brownings: Their Life and Art* [Boston: Little, Brown, 1917], p. 283).

2. See Griffin and Minchin, pp. 89–98, for an account of his first Italian journey and its effect upon the writing of *Sordello.*

very like this must have happened when Browning, intent on re-visiting Asolo and Venice, suddenly began to compose with such rapidity that his sister "refused to countenance a prolonged stay on the mountain, unless he worked at a more reasonable rate" (Orr, *Life*, p. 308).

Browning was fearful that his poetry had perhaps lost touch with common life. His critics had said, he reports in the Epilogue to *Pacchiarotto*, that his work was unconcerned with "the common heart" and that he had indulged himself in "the irremissible sin / Of poets who please themselves" (57–9). Perhaps they were right. On this trip to Venice he was reminded of the lesson he had learned four decades earlier: that ordinary men may, like bards—the subject of his last two books—be a fit theme for poetry. But what was to be the form or mode of a poetry of "the common heart"?

In contemplating a solution, Browning was doubtless reminded of Tennyson's success with the idyllic mode. The Laureate had touched ordinary life and gained praise for it. Moreover, if my speculations about "La Saisiaz" are correct, Tennyson's reputation was very much in the poet's mind. Yet it was obviously impossible for Browning to write idylls in the Tennysonian manner. As he told Miss Blagden, "We look at the object of art in poetry so differently! . . . I should judge the conflict in the . . . soul the proper subject to describe: Tennyson thinks he should describe the [scenery] . . . , anything *but* the soul" (*Dearest Isa*, p. 328). But, upon reflection, might it not be possible to compose a poem that would present the conflict in the soul and give it the added force of picturesque realization? Might, in other words, he not write a narrative related by someone other than a monologist?

Already in *Red Cotton Night-Cap Country* Browning had experimented with a narrative that recounted the incidentals of a story as well as the motives of the characters. Parenthetically he had observed:

> He thought . . .
>   (Suppose I should prefer "He said?"
> Along with every act—and speech is act—

> There go, a multitude impalpable
> To ordinary human faculty,
> The thoughts which give the act significance.
> Who is a poet needs must apprehend
> Alike both speech and thoughts which prompt to speak.
> Part these, and thought withdraws to poetry:
> Speech is reported in the newspaper.)   [IV. 23–31]

Perhaps his poetry was becoming overintellectualized. As remedy he might give the speech and acts as well as the thoughts of his characters. His first attempts in this manner—*Red Cotton Night-Cap Country* and *The Inn Album*—were found defective by his critics. Perhaps now, if he took a more purely narrative approach, tried it on a smaller scale,[3] and dealt with subjects more nearly accessible to his readers, he could succeed in bringing his poetry closer to common life. This would, of course, require an exterior method of perception. Formally it would be an idyll, that is, a short but complete story related by a narrator other than the poet. With this method and type of subject in mind he set to work on the poems published as *Dramatic Idyls*. Shortly before publication he informed a correspondent as to his understanding of the term "idyl" and why he called his dramatic:

An idyl, as you know, is a succinct little story complete in itself; not necessarily concerning pastoral matters, by any means, though from the prevalency of such topics in the idyls of Theocritus, such is the general notion. These of mine are called "Dramatic" because the story is told by some actor in it, not by the poet himself.

> [Quoted in DeVane, *Handbook*, p. 430]

As we shall see, the poet did not accurately describe what he had accomplished.

"Martin Relph" alone fits Browning's description. An introduc-

---

3. Tennyson's son reports that his father would occasionally "rally Browning playfully" on the length of his poems and say: "An artist should get his workmanship as good as he can, and make his work as perfect as possible. A small vessel, built on fine lines, is likely to float further down the stream of time than a big raft" (Hallam Tennyson, *Alfred Lord Tennyson*, II, 230). Perhaps Browning decided to take Tennyson's advice to heart and work with shorter forms.

tory quatrain provides the narrative frame that sets the story in the past; the rest of the poem consists of the tale of Martin told by himself. A young woman was suspected of being a spy against the English at the time of the 1745 Scottish uprising and sentenced to die. Having gained a reprieve, her lover hurries to prevent her execution before a firing squad. Martin is the only one to see him approach but fails to alert the English captain and so the woman is killed and her lover dies. Half admitting that the reason for his lack of action was jealousy, Martin each year tries to convince himself that he was a coward instead of a murderer. Like the Ancient Mariner, he is forced by his conscience to re-enact the crime in an attempt to exonerate himself. The story was a vague remembrance of something Browning had read as a boy.

"Pheidippides," based on material from Herodotus and other ancient historians, opens with the hero's return to Athens. What follows is a personal account, told in a measure of much metrical originality which suggests the speed and breathlessness of the runner, of his journey to Sparta to seek military aid against the Persian invaders, his failure to gain Sparta's help, and his meeting on the way back with the god Pan, who promises to fight for the Athenians in the coming battle although they had refused to honor him. Then in the last thirty-one lines a detached narrator takes up the story to finish it—first to tell how Pheidippides ran from Marathon to Athens to announce the Greek victory and fell dead from exhaustion just as he arrived with the news, and then to point up the meaning of the tale:

> He saw the land saved he had helped to save, and was suffered
>   to tell
> Such tidings, yet never decline, but, gloriously as he began,
> So to end gloriously.   [117–19]

"Halbert and Hob," suggested by a passage in Aristotle, is related entirely by an omniscient narrator, dialogue being held to only a few utterances. Almost Wordsworthian in its simplicity, the tale is of a fierce father and son who lived together in solitude. One Christmas night they became engaged in a quarrel, and the son was about to seize the old man and throw him out of doors when the latter recalled that he had proceeded also against his father in the same manner and was prevented from doing so by an inner voice. The father appeals to his son to desist as he had desisted, whereupon the son lets his father go. The two wait in silence until morning, when the father dies and the son trembles in a palsy of remorse. Even more than in "Pheidippides" the narrative commentary in "Halbert and Hob" tends to reinforce values not easily discernible from the story, which ends with the narrator's explicit summation of the moral meaning of the tale: " 'Is there a reason in nature for these hard hearts?' O Lear, / That a reason out of nature must turn them soft, seems clear!"

The narrative technique of "Ivàn Ivànovitch" is more complicated. The introduction informs us that the tale was told the narrator by a Russian friend and it prepares us for possible moral instruction:

> It scarce may be
> You never heard tell a tale told children, time out of mind,
> By father and mother and nurse, for a moral that's behind,
> Which children quickly seize.   [10–13]

The story, drawn from an old Russian folktale, is of a mother who sacrificed her three sons to a pack of wolves in order to save herself. She is beheaded by a villager, Ivàn, whose act is vindicated by the local priest and finally by the local magistrate. Ivàn is seen to be what he himself believes: an instrument of God's justice.[4] Although the story is related by a narrator detached from the action, it is in large part made up of three monologues, upon which the interest of the idyll depends. The woman's monologue is in effect much like Martin Relph's: its purpose is to convince

4. E. Warwick Slinn, "The Judgment of Instinct in 'Ivàn Ivànovitch,' " *Browning Society Notes*, 4, No. 1 (March 1974), 3–9, does not believe Ivàn is to be wholly exonerated. "The action . . . apparently suggests that man when acting instinctively is capable of either immoral or moral motivation, and that the second balances, or counters the first" (p. 7): ultimately Browning intended judgment in the poem to be "a deliberate enigma" (p. 8). Mr. Slinn's points are intelligently argued, but they do not take account of other poems by Browning in which instinctive action is praised as right action.

the monologist herself, as well as others, of the rightness of her action. Yet with the mother as with Martin we see that she cannot keep the truth from herself. The magistrate's speech is the voice of law: even if the mother were guilty, no man can take the law into his own hands, acting as judge, jury, and executioner; due legal process must be observed to prevent anarchy and Iván must be found guilty. The priest proclaims that there is a higher truth than law: there *can* be a teleological suspension of the ethical and Iván acted rightly in this case. Iván himself speaks only to say: "It had to be: / I could no other: God it was bade 'Act for me!' "; and at the end, when told of the verdict, he answers: "How otherwise?" But, even though monologue plays so large a part in this idyll, the narrator guides our sympathies and persuades us of the moral meaning of the tale.

The dreary landscape, with the black pines cropping out of the snow, serves effectively to underscore the grim realism of the idyll and also to suggest the violation of innocence resulting from the mother's deed. The rhythm builds with increasing excitement, being especially effective when the meter changes from iambs to anapests as the wolves approach. The taciturn character of Iván is well depicted, as are the fear and remorse of the mother and the sacerdotal solemnity of the priest. The poem is excellent in every detail.

"Tray," inspired by antivivisectionist controversy and founded on an actual incident witnessed by a friend of Browning's in Paris,[5] follows a simple narrative scheme. Three bards are asked to quench the soul's thirst. The first begins with a medieval tale of knights and heroic activity, whereupon he is stopped. The second commences to sing of a Byronic hero with a "sin-scathed brow" and is cut off before he can continue. The third tells of a dog who rescued a child from drowning. It is this third whose

5. Like "La Saisiaz," "Tray" owes its inception to "A Modern Symposium, The Soul and Future Life," which appeared in the *Nineteenth Century* in 1877. One of the participants, Frederic Harrison, the positivist, argued that vivisection could never explain moral and spiritual mysteries in man or even account for a dog's affection. See C. R. Tracy, "The Source and Meaning of Browning's *Tray*," *PMLA*, 55 (1940), 615–17.

"hero" is most acceptable to the narrator, who believes that compassion and spontaneous generosity cannot be accounted for by analysis of man's physical being. The gentleman who wishes to dissect the animal to learn "how brain secretes dog's soul" epitomizes all those materialists who have no knowledge of man's real life.

"Ned Bratts," based on an incident from Bunyan, is an account of two seventeenth-century sinners who have learned from Bunyan the evil of their ways and wish to be hanged immediately to cut short their wicked lives and enter straightaway into heaven. The story is told by a narrator, although a large part consists of Ned's monologue and the judgment of the Chief Justice; and it is the narrator who points out the moral of the tale—namely, that law serves best its own end and is incapable of comprehending higher values.

From this quick survey of the six idylls it can be seen that most of them do not follow Browning's description that "the story is told by some actor in it." With the exception of "Martin Relph," all are told by narrators detached from the action; in the case of "Tray" the story could not possibly be related by the main actor. In the idylls the narrator serves as the maker of the tale and alone determines its moral meaning. Unlike the narrator of *The Inn Album,* he does not so much intervene between us and his characters to prevent us from making judgments of them as to tell us in which light we should view them. This exterior method, with a strong emphasis on ethical content, is of course a complete repudiation of the dramatic monologue. Often, one is led to question whether the *Dramatic Idyls* should be called dramatic at all. For to give a story "complete in itself" is to resort more to narrative than to dramatic presentation; at least the balance between idyll and drama, which Browning's definition claims, is frequently lost —which is to say, the narrator becomes more important than the characters.

The importance of the narrator can be further gleaned when we consider the sources of the idylls. Each is based on a "fact" drawn from either history or romance and then elaborated by the "fancy" of the storyteller. The "fact" provides the act while the "fancy" provides the motive and the meaning. It is the method employed in "Of Pacchiarotto," in which the narrator says: "Thus far is a fact: I reserve fancy / For Fancy's more proper employment" (355–6). Fact is gold, we are told by the monologist of "Two Poets," and the function of fancy is "to set / Gold's inmost glint free, gold which comes up rude / And rayless from the mine" (1209–12). In the *Dramatic Idyls,* however, we frequently feel that the gold is overwrought. That is why they are so unsatisfactory. The intricacy of the narrative's technique and language encourages us to expect more than we find. Of the six idylls in this volume, "Ivàn Ivànovitch" alone has the weightiness of theme and the depth of analysis to support the complexity of both language and structure.

Although the *Dramatic Idyls* of 1879 mark a reversal in method from the poet's earlier practice, in theme they bear a decided similarity to his poems of the past two years. All of them have one central subject—judgment; and all have characters who face death in some manner or other. Browning, then sixty-seven years old, was preoccupied with his own mortality and enduring fame, and he could not repress his concern when writing these idylls, although he could for the most part disguise it. In "Tray," however, his real interest is revealed by the frame in which he tells the bathetic little tale. It is not the Tennysonian medievalizing nor the Byronic posturizing that the age requires. Rather what is needed is a poet who sees action and perceives its significance— namely, Robert Browning, the teller of "Tray."

"Tray" stands out among the 1879 idylls in that its verse form is totally unlike that of the other poems. Whereas the five other idylls are in long swinging lines, "Tray" is in octosyllabics. In most of the poems Browning attempted an English approximation of Greek hexameters, the meter of the Greek idyll, while in "Tray" he resorted to the meter of "Of Pacchiarotto," one more suitable for burlesque. We can account for this anomaly, I believe, if we view the poem not only as a serious expression of concern for antivivisectionism but also as part of the poet's continuing interest in the subject of poetic fame, which is the underlying theme of the *Dramatic Idyls*. That is why, among these poems concerned with judgment, he spoke in "Tray" more forthrightly —and in a different manner—to express his thoughts on modern poetic practice and also to suggest the superiority of his own verse. "Tray" tells of the cold-blooded, analytical dissection accorded spontaneous generosity. Read as an allegory, it adumbrates the unhappy fate of the poet who speaks to the human heart.

Dramatic Idyls was well received by both the critics and the reading public. "Praised be heaven!" the reviewer of the volume exclaimed in *Fraser's Magazine* for July 1879. "This time he comes with no basket of mud, no screech owls cry," the reviewer said, evidently referring to *Pacchiarotto and Other Poems*. "His imagination has got fitter food; he brings us a few of those heroic rhymes in which no one has surpassed him, embodying incidents which are worth telling, and inspired by that profound acquaintance with human feeling at its highest strain. . . ." Browning was so pleased with the reception of his idylls that he wrote another series of them in less than three months. The six new poems, with a prologue and epilogue, were published as *Dramatic Idyls, Second Series* in June 1880.

The formula remains the same: a certain "fact" elaborated by "fancy." The narrative technique, however, is less complex, as the narrator is not so intrusive. The underlying theme is again the role of the poet and his fame. Although commentators have found the second series of idylls inferior to the first, I personally see no evidence of "the slow subsidence of the inspiration which made the first series a new and striking volume" (DeVane, *Handbook*, p. 445). "Clive" and "Pan and Luna" are superior to almost any one of the first series, and none of this second group displays the sentimentality that characterizes "Halbert and Hob" and "Tray."

The Prologue introduces the major theme of the volume. Those persons who set themselves up as judges of all aspects of human

life see partially and thus imperfectly. Doctor A. says this and
Doctor B. says that, and both diagnose incorrectly. If they cannot
understand the parts plain to see, how then can they comprehend
that which cannot be dissected? "So sage and certain, frank and
free," they are in fact ignorant of the true vitality of life which is
"man's soul." As we observed earlier in this chapter, this was the
very quality that Browning, in his letter to Isabella Blagden,
claimed as his special province and that Tennyson's idylls were
lacking.

"Echetlos," a companion poem to "Pheidippides" and likewise
based on an account by ancient historians, opens with what may
be the poet's acknowledgment of the request of readers of the first
Dramatic Idyls who wished for more such poems. "Here is a story
shall stir you!" he begins and then tells, in a muscular rhythm of
dactyls and spondees,[6] of a nameless but valiant warrior at Marathon who, dressed in goatskin and armed only with a plowshare,
killed many Persians, proved himself a hero, and then vanished
when the battle was over. The brave man was content with the
deed and needed no praise and fame. Better to be nameless, the
narrator says, than have fame like that of Miltiades and Themis-
tocles, who proved morally deficient.

"Clive," drawn from Macaulay, follows naturally from "Echetlos" in that it too is about a person like Miltiades and Themis-
tocles whose fame was tarnished by personal misconduct. It is
told by an old man who, recalling Clive's fame, laments his own
lack of accomplishment and resulting lack of recognition. The
narrator would like to convince himself that, in the end, "Clive
turns out less wise than I" (32). He recalls how a week previously
he had asked Clive, now a broken man, to tell of the occasion on
which he had shown most courage. Clive's story is of himself as
a youth. He was playing at cards with an officer whom he caught
cheating and denounced, whereupon the captain challenged him
to a duel. Out of fear Clive fired too soon and missed. The officer

6. It is not surprising to learn that Browning read the poem with "his
foot stamping vigorously in time" (Sir Sidney Colvin, "Some Personal
Recollections," *Scribner's Magazine*, 67 [1920], 79).

then came and pointed the gun directly at Clive's head and demanded a retraction of the insult. Clive instead reiterated his charge. Facing the courage of his opponent, the captain suddenly confessed and ran away in shame. His friend's objection that Clive had met with more terrifying episodes in India is met with scorn. If the officer had thrown away his weapon, Clive says that he would have picked up the gun and shot himself. His friend, however, cannot understand that there are conditions under which a man cannot live; he believes that it takes courage to meet such a situation, not fear. "Yes—courage: only fools will call it fear," Clive replies (236). The next week he commits suicide. When he hears of Clive's death, the narrator is sure that Clive died muttering "fearfully courageous!" Even though he partially applies Clive's story and death to himself, he still, like Milton's Belial, will opt for life at any price. "I'm no Clive, nor parson either," he says in the last line; "Clive's worst deed—we'll hope condoned."

The poem is accompanied with the greatest economy. Within 240 lines Browning manages to give us two fully realized characters and, in effect, two dramatic monologues. This compactness in character portrayal is surely what Browning had hoped to achieve when he first turned to the idyllic mode. Here there is no question of an intrusive narrator manipulating his characters and his story; with the teller of the tale an actor in it, the idyll is truly dramatic. The beautiful irony of the poem is that we are permitted insight into two characters by a narrator who understands neither —that is, neither himself nor Clive. It is not surprising that Browning chose "Clive" as his best idyll (Hood, *Letters*, p. 235).

"Muléykeh," the third poem in the volume, is linked to "Clive" by its theme of integrity. Hóseyn possesses a beautiful mare, Pearl, which he loves dearly. One night Duhl steals the mare, and Hóseyn follows in hot pursuit. Duhl feels himself secure because Pearl is renowned for her speed, but he is strange to her and Hóseyn is about to overtake them, when Hóseyn's pride in her overcomes his sense of ownership and he shouts to Duhl the secret way to urge her on. Pearl bounds away and is lost to Hóseyn forever. His neighbors jeer at him upon his return home; in their eyes he has acted foolishly. Why did he not keep silent? Ah, he says, "You never have loved my Pearl."

The story, based on an old Arabian tale, is told most effectively. The narrator provides only as much as we need to know; for the rest, he is silent, allowing Hóseyn himself to supply the reason for and meaning of his action. All is shaped to bring out Hóseyn's selfless love, yielding neither to material concerns nor to his own emotional needs. He loved the thing for itself, just as an artist cares about his work for its own sake, regardless of the evaluations the world gives it.

The next idyll, "Pietro of Abano," more explicitly deals with the loneliness and scorn to which the dedicated man is subject. Pietro, a philosopher, physician, astronomer, architect, and magician, was persecuted for the power his vast knowledge gave him. Yet he grinned and bore such disgraceful usage of himself: "Somehow, cuffs and kicks and curses seemed ordained his like to suffer: / Prophet's pay with Christians, now as in the Jew's age, / Still is—stoning" (34–6). One day a young Greek, desiring for his own personal aggrandizement to acquire Pietro's wisdom and power, offers to give the mage the loving gratitude he lacks in exchange for the secret of his skill. Pietro pretends to consent and, under his spell, the young man falls asleep. In dream, the youth becomes a man of wealth, a statesman, and a churchman rising finally to the papacy; at each stage of his progress Pieto appears to him to claim the promised gratitude, which is refused. The youth awakens to see Pietro's smile and the savant's departure, left with the lesson that a genuine lover of knowledge and of mankind cannot expect thanks.

The idyll is rather tedious. It is too long, especially the part relating the young Greek's dream; and the narrator is too intrusive. The manuscript shows that "Pietro" was more worked over than any other poem in the series. Browning apparently did not know how to get straight to the story and leave it to speak for itself. For he was concerned to point up the moral—namely, the rebuffs a wise and humane person must bear and, conversely, the acclaim

the clever but unconscionable man can expect. To make sure that
the moral is appropriately understood, Browning appends a coda
and speaks in his own voice to say that there has been little
enough loving gratitude in his own life.

In the fifth idyll, "Doctor ——," which recounts an old Hebrew legend, "Browning has some fun at the expense of those
"doctors" of whom he spoke in the Prologue. If the idyll is anything more than a *jeu d'esprit,* it is the implied comment on doctors and analyzers of all types which ties it to the other poems in
the volume.

The last idyll, "Pan and Luna," is one of Browning's most exquisite poems. It relates in the most delicate and refined ottava
rima the myth, from Virgil, of the first moon eclipse, when the
white light of Luna was ensnared by the cloud fleeces of the earth
god Pan. Though for Luna it was initially a frightening experience, thereafter according to Virgil she followed Pan to the deep
recesses of his domain in the wildwood, "by no means spurning
him." As for the meaning of the myth, the narrator is willing to
let explain who may. He himself will not pronounce upon the
moral to be drawn:

> Let all else go, I keep
> —As of a ruin just a monolith—
> Thus much, one verse of five words, each a boon:
> Arcadia, night, a cloud, Pan, and the moon.

The poem has certain obvious affinities with "Numpholeptos"
in that each deals with the quest for the quintessential whiteness
of the moon's light.[7] It will be recalled that in the earlier poem the
quester was constantly unsuccessful, yet persevered. Here Browning shows the unblemished whiteness captured, but it should be
noted that it is a god who manages the feat. As for mortals, what
success can there be? Perhaps only the dream that it can be.
Perfect love and perfect beauty—in short, all the qualities sym-

---

7. See William O. Raymond, *The Infinite Moment,* pp. 193–213, for a
discussion of the imagery of "white light" versus "prismatic hues" in
Browning.

bolized by moonlight—are ideals that cannot be realized on earth. "Arcadia, night, a cloud, Pan, and the moon"—a vision of a perfect blending of earth, air, and sky—is the goal of every true seeker but, alas, one that can never be attained. The poet as well as the lover can act only as if he might find the perfection for which he strives.

The Epilogue relates the difficulty of the quest. The popular notion, inculcated by those "doctors" of the Prologue, is that the poet's work comes easily and spontaneously: "Touch him ne'er so lightly, into song he broke." The truth of the matter, however, is quite otherwise. Poetry comes only with great difficulty.[8] It is nurtured by obstacle and requires strength and persistency. Its soil is rocky and the few plants that spring up are slow growing and not soon appreciated: "What the after age / Knows and names a pine, a nation's heritage."

In summary, Browning in *Dramatic Idyls, Second Series* continues to give voice to his feeling that he had not been sufficiently appreciated and that his critics are not competent to evaluate his work. With the exception of the introductory and concluding lyrics he does not, however, display his artistic preoccupation openly in this second attempt in the idyllic mode. Nevertheless, each touches on the theme announced in the Prologue and reiterated in the Epilogue. Though he could find a modicum of comfort in the thought that "it made no sort of difference in the demand for a book of mine whether all the critics praised it or abused it" (*Learned Lady,* p. 89), it still rankled that he did not receive the applause he felt his due.

For almost three years Browning published nothing and wrote little. A year and a half after the appearance of *Dramatic Idyls,*

---

8. The lyric impulse was, however, strong in Browning. Charles Kegan Paul, the publisher, once said to him: "What your admirers wish . . . is that you should give us some more lyrics." The poet replied: "Lyrics! I could give you *buckets* of them, but they're not worth the trouble" (*A Victorian Vintage, Being a Selection . . . From the Diaries of . . . Sir Mountstuart E. Grant Duff,* ed. A. Tilney Bassett [London: Methuen, 1930], p. 181).

Second Series, he told a correspondent in reference to a rumor that a new collection of his idylls was soon to appear: "I have written a poem or two . . . which may or may not go into a new volume of Idyls," but certainly such a volume was not yet ready (Hood, *Letters,* p. 204). And to another correspondent he wrote shortly afterward: "I may print such few things as I have, along with others yet unwritten, in a new volume,—and probably shall do so—but there is nothing designed, much less accomplished" (Hood, *Letters,* p. 206).

The second series of his dramatic idylls received a poor press. This must have been something of a shock because the first had proved popular. He had thought he was composing in a manner that would make his work accessible to a wide public, but here again with the second book of idylls he ran up against the old charge of obscurity, the reviewer for the *British Quarterly,* for example, stating, in the issue for 1 October 1880, that "to any other than lovers and students of Mr. Browning it must often bear too much the aspect of a psychological puzzle." Would he ever win the acclaim to which he felt entitled? Then quite unexpectedly, almost as if in answer to the question, in the summer of 1881, some admirers proposed formation of a Browning Society and hastened to bring it into existence.[9] The poet was highly surprised. As he reflected on the society's first publication, a bibliography of his works, he was moved to say: "It makes me feel . . . as if I were dead and *begun* with, after half a century." At last he was to be vindicated. The reviews had neglected him while puffing up ephemera, and in the long run they would be proved wrong. "One fine day, we find that all the wonderful Novels, Travels, Poems, are 'puffed' into congenial air," while his poems would live (*Learned Lady,* pp. 124–5). And with forgetful hindsight he could look on the work of the Browning Society and say: "I feel a poor sinner indeed when such praises are given me: the bracing effect always came of the blame . . ." (*Learned Lady,*

9. For details about the society see William S. Peterson, *Interrogating the Oracle: A History of the London Browning Society* (Athens: Ohio University Press, 1969).

p. 132). For the time being he could rest on his laurels. That may partly account for the three-year delay between *Dramatic Idyls, Second Series* and *Jocoseria,* which appeared in March 1883.

Jocoseria is, in Browning's own words, "a collection of things grav*ish* and gay*ish*" (Hood, *Letters,* p. 213), and is a continuation in the mode of the two series of dramatic idylls. There are ten poems in all, including a prologue and an epilogue. All of them are variations on the themes of desire and frustration— which is to say that they basically have the same concerns adumbrated in the two previous collections of idylls. Although there are "gravish" matters in *Jocoseria,* the volume gives the impression of being no more than a gathering of bagatelles.

The prologue, with its first line ("Wanting is—what?") that almost invites parody,[10] announces the theme of desire elaborated in the poems following. It asks for the completeness missing in life, but it is not clear whether the "comer" addressed is divine love or its embodiment in human form.

"Donald," a companion poem to "Tray" and quite a mawkish affair, tells of the savagery and treacherous behavior that may be encountered in human life. For "sport" Donald killed a stag that trusted him so fully it presented itself defenseless before him. While committing the perifidious deed, Donald was thrown from a precipice and crippled for life. He thereafter wandered from place to place, telling his story and showing the head and hide of the stag to earn a beggar's livelihood and also to brag about his exploit. Donald, in effect, lived on as an unrepentant Ancient Mariner. The narrator sums up the story with the moral: "Rightly recorded,—Ingrate."

The ingratitude Browning felt had been his main reward during the seventies is perhaps reflected in "Donald." In "Solomon and Balkis" he speaks, through the mouth of Solomon, more directly to the issue of fame and appreciation. The Queen of

10. It has indeed been the subject of many parodies, the funniest by Swinburne. See T. J. Wise, *A Browning Library* (privately printed; London, 1931), p. 112.

Sheba, on the occasion of her visit to Solomon, discusses with the sage the kinds of courtiers they require. Balkis will admit only the good, Solomon welcomes only the wise. Suddenly and accidently, the King's truth-compelling ring is flashed, and both admit to deception in their previous conversation. Balkis confesses that she loves the good only so long as they are handsome young men; Solomon allows that he prizes the wise just so long as they admire him. In a most telling passage Solomon admits to the insubstantiality of fame but acknowledges his deep-seated need for it:

> "In heaven I yearn for knowledge, account all else inanity;
> On earth I confess an itch for the praise of fools—that's Vanity.
>
> It is naught, it will go, it can never presume to trouble me;
> But here,—why, it toys and tickles and teazes, howe'er I redouble me
> In a doggedest of endeavors to play the indifferent."

There can, I believe, be little doubt that such also were the poet's thoughts on the subject, although the "itch" evidently troubled him more than he was willing to admit.

"Cristina and Monaldeschi," a monologue, picks up the theme of ingratitude. It tells of the treacheous love of the queen's courtier and how she put him to death. Ironically comparing the fidelity of Diane de Poitiers to Francis I with the falseness of Monaldeschi, Cristina walks with her lover through the halls of Fontainebleau and intimates to him her knowledge of his perfidy, until at last she brings him to a priest who is to confess him and the soldiers who are to slay him. The poem is beautifully done and succeeds more fully than most of the tales in that it is a dramatic unfolding, without benefit of a detached narrator, by one of the actors in the story. As we have already noted, Browning best succeeds when he allows his characters to speak for themselves.

The next poem, also a monologue, is entitled "Mary Wollstonecraft and Fuseli" and purports to be the confession of a passionate but hopeless love on the part of the early feminist for the painter Henry Fuseli. Desire has been unsatisfied; all love's labors lost:

Such love has laboured its best and worst
To win me a lover; yet, last as first,
I have not quickened his pulse one beat,
Fixed a moment's fancy, bitter or sweet.

"Adam, Lilith, and Eve," which follows, considers the meaning of love and rejection. Specifically, can one really know if one is loved? does rejection not entail more than mere verbal refusal? When the two women of the title tell the truth, forced to do so somewhat in the manner of Solomon and Balkis, one confesses that she really loved the man in spite of her rejection of him, the other that she accepted him simply because another did not come along. When they realize the imprudence of their confessions, they pretend that they were only joking. The man himself pretends that he saw through the joke. All three remain as they were, the man assuring them that the truth has made him no wiser.

Taking up the theme of ingratitude and rejection, "Ixion" belongs with "Cristina and Monaldeschi" among the best poems in the volume. Most commentators see it as Browning's disavowal of the doctrine of eternal punishment.[11] It is surely more complicated. For "Ixion" makes a statement more about man's existence on earth than about his afterlife. To be human, it shows, is to suffer; and to suffer and endure is to rise to the heights of manhood. Ixion, who had been shunned by all mankind, was taken up to heaven by Zeus, who bade him live among the gods and enjoy their pleasures. Yet when Ixion attempted to do so, Zeus scornfully sent him to Hell to be bound on a wheel of fire. Zeus pretended to be his friend and then acted treacherously. Where is justice? Even assuming that he sinned in striving to become the equal of the gods, why did they not take pity on him and show him the error of his ways? And even assuming punishment necessary, why must it be eternal? As Ixion reflects on these questions, he begins to see, first, that hope can stem from suffering and,

---

11. DeVane, for example, says: "Browning's real object in *Ixion* is to set himself squarely, once and for all, against the belief in perpetual vindictive punishment by the gods" (*Handbook*, p. 470). C. R. Tracy makes this point in "Browning's Heresies," *Studies in Philology*, 33 (1936), 624.

second, that beyond Zeus, "god," there is a greater power. The gods are but phantoms of man's own creations; and rising from denunciation to prophecy, Ixion announces that mankind can rise above its conceptions of god, "past Zeus to the Potency o'er him." As Balaustion exclaimed at the close of *Aristophanes' Apology*: "There are no gods, no gods! / Glory to God."

"Ixion" is a powerful monologue in its depiction of suffering and defiance, although the speaker's transformation of Zeus from an all-too-real tormentor to a phantasmal creation of his own brain is confusing. The poem illustrates Browning's long-held belief in the virtue of striving: "Strive, my kind, though strife endure thro' endless obstruction, / Stage after stage, each rise marred by as certain a fall" (97–8). And it also iterates the poet's more recent belief that mankind's conception of the nature of God is essentially faulty. Also, I think, "Ixion" reflects some of the bitterness Browning felt when he considered the fate of his work in the seventies. Remembering his treatment of the critics in "Pacchiarotto," I cannot repress the suspicion that something of the passion of a poet wronged is revealed in such lines as these: "So did a man conceive of your passion, you passion-protesters! / So did he trust, so love—being the truth of your lie!" (89–90). Especially when we consider "Ixion" in the context of a group of poems dealing with rejection, the suspicion that it is the poet himself who is expressing his own sense of injustice begins to harden.

The lack of inventiveness that characterizes so much of Browning's poetry in the idyllic mode is evidenced by his reworking of certain materials. As, for example, "Echetlos" was a reformulation of the Greek matter of "Pheidippides," and "Donald" a variation on the subject of cruelty to animals dealt with in "Tray," "Jochanan Hakkadosh" is a remolding of two poems of *Dramatic Idyls, Second Series*. Like "Doctor ———," it takes its subject matter from rabbinical lore and recasts it as a dream vision reminiscent of "Pietro of Abano." It is the longest poem in *Jocoseria*. To Browning it was probably the most important in that it perhaps displays more of the poet's concerns than any other. DeVane says, "Browning's main intention in the poem is to expound the favorite metaphysical doctrines of his old age . . ." (*Handbook,* p. 472). Yet it is boring and occasionally difficult to follow. It is so crowded with incident—much of it unnecessary, especially the introduction, taking three hundred lines to get to the heart of the story—that it is impossible to summarize briefly. In essence, it concerns an old wise man granted an extra year of life to become, in dream, a lover, a warrior, and a statesman, only to find each stage unsatisfactory, the ideals of youth being incompatible with the wisdom of age. At the end Jochanan is vouchsafed a vision of totality in which all the antinomies of existence are harmonized and through which he learns of God's love as the means of reconciliation of good and evil. His disciple, a younger rabbi, cannot comprehend what Jochanan relates because he is too learned and abstracted to apply the old man's words to his life.

Browning turns once more to consider the poet's fame and function. Reflecting on his failure as a statesmen, Jochanan declares it better to have remained a poet. The poet is a descendentalist who does not want to reshape earth to conform to some heavenly vision: he can present a vision perhaps, but he knows that he cannot induce men to follow it.

> "Needs it irk
> Such an one if light, kindled in his sphere,
> Fail to tranfuse the Mizraim cold and murk
>
> Round about Goshen? Though light disappear,
> Shut inside,—temporary ignorance
> Got outside of, lo, light emerging clear
>
> Shows each astonished starer the expanse
> Of heaven made bright with knowledge! That's the way,
> The only way—I see it at a glance—-
>
> To legislate for earth!" [610-19]

If, as Shelley claimed, the poet is the true legislator of the world, he can legislate only by showing the truth. And Jochanan proceeds to do this at the end when he describes life as a wine-press whose yield is known only in the next state. It is precisely the point of the poem that the truth Jochanan grasps and offers to those around him is not understood and certainly not acted upon. Remembering his own experience, Browning says that if the poet is a prophet, he is but a voice crying in the wilderness. Following the narrative part of "Jochanan Hakkadosh" is a note telling of the poet's purported source for his poem, and then come three sonnets that illustrate the "pithy proverb," "From Moses to Moses arose none like Moses." DeVane calls the sonnets "pure mystification" (*Handbook,* p. 472), yet it is clear that they bear a certain relationship to those poems of the second *Dramatic Idyls* that deal with doctors, measurers, and analyzers. They have as their subject the measurements of the giant Og, whose bulk cannot be encompassed and subjected to inspection. The third sonnet is especially interesting in that it appears to refer to Browning himself. The speaker tells how he once came to a body of water and, to cool himself, was going to dive in, not fearing the depth because he saw a stork standing in the water. Suddenly a voice from heaven warns him away:

> "A man let drop
> His axe into that shallow rivulet—
> As thou accountest—seventy years ago:
> It fell and fell and still without a stop
> Keeps falling, nor has reached the bottom yet."

It may be that the man referred to is the poet himself, now seventy years old, who throughout his lifetime has explored the waters of life and has not "reached the bottom yet."

"Never the Time and the Place" returns to the longing expressed in the prologue. Desire is unrequitted in the present and can be fulfilled only in dream. Yet even in dream, circumstances oppose "with a malice that marks each word, each sign." Only within the grave, then, will the speaker find the comfort he seeks, the incomplete made whole.

Jocoseria ends, like *Dramatic Idyls, Second Series,* with a statement about the poet and his audience. Pambo, the hero of the title, spends his life pondering the first verse of Psalm 39: *"I said I will look to my ways / That I with my tongue offend not."* He finds it easy to practice the first part of the precept, but impossible to accomplish the second. The poet declares that such is the case with him:

> Brother, brother, I share the blame,
> *Arcades sumus ambo!*
> Darkling, I keep my sunrise—aim,
> Lack not the critic's flambeau,
> And *look to my ways,* yet, much the same,
> *Offend with my tongue*—like Pambo!

"Pambo" shows Browning in a better humor than does the Epilogue to *Pacchiarotto.* The poet was, as we have observed, now more assured of a wide audience than he had been in 1876. Yet evidently he still felt that he was being neglected by the critics. And despite the Browning Society and his friends' adulation he remained sufficiently convinced of the lack of proper appreciation that he made injustice a prominent theme of his new volume. The main difference between *Jocoseria* and the two earlier volumes of idylls is that he now treated the subject more gaily than he had previously.

It was with some effort, however, that Browning kept his more virulent outbursts about his supposed mistreatment under control. Originally, *Jocoseria* was to have contained eleven instead of ten poems, and it was only after the book had been set up in galley proof that he withdrew the poem entitled "Gerousios Oinos," which expressed his disdain for his contemporary fellow poets. Using the basic metaphor of the Epilogue to *Pacchiarotto,* it refers to modern poetry (other than his own, of course) as the dregs of fine vintages. Two stanzas will suffice to give some idea of the tenor of this dream vision in which the lackeys run in to finish up the feast of their masters.

> "Fill up each glass with water! Get
> Such flavor as may stick fast yet;
>   Fancy shall do the rest!
> Besides, we boast our private flasks,
> Good, stiff mundungus, home-brewed casks,
>   Beating their bottled best!

"So here's your health to watered port!
Thanks; mine is sherry of a sort.
Claret, though thinnish, clear.
My Burgundy's the genuine stuff,
Bettered and bittered just enough
By mixing it with beer."[12]

"Gerousios Oinos" ("Wine of the Elders") is a wretched affair
and Browning rightly suppressed it, not only because it reveals the
poet himself in an unattractive light but also because its tone is
out of keeping with the other poems in this "collection of things
grav*ish* and gay*ish*."

Jocoseria is the least distinguished volume of Browning's later
career. It shows him at a resting place. With the *Dramatic Idyls,
Second Series* he had thoroughly worked the idyllic vein, which
in any event was never entirely congenial to him. To take a
"fact" and elaborate on it by "fancy" meant, when using the
idyllic mode, that the poet had to undertake a kind of narrative
exposition which apparently did not greatly interest him and for
which, in addition, he had not much talent. If each of his idylls
had been "a succinct little story complete in itself . . . told by
some actor in it,"[13] they would have been superb—like "Clive."
But they turned out to be other than what their author wanted;
too frequently they became vehicles for the poet's own moralizing
—and, consequently, mawkish like "Donald" or boring like
"Jochanan Hakkadosh." In other words, the dramatic idylls of
the volumes of 1879, 1880, and 1883 are successful only to the
extent that they are dramatic. By the time of *Jocoseria*, Browning
had pretty much exhausted the possibilities of the mode. That is
why most of the poems in the collection are simultaneously
"gayish" and "gravish," neither fish nor fowl, and why one can-

12. The galley proofs of "Gerousios Oinos" were found among Browning's papers when the poet's effects were sold at auction in 1913. The
poem was first published in the *Cornhill Magazine* and the *Century Magazine* in April 1914. The text here is taken from the *Cornhill Magazine,* 36
(April 1914), 575–6.
13. The description, it will be recalled, is Browning's own. Quoted from
DeVane, *Handbook,* p. 430.

not escape the feeling that Browning published them primarily because another volume was expected of him. What he needed was a new mode more suited to his genius. At the time, however, he was resting on his laurels and pleased enough when *Jocoseria,* though "little-deserving,"[14] proved popular.

14. "This little 'Jocoseria' (joking even in the title)," Browning wrote soon after its publication, "has had the usual luck of the little-deserving . . ."(Hood, *Letters,* p. 218).

10 ❧ Ferishtah's Fancies

The day after *Jocoseria* was published in March 1883 Browning wrote to an admirer: "The poems [of *Jocoseria*] that solicit your indulgence are light enough,—probably the last of the kind I shall care to write" (Hood, *Letters*, p. 214). He realized that he had explored all the possibilities of the idyll and that it was now time to try something else. The growing activities of the Browning Society made him increasingly aware of a need to turn to graver matters and provide his adoring audience with the reflections on philosophical and religious questions expected of one acclaimed a sage in his own lifetime.

Yet he could not easily write a poem that openly and explicitly set forth his own views; although he could, as we have seen, speak out when he wanted to confront his critics, he would not willingly resort to direct statement of his own opinions on more speculative subjects. We have already noted the unhappy result of such an effort in "La Saisiaz." If he were to compose a philosophical poem, the only solution would be to assume once again a dramatic mask. The question of what kind of mask remained to be resolved. In seeking a suitable setting and persona for his intended poem, Browning perhaps thought of Goethe's *Westöstlicher Divan,* a collection of poems with a Persian backdrop divided into twelve books of unequal length.[1] At any rate, he put into verse a fable from Bidpai, which he had read as a boy, and, says

1. Mrs. Orr says that about this time, besides studying Spanish and Hebrew, Browning tried to improve his knowledge of German (*Life,* pp. 362–3).

Mrs. Orr, "It then occurred to him to make the poem the beginning of a series, in which a Dervish, who is first introduced as a learner, shall reappear in the character of a teacher" (*Handbook,* p. 331). The Persian setting would further serve the salutary purpose of allowing him to speak on religious matters outside a specifically Christian context. Browning had, we know, come increasingly to view with suspicion all dogma and, indeed, had already, in Mrs. Orr's words, "rejected or questioned the dogmatic teachings of Christianity" (*Life,* p. 353). By speaking through the disguise of a dervish he could avoid the charge of heterodoxy; address himself to fundamental religious questions without taking into account the accretions of dogma that had grown up around them; and suggest the universality of basic religious concerns.[2]

But what form was such a poem to take? For the past several years he had written poetry which began with a fact that was embellished with a fancy—his imagination, in his idylls as elsewhere, always being grounded in the actual. Such a formula would not be possible when he turned his attention to religious matter because its factuality could not be established; rather, he must begin with a question instead of a statement. What, then, if he reversed the procedure, providing first the fancy and then the fact?

As Browning reflected on such possibilities, his poem began to take shape. The twelve fancies, spoken by Ferishtah, would provide analogies and parables for considering the great theological problems, and the facts following the fancies would be lyrical treatments of the preceding meditations and would locate the speculations in man's everyday life, thus joining "things visible and invisible, / Fact, fancy" ("A Pillar at Sebzevah," 124–5). This much was settled while he was in the Italian Alps, where the Prologue was written and dated.

2. To a friend Browning wrote: "There was no such person as Ferishtah; and the stories are all inventions. The Hebrew quotations are put in for a purpose, as a direct acknowledgement that certain doctrines may be found in the Old Book which the Concocters of Novel Schemes of morality put forth as discoveries of their own" (W. R. Nicoll and T. J. Wise, *Literary Anecdotes of the Nineteenth Century* [London: Hodder and Stough, 1895], I, 470–71).

In the Prologue the poet, humorously and self-mockingly, explains the form that his work is to follow. It is, he says, to take the shape of an ortalan skewered and cooked in the Italian fashion. As the skewer contains a toasted square of bread, a sage leaf, and a bird to provide crustiness, pungency, and a pithy center in splendid combination, so will his poems be hard on the outside, piquant next, and meaty finally, in order to blend sense (the story), sight (the moral), and song (the lyrical expression of the idea), the three together being a mixture more succulent than any one alone.

Certainly by the time he wrote the playfully apologetic Prologue, Browning had a pretty good idea as to the nature of his "fancies"—that is, they would be dramatic and provided with a Persian setting and so would be Ferishtah's fancies. When he determined the nature of his lyrics we cannot be sure. Mrs. Orr says that he wrote them on consecutive days (*Life*, p. 362), although DeVane demonstrates that this could hardly be true for all of them (*Handbook*, pp. 475–6). In any case, he apparently did not compose the lyrics until after the twelve speculative parts were finished. When he finally decided that they should be love lyrics, Browning arrived at a form that was symbolic of his whole philosophy of life.

As we have seen from our examination of his poems from *Balaustion* on, Browning was increasingly discarding the forms of Christianity in an effort to penetrate to its essence. By the early eighties he presumably wished to spell out his faith to see just how much he did in fact believe. In writing *Ferishtah's Fancies,* he found that he could not go much further than he had in "La Saisiaz," when he allowed that "he at least believed in Soul, was very sure of God" (604). All that he could positively add was his credence in the goodness of creation. Yet for Browning any belief is a mere abstraction unless it is grounded in human experience. How could he be sure of anything, he must have asked himself. And whether he considered the existence of God, the efficacy of prayer, the Incarnation—no matter what religious questions he pondered—each seemed to find verification only in his own experience of love. As he had shown in *Fifine at the Fair,* the only thing of which one can be sure is the heart's affections; all else is mere shadow. That is why he found that he must conclude each of his theological speculations with a love lyric expressing in emotional terms the idea of the parable or discussion. In other words, the structure of *Ferishtah's Fancies* manifests Browning's belief that all philosophical questions can be answered only by reference to human love; or, to put it another way, the form reflects the poet's philosophy that the counsels of the intellect, which form the dialectic of the fancies, are authenticated by man's ability to love.

The parts of *Ferishtah's Fancies* are loosely joined, the connections lying mainly in verbal echoes. Yet because they all refer to love they have a kind of unity that permits us to speak of the volume as a poem, somewhat in the manner in which we can talk of the lyrics of *In Memoriam* as part of one work. The speakers in the philosophical parts are Ferishtah and his disciples, and the speakers of the lyrics, save the last, are a pair of lovers.

In the beginning Ferishtah is called to be a dervish, and in a dream God admonishes him to forgo an ascetic and contemplative existence in favor of life among men and women, where he will "work, eat, then feed who lack" ("The Eagle"). He thereupon goes to the city and, halfway to being a dervish, learns from a poor vendor of melons who had once been prime minister that it is better to be thankful to God for the joys of life than to curse Him for its sorrows ("The Melon-Seller"). Become a full dervish, Ferishtah wanders to another city, where disciples congregate round him. In sections iii–xii the master instructs his followers, dwelling not on the forms or doctrines of faith but on the basic problems of belief.

Ferishtah discourses on the historical grounds for belief in "Shah Abbas," on prayer in "The Family," on the Incarnation in "The Sun," on the problem of pain in "Mihrah Shah," on punishment in "A Camel-Driver," on asceticism in "Two Camels," on giving thanks to God in "Cherries," on the justification of sensual gratification in "Plot-Culture," on the limitations of

knowledge in "A Pillar at Sebzevah," and on the predominance
of good over evil in human existence in "A Bean-Stripe; also,
Apple-Eating." Ferishtah begins with a tabula rasa in regard to
Christianity—he is, after all, a Moslem—and induces from his
own personal needs and observations a Christian God of love who
made the earth for man's enjoyment. He is always careful to
specify that this is his own view of the matter, which others might
possibly see differently.

Ferishtah is fully aware that man's way of conceiving and talking about God is imperfect, his only means of doing so being the
use of images. Hence he can but treat of "the symbol, not the
symbolized" ("The Sun," 21), and hence his employment of
parable and analogy. When, for example, in "The Sun" he wishes
to consider with his pupils the possibility of Incarnation, he begins with the pleasure a man takes in eating a fig, for which he
gives thanks to the gardener, and then elaborates on how love is
given on an ascending scale to the Author of all creation. Ferishtah's point is that man can give love only to someone capable of
responding to love and thus he can image the divine only in
human terms: God has personality because man himself possesses
it. But the elements of personality are so incompatible with omnipotence than man's conception of God in his own image is
highly faulty. None the less, for our own human needs we can
think of deity only in this way. The Incarnation—the possibility
that "God once assumed on earth a human shape" (10)—is thus
an ideal of infinite love, an "image" just as the sun was once, in
early times, the accepted image of God. Anyone who is unable to
appreciate the beauty of such an ideal is to be pitied.

In tracing the historical grounds of belief in "Shah Abbas,"
Ferishtah maintains that an eager desire to believe, the assent of
the heart, counts for more than intellectual assent, which does not
influence life. What matters is not so much what we believe but
how we put our faith into action, it being better to distrust with
love than believe without love. The truth is that we can never
know from historical evidence what really happened. We cannot
give credence to that which we think impossible, but we can be

moved by it as an ideal. In truth there lives beauty just as in beauty there lies truth, so we must be careful in using words like "belief" and "knowledge" when we ask such questions as "it is beautiful, / But is it true?" (8–9).

Man's knowledge is forever circumscribed and worthless as an end in itself, Ferishtah says in "A Pillar at Sebzevah." Far more valuable is love. Knowledge is relative, its "prize is in the process" (22). Love, on the other hand, is absolute: "Love is victory, the prize itself" (25). Which is to say, love is the dynamic principle that makes process—sane development—possible. For man it is

> Enough to say 'I feel
> Love's sure effect, and being loved, must love
> The love its cause behind. . . .'   [51–3]

For our belief in God or the Incarnation or any of the mysteries of life we cannot claim, "Since we know, we love," but should rather say, "Since we love, we know enough" (88–9). Ferishtah, a confirmed descendentalist, counsels that a man should take only as much truth as God has vouchsafed for his individual needs and live by it, instead of seeking to prove that which can never be proven.

> Were knowledge all thy faculty, then God
> Must be ignored: love gains him by first leap.   [134–5]

Ferishtah's strictures on knowledge do not mean that he advocates mindlessness. On the contrary, reason has a very important part to play in his philosophy. "Reason aims to raise / Some makeshift scaffold-vantage midway, whence / Man dares, for life's brief moment, peer . . ." ("A Camel-Driver," 61–3). And, although man's reason is a highly individual thing, giving in different individuals different reports of the world, a man must stand or fall by reliance upon it: "Ask thy lone soul what laws are plain to thee,— / Thee and no other" ("A Camel-Driver," 87–8). Throughout his discourses Ferishtah insists on man's individual viewpoint as the means by which he knows the world. Ultimately, he says, man is alone, without direct outside help, and can rely only on himself in his pursuit of truth. That is why his last "fancy" is devoted to the importance of the individual's point of view in his perception of reality.

Illustrating with a row of black and white beans, he demonstrates that if the eye is allowed to range over the entire row the general effect is gray, although each alone is white or black. Thus is man's life balanced with joys and sorrows, each human experience taking something of its hue from those that precede or follow. To some the color may appear dun, but to Ferishtah it is gray. He can well understand that some lives may be stained with black to the extent that no intervening whiteness can affect it, and he can say only that each man must judge the color of life from his own experiences. He can speak only of how the world seems to him:

> I know my own appointed patch i' the world,
> What pleasures me or pains there: all outside—
> How he, she, it, and even thou, Son, live,
> Are pleased or pained, is past conjecture, once
> I pry beneath the semblance,—all that's fit,
> To practise with,—reach where the fact may lie
> Fathom-deep lower. There's the first and last
> Of my philosophy.   [165–72]

On the basis of his own experience he claims that though evil exists there is enough compensatory good in the world to cause him to judge life good and well worth living. As to the existence of evil allowed by a just God, he declares: "Man's impotency, God's omnipotence, / These stop my answer" (216–17).

It has long been fashionable to condemn Browning for his optimism, and "A Bean-Stripe" has been one of the chief sources for imputing to the poet a kind of mindless cheerfulness. I shall not undertake to refute the charge because the case against it has already been well argued by Philip Drew.[3] I shall say only that "A

3. *The Poetry of Browning*, pp. 233–5. Mr. Drew has an excellent chapter on Sir Henry Jones's *Browning as a Philosophical and Religious Teacher* and its pernicious influence in canonizing Browning's so-called optimism (Ch. 8, pp. 182–98).

Bean-Stripe" does not evince the heartiness of outlook usually ascribed to it. It is true that Browning allows that for every instance of darkness there is a compensatory light and that he adopts something of an evolutionary view of history. But he is careful, in using the analogy of the black and white beans, to say that Ferishtah discerns the stripe, when viewed as a whole, to be *gray*—not white or light or cream-colored, but gray; the word was very carefully chosen. In effect, the position espoused is much like that we found in "The Two Poets of Croisic," where at the end the best poet was adjudged the one who had a gladness of vision. It is an optimistic position perhaps, but an optimism colored by a knowledge of the sorrows of existence.

The Epilogue serves further to dampen the cheerful view of life expressed in "A Bean-Stripe." Throughout *Ferishtah's Fancies* to this point, the lyrics had provided a variation on the idea expressed in each discourse by bringing what otherwise might be an abstraction down to existential verification in the act of loving. The assumption from beginning to end was that love between humans is a reflection of divine love. Now there occurs to the poet the possibility that he has so confounded love with Love that he has engaged in a fiction of his own making. The first five stanzas of the Epilogue tell of the glory of creation and render a vision of the future when the darkness of mortal existence is absorbed into an eternal day unaffected by the dark of human life. Then suddenly, "at heart's utmost joy and triumph," a terror seizes him and leads him to doubt whether such a view of life is not, after all, a mirage: "What if all be error— / If the halo irised round my head were, Love, thine arms?" What if love were only love, and bore no relation to Love at all? Perhaps his own happiness was only an accident and did not signify the principle of Love at work in the universe at large.

It is significant that the question is unanswered, that *Ferishtah's Fancies*, otherwise so happy in outlook, closes with the possibility that an earlier expressed optimism was entirely unfounded. It is significant because the whole point of the poem is that none of the important questions can be answered with positive assurance.[4] All our schemes for understanding the universe, all our attempts to describe it in words, are only provisional. That is why Ferishtah, knowing full well the inadequacy of logic, offers parallel instances in his discussion of metaphysical problems. Nothing important can be proved, as logic demands proof. To know anything completely, even the smallest atom, is impossible ("A Bean-Stripe," 375–7); to deal with any metaphysical problem requires a leap of faith. Hence Ferishtah is forced to admit that at any moment his outlook is subject to change. New circumstances "may wreck / My life and ruin my philosophy / Tomorrow, doubtless" ("A Bean-Stripe," 223–5). But from his present vantage point, he can give a contingent opinion as to the goodness of creation. He will live and act *as if* there is a God of love and love the law of creation. Essentially, Ferishtah's (and Browning's) philosophy is that enunciated by Pompilia in *The Ring and the Book:*

> I am held up, amid the nothingness,
> By one or two truths only—thence I hang,
> And there I live,—the rest is death or dream,
> All but those points of my support   [vii. 598–601];

or as the speaker in the lyric following "Cherries" says:

> Love-making,—how simple a matter! No depths to explore,
> No heights in a life to ascend! No disheartening Before,
> No affrighting Hereafter,—love now will be love evermore.

Ferishtah's Fancies shows Browning in a mellow mood. After some years of discouragement, apprehensiveness for his fame, and irritability with his critics he had reached a pinnacle of esteem which he could not have dreamed possible a decade earlier. Whereas in "La Saisiaz" he was diffident about openly expressing his deepest thoughts, he was now willing to declare, through a mask, to be sure, to all who would listen just exactly what—and how much—he believed. Certainly the formation of the Browning

---

4. It is important to note that the starting point of each of Ferishtah's discourses is not a statement of belief but a question to be answered.

Society had reassured him of his eminence as a poet and given him the confidence to speak out on the most important problems that man faces. "There were several things I thought right to say —and said they are, with whatever success," he wrote to his friend Mrs. FitzGerald (*Learned Lady,* p. 183). But unaccustomed to widespread adulation, he was not completely comfortable in his new role.

The Browning Society [he wrote to another correspondent], as well as Browning himself, are fair game for criticism. I had no more to do with the founding it than the babe unborn; and, as Wilkes was no Wilkeite, I am quite other than a Browningite. But I cannot wish harm to a society of, with a few exceptions, names unknown to me, who are busied about my books so disinterestedly. The exaggerations probably come of the fifty-years'-long charge of unintelligibility against my books; such reactions are possible, though I never looked for the beginning of one so soon. That there is a grotesque side to the thing is certain; but I have been surprised and touched by what cannot but have been well intentioned, I think. Anyhow, as I never felt inconvenienced by hard words, you will not expect me to wax bumptious because of undue compliment: so enough of 'Browning.' [Hood, *Letters,* p. 212]

And in *Ferishtah's Fancies* he subtly cautioned his admirers not to exaggerate his merits:

"Why from the world," Ferishtah smiled, "should thanks
  Go to this work of mine? If worthy praise,
Praised let it be and welcome: as verse ranks,
  So rate my verse: if good therein outweighs
  Aught faulty judged, judge justly! Justice says:
Be just to fact, or blaming or approving:
But—generous? No, nor loving!
"Loving! what claim to love has work of mine?
  Concede my life were emptied of its gains
To furnish forth and fill work's strict confine,
  Who works so for the world's sake—he complains
  With cause when hate, not love, rewards his pains.
I looked beyond the world for truth and beauty:
Sought, found and did my duty."

These lines have an odd ring when we consider that they come from one (if here we may identify the poet with his speaker) who for the past seven years had been preoccupied with fame and hostile criticism of his verse.[5]

Ferishtah's Fancies may not be among Browning's very best work. It is in any case a more distinguished volume than critics have been wont to allow. Its brilliance of analogy in exposition of religious problems recalls Kierkegaard, particularly the proem to *Fear and Trembling*.[6] Its songs, devoid of that syntactical complexity which so often characterizes his late verse, express simply and clearly the poet's belief in love as the basic principle pervading all creation. Lastly, its structure—"fancy" incarnated in "fact"— is well suited to one who believed that a "poet's affair is with God," "all poetry being a putting the infinite within the finite."[7]

5. Browning, however, told Ruskin years earlier that "I shall never . . . feel other than disconcerted and apprehensive when the public, critics and all, begin to understand and approve me" (*The Works of John Ruskin,* ed. E. T. Cook and Alexander Wedderburn [London: Allen, 1909], XXXVI, xxxiv).

6. Park Honan takes an opposite view. Ferishtah, he says, "glibly and bombastically proclaims certain ideas which Browning came to believe. . . ." He suggests that "the poem is totally unreadable and pointless until we consider it as a deliberate, complex construct of hypotheses. It is a *process,* and a dramatic one at that" ("On Robert Browning and Romanticism," a review essay in *Browning Institute Studies,* 1 [1973], 170–71). Harrold, *The Variance and the Unity,* pp. 193–8, speaks more highly of the poem than any other modern critic I have discovered. Harrold discerns a cyclic structure, which is reinforced by imagery of food, especially round fruit, and the sun and by the ritual circle of the whirling dervish (this last in my judgment being somewhat farfetched).

7. From the letter to Ruskin cited in note 5.

11 §⇒ Parleyings with Certain People of Importance in Their Day

The composition of *Parleyings with Certain People of Importance in Their Day* was not quickly accomplished. Apparently it was begun during Browning's autumn holiday in Italy in 1885. "I am writing another poem," the poet confided to F. J. Furnivall, President of the London Browning Society, in early September 1885 (Hood, *Letters*, p. 239). So intensely did he become absorbed in his project that two months later he wrote to Mrs. FitzGerald that, although enjoying himself in Venice, he was counting the days until he returned to London "because I have work to finish at home" (*Learned Lady*, p. 187). Still working on the *Parleyings* a year later, he was of the opinion that the book ought to be his best (Hood, *Letters*, p. 254). Evidently, Browning had a good deal of difficulty whipping it into shape. According to Mrs. Orr, "The revision of the work caused him unusual trouble. The subjects he had chosen strained his powers of exposition . . ." (*Life*, p. 347). He knew that this was to be a work of greatest importance, one of the biggest undertakings in his life, and he wanted it to be as nearly perfect as possible. It was, in fact, to be the summation of his career. He was aware of the difficulty it would present to readers, and when he had finished it he said, only half jokingly, "I fear toughness in the fibre of the book and consequent indigestion in the case of readers . . ." (*New Letters*, p. 339). The volume was published at the end of January 1887.

In the preceding chapter I speculated that Browning wrote

Ferishtah's Fancies partly in response to the demand of his admirers that he declare himself on the great theological problems, that, in short, he state his own religious belief. William Clyde DeVane thinks that the *Parleyings* was written to satisfy the public's curiosity on biographical details concerning his career.[1] No doubt this is in part true, since the work, says Mrs. Orr, who had Browning's own authority for her statement, is "full of reminiscences" and deals with "men whose works connect themselves with the intellectual sympathies and the imaginative pleasures of his very earliest youth" (*Handbook*, p. 339). Yet Browning's intent was not solely or perhaps even primarily autobiographical. What he wished to achieve in the *Parleyings* was nothing less than an epic fullness which would show the progress of the pilgrim soul from despair to bliss and which would ultimately be no more autobiographical than the *Divine Comedy*. The *Parleyings* is, I think, the most ambitious work that Browning wrote after *The Ring and the Book*.

One wishes that we had more of the poet's own comments on his poem. Browning had been willing to discuss *The Ring and the Book* with Julia Wedgwood and others, but he made barely a mention of the *Parleyings* even to Mrs. Thomas FitzGerald, the closest epistolary confidante of his later years. One would specifically like to know how he decided on the mode of each poem and the structure of the whole. For both the mode and form are different from anything that Browning had previously done.

When he made up his mind to write a book that would be at least in part retrospective, Browning must have looked back over his career and wondered which of the many modes he had employed in the past would suit. Evidently he determined that no one alone would be adequate. For this new work was to be not

1. *Browning's Parleyings: The Autobiography of a Mind* (New Haven: Yale University Press, 1927). See especially the introduction for a discussion of the genesis of the poem. DeVane's book is the best extended treatment of the biographical nature of the *Parleyings*, and in this chapter I am particularly indebted to his work for the identification of the contemporaries with whom Browning parleys.

only a look into the past but also a summation of his art and thought in the present and of his hopes for the future. Therefore he would combine modes that he had previously perfected. He would employ exterior dialogue, interior dialogue, dramatic monologue, narrative, satire, direct statement, and lyric to build his work.

A "parleying" was to be a monologue in which a figure from the past would be summoned up to aid the speaker or to argue against him in his presentation of a certain line of thought. In the beginning of each monologue the speaker brings forth a seemingly harmless ghost from the past, but as he calls up each figure strange thoughts arise: old feelings come to life in new strength to be cast aside or embraced. The speaker, consequently, has a kind of debate—indeed, the medieval "débat" may be the closest formal analogue for the parleying—which permits him dual vision in the contemplation of an object or an idea. "How were it," asks the speaker in the parleying "With Gerard De Lairesse," "Could I . . . / Boast, with the sights I see, your vision too? / Advantage would it prove or detriment / If I saw double?" (116–19). The answer is obviously in the affirmative. Yet the speaker achieves even more than double perspective when he brings in a nineteenth-century figure to parley with also. As DeVane has shown, each parleying, save "With Charles Avison," takes into consideration a current thought or attitude with which to argue. At the very minimum, each section presents three points of view: those of the speaker, the figure summoned from the distant past, and a contemporary. More than any mode he had ever worked with, the parleying permits the most diverse simultaneous perspectives. Years earlier Browning had, through the thin disguise of the speaker in *Pauline,* said:

> I cannot chain my soul: it will not rest
> In its clay prison, this most narrow sphere:
> It has strange impulse, tendency, desire,
> Which nowise I account for nor explain,
> But cannot stifle, being bound to trust
> All feelings equally, to hear all sides:

and then had asked: "How can my life indulge them?" (593-9). At last, in the parleying he had found the best means for indulgence. Multiple perspective was a great advantage for a man who believed that "one thing has many sides" (*Balaustion's Adventure*, 2402).

The Parleyings with Certain People of Importance in Their Day is not, however, simply a series of complicated monologues.[2] On the contrary, it is a unified poem. There can be little doubt, I believe, that Browning chose the epic as a model for the structure of his work—and it may well be that he had Goethe's *Faust* and Dante's *Divine Comedy* in mind. The *Parleyings* is introduced by a Prologue analogous to the Prologue in Heaven of *Faust* or the descent into Hell in Dante, and it ends with the salvation of one John Fust, who is made the inventor of the printing press. The movement in the beginning is downward, Apollo going "down to the depths—dread hollow" to encounter the Fates (3), and works upward to the Epilogue, when Fust's friends climb "up, up, up," to what they suppose is a "chamber of dread" (1-2) but which turns out to be the abode of an apostle of enlightenment. The light imagery follows the same pattern. The Prologue is set in night and darkness (6-7), the first parleying ("With Mandeville") takes place at midnight (1), the last parleying ("With Avison") starts on "bitter morn" (2), and the Epilogue closes

---

2. Most critics have followed DeVane in stressing the diffuseness and autobiographical nature of the *Parleyings*. Park Honan, for instance, finds the poems "a medley of those ideas he [Browning] had lived with preeminently" and concludes that "confusion is apparent" (*The Book, the Ring, & the Poet*, p. 508). Robert Langbaum, Roma King, and Morse Peckham are among the few who have a high regard for the *Parleyings* and discern unity within it. Langbaum says that "the whole *Parleyings* can best be understood as Browning's verse essay on symbolism" ("Browning and the Question of Myth," p. 580). King sees a "clear relation between the parts, although their organization is thematic, psychological, and associational rather than logical and sequential" (*The Focusing Artifice*, p. 241). Peckham finds the *Parleyings* Browning's "subtlest and most penetrating examination of the identity of personality and knowledge, of the irresolvable interpenetration of the mask and the truth" (*Victorian Revolutionaries* [New York: Braziller, 1970], p. 127).

with "the comfort of sunshine" (15). As we shall see, light is the basic image of the entire work.

All of Browning's poems since the first series of *Dramatic Idyls* had been structured on facts and fancies. We have noted how in the two books of *Dramatic Idyls* and *Jocoseria* the poems begin with a fact, a bit of history or a personal experience, and then are elaborated by fancy to produce the imaginative monologue or narrative; and we remarked how *Ferishtah's Fancies* reversed the proceeding and went from a fancy, a parable to elucidate a theological problem, to a fact, the actual experience of love. In the *Parleyings* Browning complicates his structuring of facts and fancies. Each monologue begins with a fact—the calling forth of an historical figure or a personal experience—before reaching the fanciful parleying. "With Avison" provides an excellent example of the process because it begins with an explanation of it: "How strange!—but, first of all, the little fact / Which led my fancy forth." The movement in the first and last sections, on the other hand, is from fancy to fact. The work begins with a fancy, the encounter between Apollo and the Fates, and ends with a fact, the invention of printing. Hence the form of the individual parleyings is symbolic of Browning's aesthetic and moral principles, and the form of the work as a whole, from Apollo to Fust, is symbolic of his view of history, from the supernaturalism of the past to the existentialism of the present. In some ways the structure of the *Parleyings* recalls that of Goethe's *Dichtung und Wahrheit*, in which the facts of the autobiographical narrative are the "Wahrheit" and the elaboration of the facts makes up the "Dichtung."[3]

The seven monologues also have their own structure. They form a symphony of four movements, with an introduction and a coda. Thematically and imagistically, the first and second parleyings ("Mandeville" and "Bartoli") make up the first movement; the third and fourth ("Smart" and "Dodington") compose the second movement; the fifth and sixth ("Furini" and "De Lairesse") constitute the third movement; and the seventh ("Avi-

3. Harrold, *The Variance and the Unity*, sees the *Parleyings* as structured on an "Apollonian-Dionysian dichotomy" (pp. 198–224).

son") forms the last movement. There are four basic themes, or motifs, that run throughout the whole—imagination, art, religion, and knowledge. Generally speaking, the Prologue introduces the theme, the parleyings grouped as I have suggested treat it in varying ways, and the Epilogue recapitulates and resolves it. The same is true of the pattern of light imagery which underscores the different themes.

In brief, the themes are worked out in the following ways: the Prologue treats of the advent of the imagination in the person of Apollo; "Mandeville" and "Bartoli" examine its function in the perception of good; "Smart" and "Dodington" consider its moral purpose; "Furini" and "De Lairesse" deal with its use in the understanding of history; "Avison" discourses on its all-encompassing aspiration; and "Fust," the Epilogue, reflects on its inventiveness for human good. As for art, the Prologue speaks of the birth of man's art; the first movement treats of its value, the second of its altruism, the third of its truth to life, the fourth of its transformations, and the Epilogue of its dissemination. In the case of religion, "Apollo" presents a myth from the past; the first movement questions old ways of looking at the world; the second movement deals with vocation; the third considers the nature of myth; the fourth reconciles the old and new myths; and "Fust" celebrates the change that myths must undergo. Lastly, the theme of knowledge is introduced in the Prologue by a consideration of the nature of reason; it is elaborated in the first movement by an estimate of how knowledge is acquired, in the second by a questioning of its use, in the third by an examination of its advance, in the fourth by a determination of its limitations, and in the Epilogue by a declaration of man's continued desire for knowledge in spite of its bounds. Thus, in summary fashion, may the form of the *Parleyings* be described. Let us now turn to the individual poems and consider the main themes in their relation to the basic imagery of the work.

"Apollo and the Fates" serves as the prelude announcing the various themes to be developed in the composition. Apollo descends to the netherworld to intervene with the Fates on behalf of

Admetus; he asks simply that Admetus be allowed to live out his life to the usual three score and ten years. The Fates are reluctant to grant Apollo's request, wondering whether the prolongation of Admetus's life would indeed be a favor to him. For the Fates view life as essentially evil. Apollo, on the other hand, sees life as good and happy. Thereupon begins a debate as to whether life is worth living, Apollo maintaining that darkness is an unreality that can be cleared away by light, while the Fates claim that light is the illusion that soon fades and leaves the darkness: "Life mimics the sun: but withdraw such assistance, / The counterfeit goes, the reality stays— / An ice-ball disguised as a fire-orb" (88–90). If man thinks life good, he is merely deluded by Apollo's beams, which cause him "to endure—life with hope" (74); for Apollo gives man not only imaginative insight into phenomena but also hope that, no matter how wretched the present, good eventually will triumph.

Apollo "needs must acknowledge the plea" made by the Fates to the effect that "debarred / Of illusion . . . / Man desponds and despairs" (105–7), but he also argues that man has a "power in himself" that makes life meaningful as well as bearable (109–10). This is wine, the product and symbol of man's art. With the aid of art, "life's fact grows from adverse and thwart / To helpful and kindly" and makes "earth's nature sublimed" (172–4). To prove its power, Apollo persuades the Fates to drink the wine he has brought with him, and they no sooner drain the bowl than life is transformed. They perceive that age is the victory of life's earlier conflict, they discern the possibilities to which man is born. When fact and fancy are compounded through the miracle of art, they understand that man's life is "no defeat but a triumph" (221). Ultimately they experience the reconciliation of life's antinomies:

> Quashed be our quarrel! Sourly and smilingly,
>   Bare and gowned, bleached limbs and browned,
> Drive we a dance, three and one, reconcilingly,
>   Thanks to the cup where dissension is drowned,
> Defeat proves triumphant and slavery crowned. [201–5]

The poem is not allowed to close on this note of blatant optimism. Immediately upon their pronunciation of the triumph of life there comes an explosion from the center of the earth recalling them from ecstasy to sobriety. Knowledge is born among them —an "ambiguous thing"—which reveals that they cannot know absolutely what is good or bad, that life means but learning, and that the true significance of life is disclosed only by death. Apollo agrees, but asks that his plea for Admetus be granted. The Fates agree to a compromise: Admetus shall live if anyone will voluntarily die for him. "Life's term / We lengthen should any be moved for love's sake / To forego life's fulfilment" (251–3). Apollo is delighted with the bargain, convinced that friends and relatives will rush to offer themselves in place of Admetus. The Fates, knowing better, laugh sarcastically at Apollo's deluded optimism. As we know from *Balaustion's Adventure,* only one person, his wife, was willing to make the sacrifice. Hope can give as false a covering to life as can pessimism. The truth is that life is a mixture of good and bad, with darkness ever threatening to engulf the light.

The parleying "With Bernard de Mandeville" invokes the eighteenth-century philosopher to come to the aid of the speaker in his argument with another philosopher, recently dead, Thomas Carlyle, about the harmonious combination of good and evil for a beneficent purpose in life. Browning wants to use Mandeville's teaching in a certain way: to establish him as the opponent of both Enlightenment optimism and early Romantic pessimism, so as to enlist his support in the argument for a Creator who permits both good and bad.

In the fancied debate, Carlyle declares that there is no way of learning God's purpose and that man should not make the attempt to understand the infinite in terms of the finite. Agnosticism is the only possible stance that a person can assume. At this point the speaker gets to the heart of the matter, the ways in which man may attempt to understand his universe. He uses the analogy of a plan. In such a drawing one does not complain that the letter "A," which designates the house, is not the house itself. No, "look through the sign to the thing signified" (192). We learn by signs and symbols and myths. True, we can never hope wholly to comprehend the nature of the infinite, but we have the gifts of language and art, which permit us partially to discern the true reality. "A myth may teach," the speaker says (204), and then proceeds to supply a variation on the Prometheus myth.

After the creation of the world man was discontent that, though given a mind, he was not endowed with the knowledge to see behind phenomena and thus understand why they exist. Then Prometheus came to his aid, offering him an artifice by means of which the image of the sun could be obtained in little. Thereafter, by his art man was able to employ his imagination in the perception of the good of life and was reconciled to the limitations of his knowledge because he came to understand its purpose and the means by which it might grow.

From the beginning, as we see in the parleying "With Mandeville," Browning is concerned with the cultural crisis in which modern man finds himself. To those who, like the opponent in the argument, claim that man can never know anything of the infinite and should consequently confine his speculations to the physical world, Browning replies that if we take such a stance, we close our eyes to the best part of life. Certainly the infinite cannot be encompassed by man's mind, yet this is no reason to say that gleams of the infinite cannot be discovered within the finite. If we cannot look into the heart of light, we still do not have to accept the darkness of the Fates' cave as the only alternative. It is precisely the purpose of myth and of fables such as Mandeville wrote to help us with our limited vision. Yes, "a myth may teach." But myths, like all living things, change and fade. That is why new myths arise, why, perhaps, poets must assume a religious function. That is why "who better would expound it thus / Must be Euripides not Aeschylus" (205–6). It was Euripides who humanized the old myths, instead of dealing with them in their ancient literal forms as did Aeschylus; it was Euripides who taught Balaustion to say, at the close of *Aristophanes' Apology*, the "master-word": "There are no gods, no gods! / Glory to God."

And it is now Robert Browning who must summon up the shade of Euripides to declare that, though the old religious myth is losing its hold over the minds of men, a new form of the myth may arise to elucidate the teaching embedded in the old. Ironically, in parleying with Carlyle, it is Browning who attempts to respond to Carlyle's plea for "a new mythus," which had been made, in *Sartor Resartus,* more than a half-century earlier. Browning does not suffer any illusion that he has in fact provided the new myth; but he does insist upon the vitality of myth, and in his own version of the myth of Prometheus suggests the importance of artists—among whom must be included Mandeville, the "Fabulist" of the "Grumbling Hive," and Carlyle, who "himself wrote fables short and sweet" (93–4)—in the formulation of that "new mythus" which is to be:

> In little, light, warmth, life are blessed—
> Which, in the large, who sees to bless? Not I
> More than yourself: so, good my friend, keep still
> Trustful with—me? with thee, sage Mandeville!   [318–21]

In the movement of the parleying from the darkness of midnight to an image of the sun, we see that life is not a matter of either/or —either the blazing light of Apollo or the pitch blackness of the Fates' domain—but a mixture of good and evil, whose harmonious combination may be discerned through the imagination and its embodiment in art.

The second parleying, "With Daniel Bartoli," attempts a correction of what may be considered in "Mandeville" an inflated claim for the power of art. Browning would make it plain that in his opinion life is superior to art. Words, even when ordered into art, pale into insignificance before the Word as manifested in human love. The emphasis here is not on an image of God for man but on an image of God *in* man. Bartoli, a seventeenth-century moralist, serves merely as a point of departure, called forth simply to be dismissed as a hagiographer: "What legendary's worth a chronicle?" (5). While "Mandeville" questioned eighteenth-century rationalism, "Bartoli" narrates a man's mistake in love and his subsequent sorrow for that error.

The story is of a duke who loves an apothecary's daughter. He wishes to marry her, but, when faced with the loss of his dukedom in the event of the marriage, he falters in making the decision between her and his honor. The lady, on the other hand, states forthrightly that she loves him for love's sole sake and that she cannot permit his dishonoring himself on her account. When the duke proves incapable of choosing, she leaves him and her love for him behind, because he should have seen that duty was as plain to him as to her. The speaker would canonize the lady because of her self-sacrificing love, just as Balaustion had recognized Alkestis's self-sacrifice for her husband as worthy of sainted praise; and, descendentalist that he is, insists that she has far more claim for devotion than does a St. Scholastica who miraculously tamed a ferocious lion. Nothing marvelous in this story, simply a tale of human love which would yield all for love's sake:

> Saint, for this,
> Be yours the feet I stoop to—kneel and kiss!
> So human? Then the mouth too, if you will!
> Thanks to no legend but a chronicle. [257–60]

In the end the speaker even patches up a sainthood for the duke. He is said to have later been ensnared by a bewitching lady. The duke, however, claims that his real self is dead, still faithful to the old love, and that the great enchantress has but his ghost in thrall. Someday the true man will be called into life by her who left his soul "whiling time in flesh-disguise" (338).

In this parleying the contemporary antagonist is Browning himself. In the projection of the career of the duke after his lady left him the poet was probably thinking of his own relationship with Louisa Ashburton. She was the "bold she-shape" who attempted to cut him off from his love in the past. As Browning resurrects this fifteen-year-old episode of his life, his poetry, which in this section has proceeded haltingly, springs to life with the same tension marking the close of *Fifine at the Fair*, which had also covertly figured his supposed disloyalty to his dead wife in his offer of marriage to Lady Ashburton.

> Fancy's flight
> Makes me a listener when, some sleepless night,
> The duke reviewed his memories, and aghast
> Found that the Present intercepts the Past
> With such effect as when a cloud enwraps
> The moon and, moon-suffused, plays moon perhaps
> To who walks under, till comes, late or soon,
> A stumble: up he looks, and lo, the moon
> Calm, clear, convincingly herself once more!
> How could he 'scape the cloud that thrust between
> Him and effulgence?   [276-86]

The light of love shines out from the darkness to disclose the man "waiting the morn-star's re-appearance—though / You think we vanish scared by the cock's crow" (341-2). Though our knowledge be limited, it suffices if we understand "the main fact that love, when love indeed, / Is wholly solely love from first to last— / Truth—all the rest a lie" (267-9). Not in the miracles of legend but in the ordinary life of chronicles is God revealed.

Moving from a descendental manifestation of deity, the second movement of the *Parleyings* begins with a consideration of revelation attained in a visionary moment. "It seems as if . . . ," the speaker says in an unfinished sentence, the first line of "With Christopher Smart," as though he could hardly believe what he is about to say. Whereas "Daniel Bartoli" showed truth gained from the fancy of fact, this section starts with the possibility that the soul's advance might precede the body's and gain "inheritance / Of fact by fancy" (4-6). Yet the occurrence is never stated in a declarative sentence but is put into the interrogative or subjunctive. When one talks of visions, one can never be sure. Why did Christopher Smart write a single poem, "The Song of David," stamped with what seems like divine authority, and never before or after compose anything other than unexceptional verse? Though he was sane at starting, the ground gave way beneath him and "perhaps down broke / A fireball wrapping flesh and spirit both / In conflagration" (79-81). "What if, in one point only, then and there / The otherwise all-unapproachable / Allowed impingement?" (104-6). Whatever the reason, Smart once was permitted insight into undisguised nature and naked truth. And he was not only allowed to see but was also given power to express his vision in the right language. With such a gift he rose, like Adam, to assert dominion over nature, giving each thing its proper note and name

> For Man to know by,—Man who, now—the same
> As erst in Eden, needs that all he sees
> Be named him ere he note by what degrees
> Of strength and beauty to its end Design
> Ever thus operates. [157–61]

Browning's description of the power of poetry, here and in lines 113–20, leaves no doubt that that power resides in the poet's ability to act as a moral force. With an eye on Rossetti, Morris, Swinburne and the whole art-for-art school, he denounces any conception of the poet as idle singer of an empty day. "First give us knowledge, then appoint its use!" he apostrophizes Smart as the representative of all poets (216). Strength and beauty are the means and not the end. Nature was meant to be enjoyed, but it was intended to inform us of the goodness of God as well. With another eye on the poets who study the heavens before scrutinizing the rose, Browning castigates those who presume to see nothing of God in nature. It was the genius of Smart, the sole poet between Milton and Keats to pierce the screen separating thing and word, to look into nature and "tell / Us others of her majesty and might / In large, her loveliness infinite / In little" (142–5), and from him a poet should learn to begin with the little before ascending to the large. To attempt to look into the heart of light is to be blinded; it is a madness far worse than that which befell Christopher Smart. Our business is with earth, and there or nowhere will we discover "Will, Power, and Love."

The parleying with Smart unfolds in images of blazing light; the second section of the second movement, "With George Bubb Dodington," is carried on in darkness. Here the speaker is dealing with falsehood, not truth. Dodington is an entirely different kind of character from the adversary figure summoned up in the second part of the first movement, Bartoli, who was called forth simply to be dismissed. And in the parleying with Dodington the nature of the speaker changes. No longer the quester for truth, the speaker presents himself as an unprincipled observer of life whose interest lies in the clever manipulation of human beings for his own gain. He feigns this new character in order to play a role in which he can relate to the unsuccessful eighteenth-century political opportunist who was George Bubb Dodington and the successful political charlatan who was Benjamin Disraeli. The tone that the "I" adopts is as cynical as the characters whom he chooses to parley with. Instead of asking their aid or dismissing them forthright, he instructs the unsuccessful Dodington in the methods of demagoguery so successfully employed by Lord Beaconsfield, without of course mentioning Disraeli's name.

Throughout his career Browning was interested in the concept of power, political as well as poetic. His plays, for example, are for the most part studies in politics, specifically in the impossibility of embodying ideals in political reality. *Prince Hohenstiel-Schwangau,* as we have seen, was devoted specifically to the problem. "Dodington," however, is not concerned with the realization of ideals but with personal power without reference to any altruistic vision. "Yours was the wrong way," the speaker addresses Dodington at the beginning of the poem, while conceding, for the sake of argument, that his aims were right. It was wrong because his methods were wrong: he was simply not quack enough. For the rest of the parleying Browning has his speaker advise Dodington in "sham," "pretense," and "outward show."

Ironically, while pretending to teach Dodington the means of subterfuge, the speaker builds up a case for Browning's most cherished beliefs, which are presented as postulates to be somehow circumvented. The heart of his instruction lies in his insistence that man's "nature owns a Supernatural / In fact as well as phrase—which found must be" (191–2). In this doubting age, old mystery and worship have disappeared, replaced by materialism and utilitarianism. The man who could persuade the people that he acted as the agent of the supernatural could become the master statesman. Though he might shift his ground from year to year, the people would be so awestruck that they would never observe the dubiousness of his position. But not having worked this way, Dodington failed where, it is implied, Disraeli succeeded. The point that Browning wishes to make is that no matter how much a society, his own for example, may profess allegiance to material improvements, it cannot flourish without adherence to a law above the laws devised by men. Ultimately, the people recognize this fact, and a quack who has the percipiency to understand it can rule a nation according to whatever whim he may wish to indulge. If the charlatan can rule in this way for personal aggrandizement, how truly benevolent and productive would the sincere statesman prove who looked to higher law for guidance.

In Browning's eyes Disraeli, his real target in "Dodington," is condemned not because he achieved ill-gotten gains, or lied, or was a hypocrite, but because he perverted the truth to the extent that he made lies look like truth and, worse, truth look like lies. To play with truth is always reprehensible, but to debase it is loathsome. In "Dodington" the truth is so contorted that art is reduced to craft, vocation to trade, imagination to analysis, knowledge to skill. No wonder that the parleying is devoid of light and that it stands in strongest contrast to the parleying "With Christopher Smart."

The beginning of the third movement introduces a man whose aim was to reveal God's work in the world in its freshness and glory. Francis Furini was an Italian naturalistic painter of the seventeenth century whose naturalism was far different from the black and godless naturalism suggested in "Dodington." Furini painted men and women just as God made them, with "livelier colours, more attractive lines / Than suit some orthodox sad sickly saint" (551–2), such as Bartoli depicted. He did this because he recognized that the beauties of life go unnoticed unless someone, a painter perhaps, takes the trouble to point them out. He believed that "art hangs out for sign / There's finer entertainment underneath" (530–31) and endeavored to show in his pictures soul behind sense. Furthermore, he thought of art as an expression of man's best thanks to God for the joys given him. Art was a natural accompaniment to his priestly calling, because in both he saw himself fulfilling a religious function.

The speaker is glad to proclaim Furini "good priest, good man, good painter" (64), and he is quick to jump to his defense when Furini (like Pen Browning, the poet's son) is charged with indelicacy or immortality in painting female nudes. Browning is here, as previously in "Filippo Baldinucci," primarily concerned to take issue with those who subject art to exclusively moral evaluations. Opposed to poets like Swinburne who conceived of art as an end in itself, he was likewise staunch in his antagonism to those who viewed art as merely a means for the inculcation of morality. The artist's business is with God, Browning had said more than once, and hence it is beyond those who "dare advance / This doctrine that the Artist-mind must needs / Own affinity with yours" (215–17).

The scope of the parleying is even broader than this. In first a prayer and then a sermon Furini, the painter-theologian, is permitted to enlarge upon his aesthetic theory in relation to his metaphysical position. The burden of Furini's homily, addressed to "Evolutionists" in London, is very much like the closing passage of "With Christopher Smart" in its insistence that man gains knowledge by proceeding from the tangible to the abstract, from sense to soul. Whereas the evolutionists strain to the top of things until they are stopped by the question of the origin of life, Furini begins at the bottom. He professes to know just one fact—"my self-consciousness,— / 'Twixt ignorance and ignorance enisled,— / Knowledge: before me was my Cause—that's styled / God: after, in due course succeeds the rest" (351–4); and this fact he has gained from experience. His pictures are a record of his growth of consciousness and of his development in understanding the soul which lies beneath sense. Yet whatever veil is plucked from nature, the secret of the cause is never seized. All that he can surely know, and he learns it increasingly, is that the cause is external to the manifestation. From his own development he gains an understanding of history as progress in man's knowledge of good, he being always careful to say, like Ferishtah, that he speaks only from his point of vantage (259–60, 518–19). In opposition to the new science he can state that in his view good predominates over evil, that both exist to enable man to experience growth, and that he has exercised his imagination in testimony to his belief.

"Francis Furini" ends with the speaker's admission that Furini never attained to the greatest heights in painting and with praise for the vitality and joy to be found in his art. He is considered an artist most worthy to be remembered for his attempts to enlighten the darkness which obscures the manifestations of God in man's life, and he is dismissed with the speaker's suggestion that he paint Joan of Arc not in her most stately or ecstatic moments but as a young girl bathing nude in a pool with her face turned away —"that face about to burn / Into an angel's when the time is ripe" (612–13). Though Furini could not depict a transcendent vision, good descendentalist that he was, he could intimate the possibilities of revelation which lie within man's potential.

The parleying "With Gerard De Lairesse" takes up the theme of time adumbrated in Furini's sermon to the evolutionists, and, like the second section of each of the two preceding movements, deals with the opposite aspect of the dominant themes expounded in the first section. Thus, as Furini looked to the future for progress, De Lairesse looked to the past as the height of man's achievement. The light that was so brilliant at the end of "Furini" is lost in the blindness, both physical and spiritual, of the subject of the parleying "With De Lairesse." The speaker is, however, more kindly disposed toward De Lairesse than he was toward either Bartoli or Dodington, the ostensible subjects of the second sections of the previous movements, his attitude signified by the opening words "Ah, but—." Where Furini saw men and women as filled with manifestations of the Divine, De Lairesse, because of his blindness, could not be blessed "with the actual view / Of man and woman, those fair forms" (2–3).

The speaker recounts how he had once respected the Dutch painter and art historian and had felt his work as a powerful influence. This fact gives an ambivalence to the speaker's (and

Browning's) denunciation of those who claim that men of today can do no better than imitate the Ancients. For Browning, if indeed the "I" of the parleying is Browning, loved Greek literature almost better than any other—and *Balaustion's Adventure* and *Aristophanes' Apology* give ample testimony to his knowledge and love of the Greek classics. Hence it is with poignancy that he undertakes to show that for modern man the visions of the past are dead and that he must look to the present and future for his proper orientation. It was De Lairesse's book on art that the speaker valued, more than his pictures, especially the part called "The Walk," because it advised that artists can find abundant worth in the trivial commonplace: "Beyond / The ugly actual, lo, on every side / Imagination's limitless domain / Displayed a wealth of wondrous sounds and sights / Ripe to be realized by poet's brain / Acting on painter's brush!" (57–62). Yet the speaker regrets that De Lairesse was not ultimately content with the commonplace alone, but instead embellished his art with mythological fancies drawn from Greece. The speaker can understand why the painter did this even though he thinks him wrong: fancy imagined a strife between sense and soul, for sense cannot be content with mere outward things, even with mere beauty, because soul must know whence beauty springs which sense loves.

At this point, the speaker begins to consider the modern cultural condition in which man suffers a dissociated sensibility. The Great Chain of Being, "which used to bind / Our earth to heaven" (146–7), has become unlinked. Men of the nineteenth century can still fancy, but fancy has largely been pushed aside by unseen fact, which mind bids sense accept. Is mind to blame for usurpation or sense for abdication? Whatever the reason, mind has asserted its dominance and focuses on fact instead of fancy. We today could walk where De Lairesse walked and could view the rose not simply as a rose but as a flower from Venus's wreath. "Plain retrogression, this!" (165). The modern poet does not adopt an old habit of vision but perceives in a different way: he sees more deeply, possessed as he is of profounder insight.

To prove that he, a modern poet, can indeed see as De Lairesse and his predecessors saw, the speaker proposes a "walk" much in the manner of De Lairesse's "Walk." Browning's begins just before daybreak and ends at dusk to symbolize the dawning and waning of Greek culture. It is a series of vignettes in the grand manner: the first shows the struggle of Zeus and Prometheus, the ideal of love for man in conflict with the conception of God as power; the second depicts a ruthless Artemis as the spoiler by death of the happiness of marriage and symbolizes human joy and well-being at war with a cruel divinity; the third presents the pathetic story of Lyda and the Satyr, symbols of lust and ravage; the fourth departs from mythology to introduce Darius and Alexander, who represent the fierce rage for power which leaves the world in chaos; and the fifth closes the series with a voiceless and deprecating ghost, which emblemizes the death of Greek culture.

As in the previous sections, Browning has here a contemporary adversary with whom he wishes to parley. His opponent is that group of English poets who championed Hellenism in modern literature. His "walk" through Greek history includes glances at Arnold, Tennyson, Swinburne, and Morris, and perhaps, in the Prometheus episode, at Shelley, in each vignette mimicking their style in the treatment of Greek subjects. He wants to make clear, first, that the history of Greek civilization is a record of progressive dehumanization and, second, that whatever its nature, it is dead and done with. His point is that modern poets must deal with the present and the future: "Some fitter way express / Heart's satisfaction that the Past indeed / Is past, gives way before Life's best and last, / The all-including Future!" (364–7). Life does not stand still; the soul must have its eye not on the past or even on the present but on the goal of an all-reconciling future. If art does not point the way, it abnegates its duty.

"With De Lairesse" ends on a note of affirmation, the poet expressing his belief that the past, rather than dead, has marked a beginning on which men have built and will continue to build. Nothing that truly lived, whether it be literature or love or life itself, can ever die: "What here attains / To a beginning, has no end, still gains / And never loses aught: when, where, and how

— / Lies in Law's lap" (413–16). And summing up his view of the past and present intertwined, he breaks forth into a lyric of welcome to spring, which soon will emerge from the seemingly barren past into a fantasia of color and light. Though the old myths are no longer adequate to embody human aspirations, though the art of Greece cannot serve as a model for modern poets, though present knowledge has outmoded so much of Greek lore, still the present joins hands with the past in a dithyramb to the future, heralded by the recrudence of spring soon to come.

The last movement of the *Parleyings* consists of only one section, but it contains the dialectical components of the preceding ones, except that here the swing from positive to negative is reversed. The new motion is signaled by the opening words, "How strange!" On a bitter morning, the speaker looks out his window to survey the ravages worked by winter: all is torn and tattered and wrecked—no sign of beauty anywhere. Then, like the "I" of "De Lairesse" rising from the blackness of the past to greet the light of the future, he suddenly glimpses a bird which, unsatisfied with natural materials for his nest-building, has come to snatch a scrap of cloth holding up a vine: "What a life and beauty" (12). As he watches the bird tugging at "this rag of manufacture, spoiled / By art, and yet by nature near unsoiled, / New-suited to what scheming finch would breed / In comfort, this uncomfortable March" (33–6), his mind turns to another art and another "March," a tune by the eighteenth-century organist Charles Avison, which he had loved as a youth. Is Avison's music, he ponders, as dead as the winter landscape before him?

Once Avison's music had proved captivating, as had that of his contemporaries, especially the great Handel; but how simple it now seems to one accustomed to the complex harmonies of Brahms, Wagner, Dvorak, and Liszt. In its own day the music of the early eighteenth century had absorbed heart and soul as much as Wagner's does now. "Perfect from center to circumference— / Orbed to the full can be but fully orbed" (130–31)—being perfect, why does it no longer have the power that it once had? Put another way, why does art wear out? No truer truth is obtainable by man than that which music offers. Does the fact that music loses its hold over succeeding generations mean that truth itself changes?

In an attempt to answer his questions, the speaker is led to consider what music is and how it operates. To explain he must first define the words "soul" and "mind." Soul is that which underlies mind, just as a river flows under a bridge. The mind, which is the bridge, builds up our solid knowledge, while the soul, surging beneath, flows from feeling out of the deeps which cannot be understood or described. Music attempts to match and mate feeling with knowledge, to capture soul's flow and make it known, to make what we feel as hard and fast as what we know. All arts endeavor to do this, and music most nearly succeeds. Yet it too fails. Why?

Mind does not obtain knowledge from art's ministry because art literally is not creative. It arranges, dissociates, redistributes, and rearranges, producing only change, not creation. Each art would shoot liquidity into a mold and arrest the soul's movement. Poetry by its word-mesh, painting by its snare of line and color, music by its sound-net—each tries to capture the soul's evanescence. Alas, each fails; and music, which dredges deeper, is unable to give as great a permanence to its truth as its sister arts. Love, hate, joy, and fear survive, but a Handel's grasp on them soon loses its power, and then a Gluck, a Haydn, a Mozart come on the scene to recapture the hold the earlier musician once had: "So perfections tire,— / Whiten to wanness, till . . . let others note / The ever-new invasion!" (274–6).

From his laboratory of knowledge, the speaker will attempt to reinfuse with liveliness a sleep that looks like death, and crowding Avison's march with new harmonies and rhythms will recast the old piece. But he decides that no new life may be engendered in this fashion. Music's throne, sadly, seats somebody whom someone else unseats. Momentarily, he fears that the knowledge of one age is not known in the next:

> "This it was brought tears
> Once to all eyes,—this roused heart's rapture once?"
> So will it be with truth that, for the nonce,
> Styles itself truth perennial: 'ware its wile!
> Knowledge turns nescience,—foremost on the file,
> Simply proves first of our delusions.   [355–60]

Such thoughts prove, however, to be but a modulation into a minor key. For is it not possible that our present life may kindle the life of the past, that we may put ourselves in sympathy with the time that produced Avison's music and so make it live again? Answering in the bold C major of Avison's march, he reflects that truth was within man from the beginning and that, though the forms may fade, the art which captured the truth in suitable garniture for a certain age is of infinite value in the saving of truth for that time. Like all living things, art is subject to the laws of change and decay. Yet the history of art is the history of progress of truth from generation to generation. Winter comes but spring is not far behind, June boasting fruits as "not new vesture merely but, to boot, / Novel creation" (377–8). No need then for sorrow about the evanescence of art or the transience of myths: "Soon shall fade and fall / Myth after myth—the husk-like lies I call / New truth's corolla-safeguard: Autumn comes, / So much the better" (378–81).

"Charles Avison" ends with a mighty symphony of sound in which the past is recaptured and Avison with Bach, Strafford with Pym march while the dim antique grows clarion-clear. The close marks the reconciliation of all those discordant elements treated in the three previous movements. Though the Fates are allowed to speak throughout, it is Apollo who has the last word: art, knowledge, imagination, religion are shown to rise from the darkness into the light of the stars. The evil aspect that the world so often presents is perhaps not the evil it seems, but the transformation of good into a higher truth. March, the month in which the poem begins, leads on to May and June; Avison's "March," the tune from an earlier time, provides the harmonic seeds for the triumphal progress toward the future.

In the Prologue the Fates maintained that the earth "at due distance / If viewed" is only an ice ball disguised as a fire orb (86–9). In "Mandeville" the speaker held that man viewed the world only "point by point" (193–7); and in "Furini" he asked that each man "state what truth is from his point of view, / Mere pin-point though it be: since many such / Conduce to make a whole" (259–61). In "De Lairesse" he pondered whether advantage was to be gained from seeing double (118–19). Now in the final parleying the speaker rises above one and even two levels of vision to a perception of the power of imaginative sympathy as the means by which all of history may be viewed and understood, a multiperspective symbolized by the matching of words and music. He attains a more nearly comprehensive purview which shows that earth is neither an ice ball nor a fire orb but a revolving globe of "nor night nor day" (404).

The Epilogue brings the *Parleyings* to a close with a scene in a printing shop. "Fust and His Friends" presents no beatific vision such as concludes *Faust* or *The Divine Comedy,* but a comedy in which the inventor of printing is mistaken for a Faust-like mage capable of raising devils and working miracles. It is in the same verse form as "Apollo and the Fates," and with the Prologue provides the cosmic frame for the *Parleyings.* Earlier on, in "Gerard De Lairesse," the speaker had referred to Faustus's robe (50) among the marvels which he eschewed as subject matter for modern art. Here the wonder-working Faust becomes the ordinary John Fust, whose only marvel was that through imagination and diligence he made a machine capable of reproducing the written word. "The human heroes tread the world's dark way / No longer," the speaker in "De Lairesse" had said (358–9). The beatific vision of this epic is to be found in the everyday world of men and women, not in heaven. As the parleyer in "Christopher Smart" observed, "Law must be / Active in earth or nowhere; earth you see,— / Or there or not at all, Will, Power, and Love / Admit discovery" (256–9). Heaven is, in a manner of speaking, present here on earth; and all human history, as the movement of the *Parleyings* indicates, is a progress from superstition, belief in a cosmos of gods and fates removed from man, to a faith in existential reality, the divine manifested in the actual. Where previously man's fate lay in darkness, it is now illuminated by the dispersion of the word, the Word of God revealed to all who wish to see.

The seven friends who ascend "up, up, up" the spiral stair leading to Fust's chamber represent the nay-sayers of the seven preceding parleyings. They cannot believe that Fust, known to them as an ordinary man not given to piety, is capable of working any wonder without the aid of Satan. They accuse him of Faustian deeds: calling up Helen of Troy as his partner in sin, causing a vine to grow out of a table during a drinking bout, reaping strange honors for himself. Fust finally admits that he has hit upon a device that will bring man good. He has arrived at a vantage point, an Archimedean "Pou sto," which will permit him to raise the world. This, of course, is the printing press, the invention of which will redeem his sins in making restitution to truth, by fixing in print facts (as art captures the truth of a certain age) that would otherwise become lies through oral transmission, and by making truth available to the peasant as well as to the noble. Like all increases in knowledge, however, it will serve to undermine the old established formulations of truth and will even aid the dispersion of lies, in short, will be capable of producing both good and bad. Yet the heretic Martin Luther, whom Fust foresees and whom his press will benefit, will ultimately be the instrument of more good than evil. Convinced that his invention assures that "night yields to the dawn's reassurance" (268), Fust feels he has accomplished a work that has God's blessing: the forwarding of the Word's plan for men by the printed word; and he fancies he hears the Creator's benediction:

> "Be thou saved, Fust! Continue my plan,
> Who spake and earth was: with my word things began.

> "As sound so went forth, to the sight be extended
> Word's mission henceforward! The task I assign,
> Embrace—thy allegiance to evil is ended!

Have cheer, soul impregnate with purpose! Combine
Soul and body, give birth to my concept—called thine!

"Far and wide, North and South, East and West, have
    dominion
O'er thought, winged wonder, O Word!" [284–92]

At the beginning of his career Browning had a scheme for producing anonymously a series of works, *Pauline* being the first, for
the unsuspecting world, which never would guess that the authors
of "such an opera, such a speech, etc., etc., were no other than
the same individual" (quoted in DeVane, *Handbook,* p. 41). In
writing the *Parleyings,* which is so highly retrospective, he may
perhaps have wondered fleetingly whether he did indeed make
the right choice when he elected to be a poet, the comparisons of
music, painting, and poetry throughout seeming to give some hint
as to his concern. The Epilogue, nevertheless, leaves us in no
doubt. As Maisie Ward says, it brings "the message that Browning felt his own choice in life had been the right one—not art,
not music, but poetry. The written word will outlast all else."[4] It
is of no little autobiographical significance that Browning chose to
make the printing press the concluding symbol of a work that
cast a backward glance over his entire career.

The press is also a summarizing symbol of all the important
themes in the *Parleyings.* Knowledge spreads but will always have
its limitations; hope grows as the imagination is unleased from
superstitious constraints; any advance has the potential for both
good and evil; art constantly undergoes transformation; old
myths are superseded by more vital ones—all this is epitomized
by the printing press, which stands as a symbol of "life's light"
(390).

If *Fifine at the Fair* was, as Browning thought, the boldest and
most metaphysical poem he had written since *Sordello,* then
surely the *Parleyings with Certain People of Importance in Their
Day* is the boldest and most metaphysical he wrote after *Fifine.* In
conception and complexity it is grander than anything since *The*

4. *Robert Browning and His World,* p. 282.

Ring and the Book. Ranging from classical Greece through the Middle Ages and Enlightenment to the modern period, it treats of man's thought, morals, art, and religion. Browning surveyed the sweep of history leading to the modern cultural crisis, and where so many of his contemporaries found only a cause for despair he discovered a reason for hope. Though all the old patterns that once governed man's mind and conduct were in process of dissolution, Browning greeted the change with gusto. "How good is noise!" his parleyer proclaimed in "Avison," after stating that man is the cause his music champions; "What's silence but despair / Of making sound match gladness never there?" (416–17). The *Parleyings* is Browning's joyful song unto the Lord in thanks that man would not only endure but prevail.

12 ❧ Asolando

Browning's visit to Asolo in 1878 had been undertaken with a degree of apprehensiveness. He had feared to find the town radically different from his memory of it forty years earlier. Yet when he arrived he was delighted to find it almost unchanged. His holiday there proved stimulating and restorative. But he evidently had misgivings about returning a third time, because for ten years thereafter, although during the interval he vacationed in Venice, he did not go to Asolo. In 1889, however, he decided to spend part of his autumn holiday in the small city, and apparently he suffered none of the foreboding experienced a decade previously. In his letters he speaks of "the magic word . . . 'Asolo'" (*New Letters*, p. 383)', and of "Asolo, my old attraction" (Hood, *Letters*, p. 316); he recounts the old dream "of seeing Asolo in the distance and making vain attempts to reach it" until at last he "saw it again, and the dreams stopped."[1]

When he arrived he was highly pleased. The drive there "seemed to be a dream" (Orr, *Life*, p. 388); the place "remains what I first conceived it to be—the most beautiful spot I ever was privileged to see. It is seldom that one's impressions of half-a-century ago, are confirmed by present experience but so it is . . ." (*New Letters*, p. 383). He even decided to build a house there for his annual holidays. "My own desire to get the house," he wrote to his son, "is rather increased than abated by my greater experience of the country: you may take my word for it, you have not half seen the capabilities of enjoyment in the place. Every

1. Lilian Whiting, *The Brownings: Their Life and Art*, pp. 282-3.

fresh drive we take shows us new beauty" (Hood, *Letters*, p. 320). And just as a decade earlier the return to Asolo had resulted in a new burst of creative energy, so did this visit aid him in the preparation of a new volume of poems—"some few written, all of them supervised, in the comfort of your presence," he says in the dedication to Mrs. Bronson, his hostess in Asolo.

Asolando: Fancies and Facts was published on 12 December 1889, the day Browning died in Venice at the home of his son. Although it was appreciated as the last work of a great poet and went through nine reprints in a short time, the volume has not generally received the critical attention it should claim. It contains some choice lyrics, an excellent narrative, a very fine dramatic monologue, and a delightful personal poem without counterpart elsewhere in Browning. There is none of the petulance and irritability that mar his work of the late seventies and little of the moralizing that characterizes the poems from the first *Dramatic Idyls* through *Ferishtah's Fancies*. The volume may best be described as charming; it is as though Browning were consciously trying to make friends with the British public who previously had not loved him—which is not to say that he was pandering to his audience, but that he was attempting to converse with them as with old acquaintances. Browning's dedication described it as composed of "disconnected poems" united by the title, which he derived from "asolare—to disport in the open air, amuse oneself at random." But it is an important book in that it gives us the poet's last thoughts on the subject that had preoccupied him from *The Ring and the Book* on, namely, the nature of truth; and its importance is signified by the other meaning of the title, which indicates its relation to Asolo and the facts and fancies called forth by that city's name. For the return to Asolo, the city of his dreams, symbolized the changes his conception of truth had undergone in the past half-century.

The change is outlined in the Prologue, which recalls Wordsworth's "Tintern Abbey," "Stanzas on Peele Castle," and "Intimations Ode." Though Asolo has remained the same, the poet himself has changed. Once the natural world seemed to take a coloring from his eye: "Natural objects seemed to stand / Palpably fire-clothed"; over all he cast a haze of fancy. It was a terrible beauty he saw and in its presence he could not speak. But the flame has disappeared, the burning bush is bare: God is no longer where the poet once had thought to find Him. Yet he does not regret the loss of an old habit of vision because now he has learned a new, truer way of seeing: he views things as they are, no longer draped in fancy but as they in themselves are: "Hill, vale, tree, flower—they stand distinct, / Nature to know and name." He now understands "earth's import": he and nature are separate entities, "God is it who transcends." If nature is to be redeemed, it is God and not the poet who will do it.

Browning, in this very personal poem, does not despair of the changes that the years bring: no disillusionment, despondency, or madness for him but rather gladness for his ability to perceive more nearly the truth uncovered from its draperies, "the naked very thing." He takes up here the theme elaborated in the *Parleyings*, especially in "With Gerard De Lairesse." Whereas the older poets (and, by implication, he himself earlier) had urged, "Push back reality, repeople earth / With vanished falseness, recognize no worth / In fact new-born unless 't is rendered back / Pallid by fancy," he counsels, "Let things be—not seem, / . . . do, and nowise dream" ("De Lairesse," 384-7, 389-90). To leave off dreaming is, in one sense, to forswear one's youth. There is a brief note of sadness in both "De Lairesse" and the Prologue, as Browning reflects on the joys of the past, illusory though in part they were:

> And now? The lambent flame is—where?
>   Lost from the naked world: earth, sky,
> Hill, vale, tree, flower,—Italia's rare
>   O'er-running beauty crowds the eye—
> But flame? The Bush is bare.

The poet who in youth had been aware of an intense consciousness of self and believed that his self "exists, if tracked, in all: / But linked, in [him], to self-supremacy, / Existing as a centre to all things, / Most potent to create and rule and call / Upon all things to minister to it"—this person, who "would be all, have see, know, taste, feel, all" (*Pauline*, 268–78), had believed that God exists behind every thing or person and that to reach Him one should possess the phenomenal world as fully and intensely as possible. Yet as he matured he witnessed "dwindling into the distance" the star of God's presence on earth (Epilogue to *Dramatis Personae*) until God became like an "unseen friend" who does not show himself: "He keeps absent,—why I cannot think" ("Fears and Scruples"). Finally, God disappears entirely from nature— "The Bush is bare"—and a voice says: "At Nature dost thou shrink amazed? / God is it who transcends." There is surely a sense of loss expressed in the Prologue, but the sadness of the loss is mitigated by a more than compensatory gain. Better plain fact, Browning says, than embellished fancy.

Although the Prologue recounts the history of the poet himself, it aptly serves to introduce the other pieces in the collection, which are not so personal but nevertheless have a personal relevance. In *Asolando* Browning is relating his own experience but he intends it to have a wider application. For he attempts in this volume, as he did in the *Parleyings*, to trace the history of mankind in terms of his own development. "What law prevails alike through great and small, / The world and man—world's miniature we call?" he asks in "Beatrice Signorini" (94–5). Or as he states more directly in "Reverie":

> I for my race and me
>   Shall apprehend life's law:
> In the legend of man shall see
>   Writ large what small I saw
> In my life's tale: both agree.   [26–30]

The tale he undertakes to tell—the effort to find "life's law" for himself and the race—is recounted in reference to the facts and fancies of the title.

In the Prologue, as well as in the other poems of the book, Browning leaves us with no doubt that fact is to be preferred to fancy, which includes both dreams and visions. "Poetics" illustrates how even figurative language can falsify and hence debase

the thing itself. "Rose," "swan," "moon," the conventional metaphors drawn from the inanimate or lower animal world, cannot
fitly celebrate the loved one: "What is she? Her human self,—no
lower word will serve." "Speculative" evinces the poet's craving
to possess even in heaven the real love he knew on earth, in
preference to dreamed-of new life for man, nature, and art.
"Beatrice Signorini" shows a husband returning from a voyage of
fancy in art to the fulfillment to be found in the facts of the heart
at home. "Rosny" portrays a maiden who would prefer dreams to
reality and so would be left without her lover. "Inapprehensiveness" depicts a lady absorbed in a fancy about the landscape
while the man, longing for her to give him some sign of her affection, is left to ponder "fancies that might be" and "facts that are."

But, the question remains, what is fact? Certainly it is not
synonymous with truth. It is not merely something observable and
hence provable. In "La Saisiaz" the speaker had observed:
"Facts? that they o'erpass my power of proving, proves them
such" (223). Nor is fact necessarily divorced from fancy. In *The
Ring and the Book* the poet had proclaimed: "Fancy with fact is
just one fact the more" (I. 458). Fact is but a step toward truth,
which frequently cannot be grasped without the aid of fancy, so
that fact and fancy are natural allies in human development.
Nowhere is this made more explicit than in "Development," a
delightful poem about Browning's own education.

When the poet was a child, his father taught him a game illus-
trative of the siege of Troy, then a little later gave him Pope's
version of the *Iliad* to read, and finally turned him loose on
Homer in the original Greek; at each stage of his growth he was
provided with the proper means for his understanding, his father
knowing "better than turn straight / Learning's full flare on
weak-eyed ignorance." By young adulthood, then, he had all the
"facts" about Homer: "nothing more remains to know." "Thus
did youth spend a comfortable time," until he learned of the German higher criticism. He was told that there never was a Homer
or a Trojan War: "No warrant for the fiction I, as fact, / Had
treasured in my heart and soul so long." Yes, even the "facts"

change. Nevertheless, "as fact held still, [I] still hold, / Spite of new knowledge, in my heart of hearts / And soul of souls, fact's essence freed and fixed, / From accidental fancy's guardian sheath."

In dealing with the higher criticism of Homer, Browning is of course also dealing with the parallel instance of the higher criticism of the Bible. During the course of his development he comes to realize that "facts" as well as myths are but provisional constructs, never to be taken as truth itself since, as the Pope in *The Ring and the Book* pointed out, truth is always in advance of any formulation of it. Facts are, as it were, but points of view that can never encompass the truth itself. They are, furthermore, signs that suggest the ways to truth. "Look through the sign to the thing signified," Browning admonished in "With Bernard de Mandeville" (192). And that is exactly what he proposes in the case of Homer. He will attempt to pass beyond the accidentals of both fact and fancy to grasp the essence of the Greek epics: Helen, Ulysses, Hector, Achilles will remain in "the shrine my precious tenantry." As with Homer so with religion: no matter what the scholars teach concerning the historical inaccuracies of the Bible, he will cling to essential Christianity and guard the Christ in his shrine.

Fancies are as necessary as facts, Browning explains in "Development." His father did right to let him approach Homer in the way appropriate to each stage of his growth. One might argue, like a Gradgrind, that it was misguided on his parent's part to allow the child ever to read about the "fiction" of the Trojan War at all. I might have, he suggests,

> Been taught, by forthrights not meanderings,
> My aim should be to loathe, like Peleus' son,
> A lie as Hell's Gate, love my wedded wife,
> Like Hector, and so on with all the rest.
> Could not I have excogitated this
> Without believing such men really were?   [99–104]

His father could have given him straight off the *Nicomachean Ethics*. But what good would it have served? Now that he is gray he finds it hard to understand Aristotle. What would he have made of it as a child? No, a person must learn by degrees, and often this means the employment of fancy to reach the truth hidden beneath the surface. Although reason is ultimately superior to dream or fancy, it cannot be called into function until the person is capable of making use of it.

"A myth may teach," Browning had said in the parleying "With Mandeville" (204); but myths become outmoded and are replaced by new myths, he observed in "With Avison." In the brilliant monologue "Imperante Augusto Natus Est——" he returns to the efficacy of myth and its changing nature. The speaker tells of his attendance at the baths the previous day when a poet read a panegyric on the Emperor, proclaiming him a god. With his head full of Augustus's glory he leaves the baths and strolls through the city of Rome, finding everywhere monuments testifying to the splendor of the Emperor. He comes upon a beggar and recognizes Augustus under the disguise. He remembers a rumor that once a year the Emperor plays the beggar to disarm Fate's envy, and he is struck by the thought that even gods are not safe.

> Who stands secure? Are even Gods so safe?
> Jupiter that just now is dominant—
> Are not there ancient dismal tales how once
> A predecessor reigned ere Saturn came,
> And who can say if Jupiter be last?
> Was it for nothing the gray Sibyl wrote
> "Caesar Augustus regnant, shall be born
> In blind Judæa"—one to master him,
> Him and the universe?   [152–60]

The insufficiency of the myth of the Emperor-god is indicated by the last three lines of the monologue:

> Bath-drudge! Here, slave! No cheating! Our turn next.
> No loitering, or be sure you taste the lash!
> Two strigils, two oil-drippers, each a sponge!

Browning welcomes the decay of old myths and the growth of new ones: "Soon shall fade and fall / Myth after myth . . . / So much the better," he had said in the *Parleyings* ("With Avison,"

378–81). He greets new stages of development in the race as well as in his own life because he detects at work in history an unfolding of ever greater possibilities by which good may be perceived and hence acted upon. This is his concern in "Reverie," probably the most difficult poem in the volume.[2] In his youth, as in the childhood of the race, power was easily discerned, not so love. To find this love and to reconcile it with power was, according to Browning, his life-long quest and also that of human history: "Even as the world its life, / So have I lived my own— / Power seen with Love at strife" (171–3). And looking over his life and the history of mankind he has learned "that, strive but for closer view, / Love were as plain to see" (214–15). Perhaps on this earth the full reconciliation of power and love will never be revealed, but he has faith that it will be so in the world beyond.

Finite minds are necessarily limited in their understanding of God's purpose. Browning told Mrs. Orr that in his opinion divine love "could only reveal itself to the human heart by some supreme act of *human* tenderness and devotion; the fact, or fancy, of Christ's cross and passion could alone supply such a revelation."[3] Possessed of such a fact or fancy, Browning was assured of the love as well as the power of God, and he was convinced, as we have seen in *Ferishtah's Fancies* and the *Parleyings*, that evil is allowed to exist for a very definite purpose—as a condition for good. Man's thought must be projected toward the future and toward heaven; and so, the poet says in "Reverie," life means not resting and having, but being and becoming, aspiring to the heights of heaven where power and love are one. Human life as the battleground between good and evil is developed in "Rephan," in which a being on another planet could not exist where all was perfection, everything merging in a neutral best, but longed for the imperfection, pain, growth, doubt, and change which would startle him up to the infinite. When he became

2. See Philip Drew, *The Poetry of Browning*, pp. 170–74, for a careful reading of the poem and also an account of its difficulties.

3. "The Religious Opinions of Robert Browning," *Contemporary Review*, 60 (1891), 879.

aware that he could not rest content with the perfection of Rephan, he was told:

> Burn and not smolder, win by worth,
> Not rest content with a wealth that's dearth?
> Thou art past Rephan, thy place be Earth!

Browning's essentially Christian interpretation of history is disclosed by a comparison of "Imperante Augusto Natus Est——"
and "The Bean-Feast." It will be recalled that the Emperor disguised himself as a beggar out of fear that Fortune would turn
spiteful and strike low one who stood so high. The Pope in "The
Bean-Feast" also undertakes to play the mendicant, but he does
so out of joy rather than fear. Wishing to learn better how his
people live, he wanders to a humble home and happily and with
relish joins the family in a dish of beans. The descendental thrust
of the Pope's nature, to use the Carlylean term we have employed in earlier chapters, is toward the plenitude of God's creation and hence results in exaltation, praise, and joy; while the
Emperor's turning toward the lowly is but self-abasement undertaken to escape Fate's envy and issuing forth in despair. What is
missing in Augustus's world is the joy derived from the knowledge
that God has provided for man, for which the Pope returns thanks:

> Thy care extendeth to Nature's homely wants,
> And, while man's mind is strengthened, Thy goodness nowise
> scants
> Man's body of its comfort,—that I whom kings and queens
> Crouch to, pick crumbs from off my table, relish beans!
> The thunders I but seem to launch, there plain Thy hand
> all see:
> That I have appetite, digest, and thrive—that boon's for me.

The Pope is another embodiment of the Heraklean ideal, which
Browning had first delineated in *Balaustion's Adventure*, while
the Emperor is another in that succession of mournful pagan figures whose type was established in "Cleon."

What convinces Browning that Power is also Love—what, in
other words, makes him a Christian, doctrinally heterodox though
he might be—is his own experience of love. In *Asolando*, as in all

the poems of his later career, human love is the one unchanging fact of which man can be certain. It is "life's law" spoken of in "Reverie." More than half the poems of the volume deal specifically with love and the truth to be discovered in the disclosure of one heart to another.

> The moment eternal . . .
> When ecstasy's utmost we catch at the core.   ["Now"]

> Brightest truth, purest trust in the universe—all were for me
> In the kiss of one girl.   ["Summum Bonum"]

The truest fancy, the flame in the bush alluded to in the Prologue, is to be found in the fact of love:

> I am wrapt in blaze,
> Creation's lord, of heaven and earth
> Lord whole and sole—by a minute's birth—
> Through the love in a girl.   ["A Pearl, A Girl"]

Once experience the rapture, and one's life is forever transformed. "No dream, more real by much" ("Dubiety"), the "moment eternal" is a truth never to be doubted. Others may require new life in heaven, but the speakers in Browning's love lyrics need only "earth's old life" when a man and woman loved ("Speculative").

To lay claim to the eternal moment means that in love, as in religion, one must look through the accidentals to the heart of the matter. Two poems of *Asolando*, both dialogues, deal with the lack of recognition of a situation in which love might be realized. The pair in "Inapprehensiveness" discuss trivia, while the man longs for some look or gesture that would allow "dormant passion . . . / To burst into immense life." In "Flute-Music, with an Accompaniment" a man and a woman discuss the music they hear wafted over the treetops from some unseen flutist. He fancies that the music proceeds from an unusual passion in love. She replies that his observation is but "fancy-spinning," the "fact" being that a poor clerk is practicing musical exercises during his lunch hour and playing very badly. The man, however, insists that whatever the flutist's competency, "he could surprise one / Well-

nigh into trusting / Here was a musician / Skilled consummately"
(88–91). The woman's companion rebukes her:

> as you explain things,
> All's mere repetition,
> Practise-pother: of all vain things
> Why waste pooh or pish on
> Toilsome effort—never
> Ending, still beginning—
> After what should pay endeavour
> —Right-performance? winning
> Weariness from you who,
> Ready to admire some
> Owl's fresh hooting—Tu-whit, tu-who—
> Find stale thrush-songs tiresome.   [109–20]

The man is irked that she does not lend a sympathetic ear to the
music, does not hear what it tries to convey rather than criticize
the wrong notes; he tells that he laments such warning of ill below
the surface, the doubting of passion in music or the distrust of
expressions of love. While she maintains that it is the distance that
has caused him to misinterpret the music, he insists that in music
as in love distance brings things into true perspective.[4] He would
believe in the music as he believes in love. If it be a dream, then
let him sleep on. Besides, he asks, "What if all's appearance? / Is
not outside seeming / Real as substance inside? / Both are facts,
so leave me dreaming" (184–7). As Browning says in "Development," "No dream's worth waking" (84). Better to love in fancy
than in fact not love at all.

Another poem closely related to the two just discussed is "Beatrice Signorini," which Browning thought the best in *Asolando*
(DeVane, *Handbook*, p. 544). The artist Francesco Romanelli

---

4. George M. Ridenour, "Browning's Music Poems: Fancy and Fact,"
notes that in this poem "appearances are realities, and are part of the
experienced being of the person or thing, the woman or the song. And implicitly here the woman is the song. Or rather, the flute music as accompanied by the structuring commentary of the man and the woman all
together make up the song, a fact which is a joke on the woman. It is a
song played on a flute: light, witty, playful . . ." (p. 373).

was working in Rome and was attracted by Artemisia, an artist more gifted than he, who would not give herself to him. She sends him back to his wife in Viterbo and as a parting present gives him a canvas with a frame of flowers, the central space to be filled in by him with a portrait of the woman he loves best. Francesco chooses to paint in the face of Artemisia. Once home, he shows the portrait to Beatrice, his wife, assuming that she will docilely accept anything at his hands, and mentally contrasting her tame acquiescence with Artemisia's proud spirit. Beatrice calmly criticizes the floral frame and then suddenly stabs the portrait and slashes it to bits. Realizing the unsuspected passion in her character and her profound love for him, Francesco yields to new admiration of his wife. The acknowledgment of her passion for him causes him to say that, in this moment, they have become one in soul and body; and "thus he loved / Past power to change, until his dying day" (334–5). The rushing together of souls became an eternal moment to be treasured forever.

When Browning composed the Epilogue, he could not have known that it was to be his last word to the world. We can only regret that it stands as the poet's valediction. For the Epilogue is little more than rhetoric, apparently designed not only to exculpate the poet from all transgressions but to force his beliefs upon his readers as well.[5] The burden of his argument is that since he has always been an undoubting fighter and striver, he will find happiness in the hereafter, fighting and striving "there as here." David Shaw remarks, "The call to battle is a false alarm. He is simply making an exchange between fighting 'here' and fighting 'There,' with no real transformation of his moral terms."[6] Furthermore, the blustering yea-saying is untrue. As we have noted previously in such poems as "La Saisiaz," Browning's doubt

5. A remark made by Browning just before his final illness leaves no doubt that the poet is the speaker. While reading proof of his last volume, Browning said to his sister and daughter-in-law about the Epilogue: "It almost sounds like bragging to say this, and as if I ought to cancel it." But alas, he convinced himself that "it's the simple truth; and as it's true, it shall stand" (quoted in DeVane, Handbook, p. 553).
6. The Dialectical Temper, p. 220.

and occasional despair run like counterpoints to his cheerfulness all through these later years.

Far more appropriate would it have been, both aesthetically and symbolically, had Browning concluded *Asolando* with "Bad Dreams." Park Honan finds that several poems in the volume suggest "the difficulty of maintaining determined attitudes and of disciplining one's deepest feelings."[7] Instead of the conscious affirmation of the speakers' constancy in love expressed elsewhere, we find in "Bad Dreams" a series of nightmarish encounters between a man and a woman in which are revealed their doubts and fears about themselves as well as about each other: their confidence in their relationship is belied by their unquiet sleep. The architectural images, which recall those of *Fifine* and *Night-Cap Country*, are especially striking in their fantastic horror:

> I saw a lucid City
> Of architectural device
> Every way perfect. Pause for pity,
> Lightning! nor leave a cicatrice
> On those bright marbles, dome and spire,
> Structures palatial. . . .
>
> Ah, but the last sight was the hideous!
> A City, yes,—a Forest, true,—
> But each devouring each. Perfidious
> Snake-plants had strangled what I knew
> Was a pavilion once: each oak
> Held on his horns some spoil he broke
> By surreptitiously beneath
> Upthrusting: pavements, as with teeth,
> Griped huge weed widening crack and split
> In squares and circles stone-work erst.
> Oh, Nature—good! Oh, Art—no whit
> Less worthy! Both in one—accurst! ["Bad Dreams.III"]

Yet whatever doubts and fears the dreams express—and it may well be that here Browning was once again thinking of his "disloyalty" to his wife in proposing marriage to Lady Ashburton—in the end the love proves true. In "Bad Dreams.IV" the man is

7. *The Book, the Ring, & the Poet*, p. 517.

discovered shedding tears over the woman's grave, their love continuing even after their lives are separated. We feel that the ambivalences of these dreams are more expressive of the complex nature of Robert Browning than is the strident affirmation of the Epilogue. The subconscious "fancies" could be truer than the waking "facts."

It is fitting that *Asolando* is Browning's last publication. Asolo, which recalled all the facts and fancies of a lifetime and which came to symbolize the changes that his conception of truth had undergone during the previous fifty years—the return to Asolo set the poet to casting a backward glance over his past and encouraged the writing of what was to be his farewell. He had witnessed fancies blend into facts and facts become fancies; and what was true of him was also true of the race. He had learned that living means shedding the old and taking on the new, one mode of vision yielding to a new way of seeing. *Asolando: Fancies and Facts* expresses Browning's acceptance of conflict and change.

ᔰ Conclusion

As we look back over the poetry Browning wrote after *The Ring and the Book*, we can identify three distinct periods of his later career. The first covers the four years 1871–1875 and includes the six long poems beginning with *Balaustion's Adventure* and ending with *The Inn Album*. During this time Browning was concerned to examine the polarities in man's nature and to show that a healthy existence means acceptance of the antinomies of life. Personality, he shows, is founded in the dialectic tension between body and soul, sense and spirit, good and evil. Though always aspiring higher, man is prevented from soaring upward by his finite limitations. Yet the infinite can be experienced in human love, which partakes of the divine nature. In *Balaustion* Browning's vision of mankind redeemed by love is at its brightest. But as we follow Hohenstiel-Schwangau torn between practicality and idealism, Don Juan attracted by both Fifine and Elvire, Miranda ripped apart by his inability to choose between turf and tower, Aristophanes made the creature of sense, and the nobleman in *The Inn Album* turned into a contemptible blackguard—as we follow this progression, Browning's vision darkens. This was a time of radical formal experimentation and innovation, during which the poet reached the limits of expansion of the dramatic monologue in *Aristophanes' Apology* and attempted two narratives using some techniques of prose fiction in *Red Cotton Night-Cap Country* and *The Inn Album*.

In the second period—from 1876 to 1883, from *Pacchiarotto* through *Jocoseria*—Browning displays bitterness toward the un-

favorable critical reception of his work. Nearly all the poems of
this time are concerned, either explicitly or implicitly, with judgment, justice, and fame. The only formal innovation was made in
the idyllic mode and this not very successfully. During his later
years Browning was intrigued by the long poem and apparently
had lost most of his earlier interest in shorter forms.

The third period dates from 1884 and includes the poet's three
last volumes. Beginning with *Ferishtah's Fancies,* Browning by
and large sheds fears for his fame and writes in a mellow mood of
affirmation. In the *Parleyings* he shows the very nature of truth
to be ever changing, any vesture of it being but short-lived; and
in *Asolando* he considers further how truth may evolve from
falsehood. In this final period the poet, no longer disturbed by
transiency, welcomes with a glad heart the changes that time
brings. It is fitting that in his last years he achieved in the *Parleyings* the largeness of vision for which he had been seeking all
his life.

As early as *The Ring and the Book* Browning had despaired of
any system, either religious or political, as a means of universal
salvation. In the poems we have studied he noted his increasing
awareness of the gap between individual and universal values. To
no institution can man appeal for help; he can save only himself,
and to delude himself that he can save others is to follow an *ignis
fatuus* through a quagmire. In an environment that Browning
increasingly saw as hostile man is left with himself alone. All
around him is false and fleeting; only the self, as Don Juan says, is
true. Man's problem is to work through the morass of meaningless
phenomena to approach the truth that lures him on.

During the first period of his later career, Browning character-
istically uses the terms "sense" and "soul" to denote falsehood and
truth and comes to the conclusion that, though there is a distinc-
tion to be made between the two constituent elements of man's
selfhood, the opposition is more apparent than real. This is indicated by his change in nomenclature from 1876 on, when he prefers to talk more about "fact" and "fancy" than "soul" and
"sense." Truth is to be identified with neither pole of the implied

dialectic. For the apprehension of truth on earth is an illusion or, if not illusive, then so fleeting that truth vanishes almost the moment it is crystallized. In the terrestrial sphere there are only partial truths, fragments of the real truth, on which man builds in hopes of finding that reality hidden by the appearances of the world.

This perception leads Browning to the formulation of what we might call his doctrine of evanescence, the only aspect of his thought that can be characterized as doctrinaire. All is in a state of flux; whatever we seek to grasp melts in our hands or is seen to be something other than we had hoped to find; fact turns out to be fiction and sometimes fiction is disclosed as fact. At best, our finest acts and insights—our language, our art, our myths—are but provisional constructs. During the first phase Browning occasionally finds this a cause for sadness. During the final phase, however, he accepts it unquestioningly.

The universe of Browning's later poetry is very nearly one of absurdity, where man is depicted dealing with fictions in order to reach the "Truth," which in itself may be only the supreme fiction. Almost everything takes on an "as if" quality. A man works as if he were accomplishing something; he lives as if life were meaningful—and because he does, it is. What ultimately saves this world from total absurdity is the experience of love, the one sure manifestation of truth; yet at times, as in the Epilogue to *Ferishtah's Fancies,* the poet speculates that even this may be an illusion. On the whole, however, Browning sees the love between men and women as paradigmatic of the love between God and man.

During his later years Browning repeatedly studies the role of art. Although it is not wholly redemptive, as *Balaustion* almost suggests, it is, as we learn in the *Parleyings,* an instrument of redemption: a power and a moral force that teaches man how aspects of truth may be apprehended. To be sure, it wears out and loses its vitality, like everything else. But art serves to disturb men's assumptions about the nature of truth and, by dissociating and rearranging it, temporarily shoots liquidity into a mold and captures certain truths for a certain period of time.

What is true of art is likewise true of myth. Throughout his later career Browning is preoccupied with the evanescence of religious myth. He speaks to all those who, like his Aristophanes, fear that if there is no "God," the deity of institutionalized religion, then all is permitted. Browning's purpose was to show that men's concepts of divinity change: if the Jehovah of the Old Testament fades into the distance, Ultimate Truth remains. Myth, as well as art, is a focusing artifice like that described in the *Parleyings;* which is to say, myth and art are symbolic representations of truth, not truth itself. And since man is man and not God, the artifice becomes a means of saving his soul. Balaustion's words "There are no gods, no gods! / Glory to God" echo throughout the later poems.

Love, art, and religion—these are the three basic and interconnected concerns of the verse we have studied. Frequently, perhaps more often than not, Browning talks about one in terms of the others. All three individually and collectively are subsumed for Browning in the Incarnation, the ideal of "God, man, or both together mixed" (*Fifine,* LIX). For Browning the Incarnation offers a pattern for movement into ever new spheres of being, God being most God when He becomes man and realizing the greatest potentiality of manhood when He assumes again His Godhood. It is a pattern of abasement and elevation symbolizing the descendental and transcendental thrusts of the human condition in time. Browning's belief in the Incarnation was not that of orthodox Christianity; rather, the Incarnation was for him a basic pattern of existence by which truth is vouchsafed to the phenomenal world and which, as a necessary surmise, the poet accepted as the example for love, art, and religion.

One hardly dares hope that the later Browning will soon be popular. For one reason, the greatest achievements of the last two decades of his life are long poems, and apparently the taste for the long poem has become dulled in the twentieth century. For another reason, the later works reflect Browning's curious erudition. *Aristophanes' Apology* requires at least a modicum of knowledge about fifth-century Athens, and, to take another example, a poem like the *Parleyings* demands that a reader be acquainted not only with a number of minor historical personages, but also with particular nineteenth-century figures and topics of interest. For still another reason, the language is complex, the syntax especially a source of confusion. The dash and the exclamation point, the compound word, the absolute phrase or interjected clause: these are the salient characteristics of the language and they do not make for easy reading.[1] These are, of course, surface difficulties and there is no reason why, for serious students of poetry, they cannot be overcome. There is some sign that evaluation of the later work is slowly beginning to change. Roma King and Morse Peckham have within recent years spoken out strongly in its favor, and Philip Drew has treated it sympathetically.[2] In addition, a growing number of doctoral dissertations and of published articles and essays is being devoted to works written after 1869. But critical judgment has been set for so long against the later Browning that one cannot be optimistic that the received opinion will soon be substantially altered.

There is, admittedly, something of the "grotesque" in the later Browning, as his critics claim.[3] But far from being a defect, its

1. Swinburne's remarks on the difficulty of Browning's later poetry and his supposed obscurity are worth recalling:

To charge him with obscurity is about as accurate as to call Lynceus purblind or complain of the sluggish action of the telegraphic wire. He is something too much the reverse of obscure; he is too brilliant and subtle for the ready reader of a ready writer to follow with any certainty the track of an intelligence which moves with such incessant rapidity, or even to realise with what spider-like swiftness and sagacity his building spirit leaps and lightens to and fro and backward and forward as it lives along the animated line of its labour, springs from thread to thread and darts from centre to circumference of the glittering and quivering web of living thought woven from the inexhaustible stores of his perception and kindled from the inexhaustible fire of his imagination. . . . the proper mood in which to study for the first time a book of Mr. Browning's is the freshest, clearest, most active mood of the mind in its brightest and keenest hours of work. [*The Complete Works of Algernon Charles Swinburne,* ed. Edmund Gosse and Thomas J. Wise (London: William Heinemann, 1926), XII, 145–6]

2. King, *The Focusing Artifice;* Peckham, *Victorian Revolutionaries,* Ch. 3; Drew, *The Poetry of Browning.*

3. It might be argued that the grotesque element in Browning's poetry

radical and often rough-hewn quality is, in my estimation, a source of its vitality. Realizing that he could not capture the pure white light of truth unstained and unblemished, he sought to find a means for circumscribing the reality that cannot be got at directly. Hence his increasingly complex use of perspective as a strategy for bringing an object into fuller view: "So as to take in every side at once, / And not successively" (*Aristophanes' Apology*, Concl., 58–9). Hence also his increasingly elaborate use of language, talking about and around a subject as a strategy for hemming in an elusive truth: "Words have to come," even though "somehow words deflect" (*Hohenstiel-Schwangau*, 2133).[4] If, therefore, the later poetry is grotesque, the grotesqueness—both formal and linguistic—is part of the meaning: "Art's response / To earth's despair" ("With Christopher Smart," 52–3). We should recognize in the contrivances of his art—his quirkish diction, his manner of proceeding by fits and starts, his arbitrary shifts of direction—a way of signaling us that art is play and only

---

is a sign of his modernity. Consider, for example, these observations from Benjamin Nelson's essay "The Omnipresence of the Grotesque": "From one point of view, there is nothing more grotesque in the world than what we call 'normal,' everyday reality.' . . . Are there circumstances when 'normal reality' takes a more than normally grotesque appearance? The answer is yes—when times are unusually stressful. . . . *The omnipresence of the grotesque* is the very hallmark of our time" (*The Discontinuous Universe*, ed. Sallie Sears and Georgianna W. Lord [New York: Basic Books, 1972], pp. 174, 175, 183).

4. Morse Peckham has a stimulating essay on Browning's use of language in his *Victorian Revolutionaries*, pp. 84–129. For Browning, Peckham says, "It is not that man uses language; rather, language uses man. Or better, man is language" (p. 92). George M. Ridenour has an excellent essay on Browning's use of music as a means for dealing with the limits of language: "Browning's Music Poems: Fancy and Fact." Although they deal mainly with the earlier poetry, William Cadbury, "Lyric and Anti-Lyric Forms: A Method for Judging Browning," *University of Toronto Quarterly*, 34 (1964), 49–67, and Robert Preyer, "Two Styles in the Verse of Robert Browning," *ELH*, 32 (1965), 62–84, suggest that so-called cacophony and obscurity may be functional in Browning's art. A thoroughgoing study of the language and style of the later Browning is very much needed.

a feigned image of things, that speech is a precious gift which nevertheless belies the ineffable.

In his later work Browning constantly attempted to transcend the boundaries of art, to "break through Art and rise to poetry" (*Night-Cap Country,* IV. 775). If this meant that his verse were deemed unmusical, what matter, so long as "his own outburst / . . . grew song which was mere music erst" (*Aristophanes' Apology,* Concl., 173–5). If this meant that his poetry were judged formally unfinished, what matter, so long as "the incomplete / More than completion, matches the immense" (*Night-Cap Country,* IV. 778–9).[5] "*Omnia non omnibus,*" the poet had observed at the end of the parleying "With Furini." He was concerned only to work through the false and fleeting, "And reach at length 'God, man, or both together mixed' " (*Fifine,* CXXIV).

5. On this point Chesterton evinces the sound judgment that characterizes his book on Browning: "If we study Browning honestly, nothing will strike us more than that he really created a large number of quite novel and quite admirable artistic forms. It is too often forgotten what and how excellent these were. . . . The thing which ought to be said about Browning by those who do not enjoy him is simply that they do not like his form; that they have studied the form, and think it a bad form" (*Robert Browning,* pp. 137–8).

§➤ Bibliography

I. WORKS BY BROWNING (ARRANGED CHRONOLOGICALLY)

1. *Editions*

Complete Works of Robert Browning. Ed. Charlotte Porter and Helen A. Clarke. Camberwell Edition. 12 vols. New York: Thomas Y. Crowell, 1898.

The Works of Robert Browning. Ed. Frederick G. Kenyon. Centenary Edition. 10 vols. London: Smith, Elder, 1912.

New Poems by Robert Browning and Elizabeth Barrett Browning. Ed. Sir Frederick G. Kenyon. New York: Macmillan, 1915.

"The Texts of Fifteen Fugitives by Robert Browning." Ed. Park Honan. *Victorian Poetry,* 5 (1967), 157–69.

2. *Individual Works (First Publication)*

A. Volumes

Balaustion's Adventure: Including a Transcript from Euripides. London: Smith, Elder, 1871.

Prince Hohenstiel-Schwangau, Saviour of Society. London: Smith, Elder, 1871.

Fifine at the Fair. London: Smith, Elder, 1872.

Red Cotton Night-Cap Country or Turf and Towers. London: Smith, Elder, 1873.

Aristophanes' Apology: Including A Transcript from Euripides, Being The Last Adventure of Balaustion. London: Smith, Elder, 1875.

The Inn Album. London: Smith, Elder, 1875.

Pacchiarotto and How He Worked in Distemper: With Other Poems. London: Smith, Elder, 1876.

The Agamemnon of Aeschylus. London: Smith, Elder, 1877.

La Saisiaz: The Two Poets of Croisic. London: Smith, Elder, 1878.

Dramatic Idyls. London: Smith, Elder, 1879.

Dramatic Idyls, Second Series. London: Smith, Elder, 1880.

Jocoseria. London: Smith, Elder, 1883.

Ferishtah's Fancies. London: Smith, Elder, 1884.

Parleyings with Certain People of Importance in Their Day. London: Smith, Elder, 1887.

Asolando: Fancies and Facts. London: Smith, Elder, 1890.

B. Fugitives, Periodical Writings, Posthumous Verses

"Hervé Riel." *Cornhill Magazine,* 23 (1871), 257–60.

"To My Critics." *Examiner,* 5 August 1876, p. 879.

"Oh Love, Love, thou that from the eyes diffusest" (a lyric from Euripides). *Euripides,* by J. P. Mahaffy. London: Macmillan, 1879. P. 116.

"The Blind Man to the maiden said" (a translation from the German). *The Hour Will Come,* by Wilhemine von Hillern. Transl. by Clara Bell. Leipzig: Tauchnitz, 1879. II, 174.

"Thus I Wrote in London, musing on my betters" (ten new lines to "Touch him ne'er so lightly"). *Century Magazine,* 25 (1882), 159–60.

Sonnet on Goldoni. *Pall Mall Gazette,* 8 December 1883.

"All Singers, trust me, have this common vice" (a paraphrase from Horace). *Pall Mall Gazette,* 13 December 1883.

"Helen's Tower." *Pall Mall Gazette,* 28 December 1883.

Sonnet on Rawden Brown. *Century Magazine,* 27 (1884), 640.

"The Founder of the Feast." *The World,* 16 April 1884. Another version, in form an Italian sonnet, may be found in *New Poems,* 1914, pp. 49–50.

"The Names (To Shakespeare)." *The Shakesperian Show-Book,* May 1884.

"Why I am a Liberal." *Why I Am a Liberal, Being Definitions by the Best Minds of the Liberal Party.* Ed. Andrew Reid. London: Cassell, 1885. P. 11.

"A Spring Song" ("Dance, yellows and whites and reds!"). *The New Amphion,* "The Book of the Edinburgh University Fancy Fair." Edinburgh, 1886. P. 1.

"Jubilee Memorial Lines." In a pamphlet prepared for the Memorial ceremonies commemorated by the great Jubilee window at St. Margarets, Westminster; and in *Pall Mall Gazette,* December 1887.

"The Isle's Enchantress." *Pall Mall Gazette,* 26 March 1889.

"To Edward FitzGerald." *The Athenaeum,* 13 July 1889, p. 64.

"Lines for the Tomb of Levi Lincoln Thaxter." *Poet Lore,* 1 (1889), 398.

"Lines to Accompany G. D. Giles' Pencil Sketch." W. M. Rossetti, "Portraits of Robert Browning.—III," *Magazine of Art,* 13 (1890), 266.

Response to a Translation by Longfellow. *Recollections of Louisa May Alcott, John Greenleaf Whittier, and Robert Browning,* by Maria S. Porter. Boston: Published for the author by the New England Magazine Corporation, 1893. P. 48.

"Yellow and Pale as Ripened Corn." *Sir Frederick Leighton,* by Ernest Rhys. London: George Bell, 1895. P. 51.

Variation on a Description by Moscheles for "The Isle's Enchantress." *Fragments of an Autobiography,* by Felix Moscheles. London: J. Nisbet, 1899. P. 335.

"Epps." *Cornhill Magazine,* 35 (1913), 433–5.

"Aeschylus' Soliloquy." *Cornhill Magazine,* 35 (1913), 577–81.

"Gerousios Oinos." *Cornhill Magazine,* 36 (1914), 575–6.

"Dialogue Between Father and Daughter." *New Poems,* 1914. P. 72.

"The Dogma Triumphant." *New Poems,* 1914. P. 73.

Replies to Challenges to Rhyme. *New Poems,* 1914. Pp. 71–2.

Reply to a Telegraphic Greeting. *New Poems,* 1914. P. 70.

"A Scene in the Building of the Inquisitors at Antwerp." *New Poems,* 1914. P. 69.

Translation from Pindar's Seventh Olympian, Epode III. *New Poems,* 1914. P. 39.

Rhyme for a Child on a Painting of Venus and Paris. *Memories and Reflections,* by Lady Laura Troubridge. London: Heinemann, 1925. P. 45.

Quatrain on Richard Wagner. In American Art Association's Sales Catalogue (New York) for 16 December 1929, lot 3.

Couplet for Furnivall on Two Publishers. *Letters of Robert Browning.* Ed. Thurman L. Hood. London: John Murray, 1933. P. 226.

Quatrain for Mrs. Pattison on Charles Dickens. *University of Toronto Quarterly,* 21 (1952), 181.

3. *Letters*

Letters of Robert Browning, Collected by Thomas J. Wise. Ed.
Thurman L. Hood. London: John Murray, 1933.
*Robert Browning and Julia Wedgwood. A Broken Friendship as
Revealed by Their Letters.* Ed. Richard Curle. London: John
Murray and Jonathan Cape, 1937.
Dearest Isa: Robert Browning's Letters to Isabella Blagden. Ed.
Edward C. McAleer. Austin: University of Texas Press, 1951.
New Letters of Robert Browning. Ed. William Clyde DeVane and
Kenneth L. Knickerbocker. London: John Murray, 1951.
Letters of the Brownings to George Barrett. Ed. Paul Landis with
the assistance of Ronald E. Freeman. Urbana: University of
Illinois Press, 1958.
*Browning to His American Friends: Letters between the Brownings,
the Storys, and James Russell Lowell.* Ed. Gertrude Reese Hudson.
London: Bowes and Bowes, 1965.
*Learned Lady: Letters from Robert Browning to Mrs. Thomas
FitzGerald.* Ed. Edward C. McAleer. Cambridge: Harvard University Press, 1966.

II. SELECTED BIOGRAPHIES, STUDIES, AND CRITICISM

Allingham, William. *A Diary.* Ed. H. Allingham and D. Radford.
London: Macmillan, 1907.
Broughton, Leslie N., and B. F. Stelter. *A Concordance to the
Poems of Robert Browning.* 2 vols. New York: G. E. Stechert,
1924–5.
Broughton, Leslie N., Clarke Sutherland Northrup, and Robert
Pearsall, comps. *Robert Browning: A Bibliography, 1830–1950.*
Ithaca: Cornell University Press, 1953.
Cadbury, William. "Lyric and Anti-Lyric Forms: A Method for
Judging Browning." *University of Toronto Quarterly,* 34 (1964),
49–67.
Chesterton, G. K. *Robert Browning.* New York and London:
Macmillan, 1903.
Clarke, Helen A. "A Defence of Browning's Later Work." *Poet Lore,*
12 (1900), 284–304.
Cohen, J. M. *Robert Browning.* London: Longmans, Green, 1952.
Collins, Thomas J. "The Poetry of Robert Browning: A Proposal

for Reexamination." *Texas Studies in Literature and Language,* 15 (1973), 325–40.

Columbus, Claudette Kemper. *"Fifine at the Fair:* A Masque of Sexuality and Death Seeking Figures of Expression." *Studies in Browning and His Circle,* 2, No. 1 (Spring 1974), 21–38.

Columbus, Robert R., and Claudette Kemper. "Browning's Fuddling Apollo, or The Perils of Parleying." *Tennessee Studies in Literature,* 12 (1967), 83–102.

Davies, Hugh Sykes. *Browning and the Modern Novel.* Hull: University of Hull Publications, 1962.

DeVane, William Clyde. *A Browning Handbook.* 2nd ed. New York: Appleton-Century-Crofts, 1955.

——. "Browning and the Spirit of Greece." *Nineteenth-Century Studies,* ed. H. Davis, W. C. DeVane, and R. C. Bald. Ithaca: Cornell University Press, 1940.

——. *Browning's Parleyings: The Autobiography of a Mind.* New Haven: Yale University Press, 1927.

——. "The Harlot and the Thoughtful Young Man." *Studies in Philology,* 29 (1932), 463–84.

Domett, Alfred. *The Diary of Alfred Domett, 1872–1885.* Ed. E. A. Horsman. London, New York, and Toronto: Oxford University Press, 1953.

Drew, Philip. *The Poetry of Browning: A Critical Introduction.* London: Methuen, 1970.

Duckworth, Francis R. G. *Browning: Background and Conflict.* London: Ernest Benn, 1931.

Duffin, Henry Charles. *Amphibian: A Reconsideration of Browning.* London: Bowes and Bowes, 1956.

Friend, Joseph H. "Euripides Browningized: The Meaning of *Balaustion's Adventure." Victorian Poetry,* 2 (1964), 179–86.

Gridley, Roy E. *Browning.* London: Routledge & Kegan Paul, 1972.

Griffin, W. Hall, and H. C. Minchin. *The Life of Robert Browning.* Rev. ed. London: Methuen, 1910; rpt. Hamden, Conn: Archon, 1966.

Harrold, William E. *The Variance and the Unity.* Athens: Ohio University Press, 1973.

Herford, C. H. *Robert Browning.* Edinburgh and London: William Blackwood, 1905.

Hitner, John Meigs. *Browning's Analysis of a Murder: A Case for*

THE INN ALBUM. Marquette: Northern Michigan University Press, 1969.

——. "Browning's Grotesque Period." *Victorian Poetry,* 4 (1966), 1–13.

Honan, Park. *Browning's Characters: A Study in Poetic Technique.* New Haven and London: Yale University Press, 1961.

——. "On Robert Browning and Romanticism." *Browning Institute Studies,* 1 (1973), 147–72.

Irvine, William, and Park Honan. *The Book, the Ring, & the Poet: A Biography of Robert Browning.* New York: McGraw-Hill, 1974.

Kendall, J. L. "Browning's *Fifine*—Meaning and Method." *Victorian Newsletter,* No. 22 (Fall 1962), 16–18.

King, Roma A., Jr. *The Focusing Artifice.* Athens: Ohio University Press, 1968.

——. "The Necessary Surmise: The Shaping Spirit of Robert Browning's Poetry." *Romantic and Victorian: Studies in Memory of William H. Marshall,* ed. W. Paul Elledge and Richard L. Hoffman. Rutherford, Madison, and Teaneck, N.J.: Fairleigh Dickinson University Press, 1971. Pp. 346–61.

Knickerbocker, Kenneth L. "Browning and His Critics." *Sewanee Review,* 43 (1935), 283–91.

Langbaum, Robert. "Browning and the Question of Myth." *PMLA,* 81 (1966), 575–84.

——. *The Poetry of Experience: The Dramatic Monologue in Modern Literary Tradition.* New York: Random House, 1957.

Litzinger, Boyd. *Time's Revenges: Browning's Reputation as a Thinker, 1889–1962.* Knoxville: University of Tennessee Press, 1964.

Litzinger, Boyd, and Kenneth L. Knickerbocker, eds. Bibliography of Browning Studies from 1951 through May 1965. *The Browning Critics.* Lexington: University of Kentucky Press, 1965.

Litzinger, Boyd, and Donald Smalley, eds. *Browning: The Critical Heritage.* London: Routledge and Kegan Paul, 1970.

Melchiori, Barbara. *Browning's Poetry of Reticence.* Edinburgh and London: Oliver and Boyd, 1968.

Miller, Betty. *Robert Browning.* London: John Murray, 1952.

Miller, J. Hillis. *The Disappearance of God: Five Nineteenth-Century Writers.* Cambridge: Harvard University Press, 1963; rpt. New York: Schocken Books, 1965.

Nettleship, John T. *Robert Browning: Essays and Thoughts.* 2nd ed. London: Elkin Matthews, 1890.

Orr, Mrs. Sutherland. *A Handbook to the Works of Robert Browning.* 6th ed. London: G. Bell, 1927.

———. *Life and Letters of Robert Browning.* Rev. and in part rewritten by Frederick G. Kenyon. Boston: Houghton, Mifflin, 1908.

———. "The Religious Opinions of Robert Browning." *Contemporary Review,* 60 (1891), 876–91.

Peckham, Morse. *Victorian Revolutionaries.* New York: George Braziller, 1970.

Peterson, William S. *Interrogating the Oracle: A History of the Browning Society.* Athens: Ohio University Press, 1969.

Preyer, Robert. "Two Styles in the Verse of Robert Browning." *ELH,* 32 (1965), 62–84.

Priestley, F. E. L. "A Reading of *La Saisiaz.*" *University of Toronto Quarterly,* 25 (1955), 47–59.

Raymond, William O. *The Infinite Moment, and Other Essays in Robert Browning.* 2nd ed. Toronto: University of Toronto Press, 1965.

Ridenour, George M. "Browning's Music Poems: Fancy and Fact." *PMLA,* 78 (1963), 369–77.

Santayana, George. "The Poetry of Barbarism." *Interpretations of Poetry and Religion.* New York: Scribner, 1900. Pp. 188–216.

Shaw, David. *The Dialectical Temper: The Rhetorical Art of Robert Browning.* Ithaca: Cornell University Press, 1968.

Slinn, E. Warwick. "The Judgment of Instinct in 'Ivàn Ivànovitch.'" *Browning Society Notes,* 4, No. 1 (March 1974), 3–9.

Smalley, Donald, ed. *Browning's Essay on Chatterton.* Cambridge: Harvard University Press, 1948.

———. "A Parleying with Aristophanes." *PMLA,* 55 (1940), 823–38.

Spindler, Robert. *Robert Browning und die Antike.* Leipzig: B. Tauchnitz, 1930.

Swinburne, Algernon Charles. *Essays and Studies.* London: Chatto and Windus, 1875.

Symons, Arthur. *An Introduction to the Study of Browning.* New rev. ed. London: Cassell, 1906.

Szladits, Lola L. "Browning's French Night-Cap." *Bulletin of the New York Public Library,* 61 (1957), 458–67.

Tracy, C. R. "The Source and Meaning of Browning's *Tray.*" *PMLA,* 55 (1940), 615–17.

Ward, Maisie. *Robert Browning and His World: Two Robert Brownings? (1861–1889).* London: Cassell, 1969.

Watkins, Charlotte Crawford. "The 'Abstruser Themes' of Browning's *Fifine at the Fair.*" *PMLA,* 74 (1959), 426–37.

——. "Browning's *Red Cotton Night-Cap Country* and Carlyle." *Victorian Studies,* 7 (1964), 359–74.

Whiting, Lilian. *The Brownings: Their Life and Art.* Boston: Little, Brown, 1917.

Whitla, William. "Browning and the Ashburton Affair." *Browning Society Notes,* 2, No. 2 (July 1972), 12–14.

——. *The Central Truth: The Incarnation in Robert Browning.* Toronto: University of Toronto Press, 1963.

Wilson, F. Mary. *A Primer on Browning.* London: Macmillan, 1891.

ᔍ Index

Italicized numerals indicate a major discussion.

Aeschylus, 31, 32n., 77, 83, 143, 144-5, 209
  Agamemnon, 104, 143, 144n., 166
  Prometheus Bound, 77
Alciphron, 102
Allingham, William, 103n., 105n., 166n.
Altick, R. D., 26n.
Aristophanes, 83, 101-18, 241, 244
  The Frogs, 115
Aristotle, 169, 233
  Nicomachean Ethics, 232
Arnold, Matthew, 143-5, 219
  Preface to *Poems* (1853), 143, 145
Ashburton, Louisa Lady, 46-7n., 60, 61, 211, 239
Athanasius, 155
Athenaeus, 102
Auden, W. H., 64
Austin, Alfred, 37n., 133, 142
Avison, Charles, 220-23

Bach, J. S., 129, 222
Bailey, J. O., 15n.
Bald, R. C., 29n.
Baldinucci, Filippo, 136
Balzac, Honoré de, 100n.
Bartoli, Daniel, 210, 213, 217
Bassett, A. Tilney, 179n.
Baudelaire, Charles, 60
Bergman, Ingmar, 60
Berlioz, Hector, 100
Bidpai, 190
Blagden, Isabella, 27n., 28, 43, 47, 59, 60, 133, 167, 175

Brahms, Johannes, 129, 220
Bronson, Katherine de Kay, 228
Broughton, L. N., 54
Brown, E. K., 15n.
Browning, Elizabeth Barrett, 18, 21, 27n., 28, 31, 32n., 36, 37n., 41 and n., 45, 47n., 61-2, 103n., 149, 151, 157, 163-4, 165, 211, 239
Browning, Robert
  "Adam, Lilith, and Eve," *183*
  Agamemnon of Aeschylus, The, 132, *143-6*
  "Amphibian" (Prologue), *62-4,* 67, 68, 72, 74, 79, 81-2
  "Any Wife to Any Husband," 61
  "Apollo and the Fates," 204, 205, *206-8,* 223
  Aristophanes' Apology, 101-18, 119, 143, 144, 184, 209, 218, 241, 245, 246, 247
  Asolando, 227-40, 242
    Prologue, *228-30*
    Epilogue, *238,* 240
    See also titles of individual poems
  "At the 'Mermaid'," 137, 142, 148, 163n.
  "Bad Dreams," *239-40*
  Balaustion's Adventure, 28-41, 42, 44, 45n., 47n., 56n., 101-2, 104 and n., 107, 132, 192, 204, 208, 211, 218, 235, 241, 243
  "Bean Feast, The," *235*
  "Bean-Stripe, A," 194, *196-7,* 198

Browning, Robert (*cont.*)
"Beatrice Signorini," 230, 231, *237-8*
"Bifurcation," 132, 138
"Camel-Driver, A," 193, 195
"Cenciaja," 141
"Cherries," 193, 198
Christmas-Eve and Easter-Day, 18, 44
"Cleon," 143, 235
"Clive," 174, *175-6*, 188
"Christina and Monaldeschi," *182*, 183
"Death in the Desert, A," 21, 22 and n.
"Development," *231-3*, 237
"Dis Aliter Visum," 65
"Doctor ——," *178*, 184
"Donald," *181*, 184, 188
Dramatic Idyls (First Series), *165-74*, 175, 188, 205, 228
See also titles of individual poems
Dramatic Idyls, Second Series, *174-9*, 184, 186, 188, 205
Prologue, *174-5*, 178, 179
Epilogue, *179*
See also titles of individual poems
Dramatis Personae, 21, 22, 132
Epilogue, 21, 230
"Dubiety," 236
"Eagle, The," 193
"Echetlos," *175*, 184
Essay on Shelley, 19-20, 24, 25, 41, 44, 116, 161
"Family, The," 193
"Fears and Scruples," 139, 230
Ferishtah's Fancies, *190-200*, 202, 205, 216, 228, 234, 242
Prologue, 191, *192*
Epilogue, *197*, 243
See also titles of individual poems
Fifine at the Fair, 46n., *59-82*, 83, 84, 87, 101, 135, 141, 159n., 163n., 193, 211, 225, 239, 241, 244, 247
"Filippo Baldinucci on the Privilege of Burial," 140, 216

"Flute-Music, with an Accompaniment," *236-7*
"Forgiveness, A," 138, 141n.
"Fust and His Friends," 204, 205, 206, *223-5*
"Gerousios Oinos," *187-8*
"Gold Hair," 21
"Grammarian's Funeral, The," 46
"Halbert and Hob," *169-70*, 174
"Hervé Riel," 132n., 137-8
"House," 132n., 134n., 136, 142
"Householder, The," *80-81*, 82
"Imperante Augusto Natus Est ——," *233*, 235
"Inapprehensiveness," 231, 236
Inn Album, The, *119-31*, 132, 143, 152, 168, 172, 241
"Iwàn Iwànovitch," 51, *170-1*, 173
"Ixion," 183-5
"Jochanan Hakkadosh, 184-6, 188
Jocoseria, 181-9, 190, 205, 241
Prologue, 181, 186
See also titles of individual poems
"Magical Nature," 132n., 138
"Martin Relph," *168-9*, 170-71, 172
"Mary Wollstonecraft and Fuseli," *182-3*
"Melon-Seller, The," 193
Men and Women, 16, 18, 43
"Mihrah Shah," 193
"Muléykeh," *176-7*
"Natural Magic," 132n., 138
"Ned Bratts," *172*
"Never the Time and the Place," *186*
"Now," 236
"Numpholeptos," *139*, 141, 178
"Of Pacchiarotto, and How He Worked in Distemper," *135-6*, 140, 148, 173, 184
"Old Pictures at Florence," 19
"One Word More," 148
Pacchiarotto and How He Worked in Distemper, *132-42*, 143, 163n., 174, 241
Prologue, 132n., 135, 139
Epilogue, 141, 142, 148, 163n., 167, 187

Browning, Robert (*cont.*)
  *See also titles of individual
    poems*
"Pambo," *186-7*
"Pan and Luna," 174, *178-9*
Paracelsus, 16, 18 and n., 46
*Parleyings with Certain People of
    Importance in Their Day,* 16,
    44, 56, *201-26,* 229, 230,
    242, 243, 244, 245
  *See also titles of individual
    poems*
Pauline, 16, 17, 46, 203-4, 225,
    229-30
"Pearl, A Girl, A," 236
"Pheidippides," *169,* 170, 175,
    184
"Pietro of Abano," *177-8,* 184
"Pillar at Sebzevah, A.," 191, 194,
    195
"Pisgah Sights, I, II," 137
"Plot-Culture," 193
"Poetics," 230-1
Prince Hohenstiel-Schwangau, 12,
    42-58, 59, 69n., 89, 101,
    153, 163n., 214, 241, 246
"Rabbi Ben Ezra," 110
Red Cotton Night-Cap Country,
    46n., *83-100,* 101, 119, 135,
    143, 150, 159, 167, 168, 239,
    241, 247
"Rephan," 234-5
"Reverie," 230, *234,* 236
Ring and the Book, The, 15, 23,
    25, 26, 27n., 28, 29 and n.,
    30-32, 37, 39, 44n., 46, 101,
    102, 116, 130, 131, 148, 161,
    198, 202, 226, 228, 231, 232,
    241, 242
"Rosny," 231
"St. Martin's Summer," 138
"Saisiaz, La," 137n., *147-57,* 158,
    159, 160, 163n., 165, 166,
    167, 171n., 190, 192, 198,
    231, 238
*Saisiaz, La: The Two Poets of
    Croisic, 147-64*
"Saul," 18, 20
"Shah Abbas," 193, *194-5*
"Shop," 132n., 139, 142
"Solomon and Balkis," *181,* 183

Sordello, 16-17, 23, 31, 73, 83,
    102, 148, 163, 166, 225
"Speculative," 231, 236
"Statue and the Bust, The," 46,
    94, 127
Strafford, 30
"Summum Bonum," 236
"Sun, The," 193, *194*
"Thamuris Marching," 102, *117-
    18*
"To My Critics," 142
"Touch him n'er so lightly." See
    *Dramatic Idyls, Second Ser-
    ies,* Epilogue
"Tray," *171-2, 173-4,* 181, 184
"Two Camels," 193
"Two Poets of Croisic, The,"
    158-64, 165, 173, 197
"With Bernard de Mandeville,"
    31, 161, 204, 205, 206, *208-
    10,* 223, 232, 233
"With Charles Avison," 203, 204,
    205-6, *220-23,* 226, 233
"With Christopher Smart," 205,
    206, *212-13,* 215, 216, 223,
    246
"With Daniel Bartoli," 205, 206,
    210-12
"With Francis Furini," 205, 206,
    215-17, 223, 247
"With George Bubb Dodington,"
    205, 206, *213-15*
"With Gerard De Lairesse," 203,
    205, 206, *217-20,* 223, 229
Browning, Robert, Sr., 61
Browning, Robert Wiedemann Bar-
    rett ("Pen"), 47n., 216, 227,
    228
Browning, Sarianna, 147, 165
Browning Society (London), 26,
    180, 187, 190, 199, 201
Bunyan, John, 172
Buñuel, Luis, 60
Bush, Douglas, 29n.
Byron, George Gordon, Lord, 65,
    73, 129, 155, 156, 163n., 171,
    173
Beppo, 163
"The Vision of Judgment," 163n.

Cadbury, William, 246n.

Carlyle, Thomas, 20 and n., 73, 79n., 86 and n., 104n., 117, 121, 136, 143, 208-10, 235
"Characteristics," 79n.
Sartor Resartus, 20n., 210
Cavour, Count C. B. di, 46
Charlton, H. B., 13
Chesterton, G. K., 58n., 99n., 247n.
Clarke, Helen, 157n.
Cohen, J. M., 43 and n.
Colenso, J. W., 21
Collins, Thomas C., 18n.
Colvin, Sidney, 175n.
Comicorum Graecorum Fragmenta, 102
Comte, Auguste, 51 and n.
Conrad, Joseph, 84
Cook, E. T., 24n., 200n.
Correggio, 129
Cowper, Countess Anne, 28
Cressman, E. D., 29n.
Curle, Richard, 27n.
Czerny, Karl, 128

Dante, 151, 204
Divine Comedy, 129, 202, 204, 223
Davies, H. Sykes, 100n.
Davis, Herbert, 29n.
DeVane, W. C., 29n., 43n., 62, 66n., 80n., 83, 102 and n., 119n., 131, 132n., 134n., 142n., 151n., 168, 174, 183n., 184-5, 186, 188n., 192, 202, 203, 204n., 225, 238n.
Disraeli, Benjamin, 214-15
Dodington, George Bubb, 216-18, 220
Domett, Alfred, 83, 117n., 119n., 144n.
Doré, Gustave, 70
Doughty, Oswald, 28n.
Drew, Philip, 14n., 58n., 100n., 119n., 154n., 163n., 196 and n., 234n., 245
Dvorak, Anton, 220

Eliot, George, 120
Elledge, W. Paul, 22n.
Essays and Reviews, 21

Euripides, 28-41 passim, 44, 101-18 passim, 209
Alkestis, 28-40 passim, 42, 104, 105n., 113
Elektra, 112
Herakles, 42, 104, 112-15, 144
Hippolytus, 107

Fairchild, H. N., 22n.
Faverty, F. E., 13n.
FitzGerald, Mrs. Thomas, 133, 165, 199, 201, 202
Flaubert, Gustave, 100n.
Forster, John, 132
Fourier, François C., 51 and n.
Freeman, R. E., 127n.
Friend, J. H., 41n., 47n., 103n.
Furini, Francis, 215-17
Furnival, F. J., 201
Fuseli, Henry, 183
Fust, Johann, 223-5

Gainsborough, Thomas, 129
Gentilhomme, René, 160-61
Gladstone, W. E., 121
Gluck, C. W., 221
Goethe, J. W. von, 156, 190, 205
Dichtung and Wahrheit, 205
Faust, 204, 223
Westöstlicher Divan, 190
Gosse, Edmund, 245n.
Gridley, R. E., 100n.
Griffin, W. Hall, 142n., 143, 166n.

Hair, D. S., 27n.
Handel, G. F., 220, 221
Harrison, Frederic, 171n.
Harrold, W. E., 158n., 200n., 205n.
Hayden, Josef, 221
Herodotus, 169
Hitner, J. M., 15n., 99n., 119n.
Hoffman, R. L., 22n.
Homer, 231-2
Iliad, 231
Honan, Park, 13, 32n., 37n., 45n., 57 and n., 117, 118n., 163n., 200n., 204n., 239
Hood, T. L., 20n., 26, 29n., 43, 45, 47n., 58, 84, 102 and n., 103, 141n., 142n., 143, 149, 176,

Hood, T. L. (*cont.*)
  180, 181, 189n., 190, 199, 201,
  227
Houghton, W. E., 13n.
Hugo, Victor, 52
Hunt, Holman, 130

Irvine, William, 32n., 37n., 117n.,
  163n.

Jackson, C. N., 102n.
James, Henry, 26n., 134
Joan of Arc, 217
Jones, Henry, 196n.
Jowett, Benjamin, 14, 143, 144

Keats, John, 213
Kegan Paul, Charles, 179n.
Kenyon, F. G., 60n.
Kierkegaard, Sören, 136, 161, 200
  Fear and Trembling, 202
King, R. A., Jr., 14n., 21, 57 and n.,
  103 and n., 151n., 204n., 245
Kintner, Elvan, 149n.
Knickerbocker, K. L., 15n., 133n.
Korg, Jacob, 13n.

Lairesse, Gerard De, 217-19
Landis, Paul, 127n.
Landseer, Edward, 130
Lang, Cecil Y., 29n., 102n.
Langbaum, Robert, 13n., 18n., 29n.,
  66, 204n.
Liszt, Franz, 220
Litzinger, Boyd, 15n.
Lord, Georgianna, 246n.
Luther, Martin, 224

Macaulay, T. B., 175
Maillard, Paul, 161
Mandeville, Bernard de, 208-9
Marsh, Virginia, 147
Marshall, Andrew, 103n.
McAleer, E. C., 27n., 133n.
Melchiori, Barbara, 15n., 60 and n.,
  67
Michelangelo, 70, 99
Millais, John, 130
Miller, Betty, 47n.
Miller, J. Hillis, 22, 100

Milton, John, 52, 128, 141, 149-50,
  176, 213
  Comus, 119n.
  "Lycidus," 149-50
  Paradise Lost, 128, 129, 149
  Paradise Regained, 128
Minchin, H. C., 142n., 143, 166n.
Molière, 64, 65n., 81, 89
  Don Juan, 64, 65n., 81
Morris, William, 213, 219
Mozart, W. A., 221

Napoleon III, 42, 43-4, 45-6, 47n.,
  51n., 52n., 55n., 56
Nelson, Benjamin, 246n.
Nettleship, J. T., 66n.
Never on Sunday, 36
Nicoll, W. R., 191n.

Orr, Mrs. Sutherland, 48n., 54, 60
  and n., 99n., 144n., 167, 190n.,
  191, 192, 201, 202, 227, 234

Pater, Walter, *The Renaissance,* 152
Peckham, Morse, 204n., 245, 246n.
Peterson, W. S., 180n.
Pius IX, Pope, 99
Plutarch, 32
Pope, Alexander, 155, 156, 231
  Essay on Man, 155
  Iliad, 231
Porter, Charlotte, 157n.
Pound, Ezra, 29n.
Preyer, Robert, 246n.
Priestley, F. E. L., 153
Prothero, R. E., 15n.
Proudhon, P. J., 51 and n.
Pym, John, 222

Raff, Joachim, 128
Raphael, 70
Raymond, W. O., 15n., 48n., 60 and
  n., 178n.
Renan, Ernest, *La Vie de Jésus,* 21
Ridenour, G. M., 118n., 237n., 246n.
Rimbaud, Arthur, *Une Saison en
  Enfer,* 26
Ritchie, Annie Thackeray, 98n.
Rossetti, D. G., 28-9, 134 and n.,
  213
  The House of Life, 134 and n.

Rousseau, J. J., 155, 156, 161
Ruskin, John, 24, 121, 200n.

Santayana, George, 15n.
Schumann, Robert, *Carnaval*, 74
Sears, Sallie, 246n.
Shaffer, Elinor, 22
Shakespeare, William, 137 and n.,
    141
Shaw, W. David, 103 and n., 238
Shelley, P. B., 20, 61, 63, 141, 149,
    154, 185, 219
    "Adonais," 149
    A Defense of Poetry, 63
    Prometheus Unbound, 154
Slinn, E. W., 170n.
Smalley, Donald, 15n., 116n.
Smart, Christopher, 212-13
    "The Song of David," 212
Smith, Anne Egerton, 147-57 pas-
    sim, 165
Spindler, Robert, 29n.
Stange, G. Robert, 13n.
Stelter, B. F., 54
Story, Edith, 43, 47n.
Strafford, T. Wentworth, Earl of,
    222
Swinburne, A. C., 29, 102, 119n.,
    181n., 213, 216, 219, 245n.
Symons, Arthur, 99n.

Tennyson, Alfred, 37n., 64, 119n.,
    121, 132, 137n., 149, 156, 157-
    8, 167, 168n., 175, 219
    "Enoch Arden," 158n.
    "The Epic," 149
    "The Holy Grail," 158n.

Idylls of the King, 64
    In Memoriam, 149, 158, 193
    "Locksley Hall," 157
    Queen Mary, 119n.
Tennyson, Hallam, 14n., 168n.
Thackeray, W. M., *Vanity Fair*, 120
Thiers, L. A., 52
Tisdel, Frederick, 102n.
Tracy, C. R., 118n., 171n., 183n.
Trollope, Anthony, 127n., 128
    Framley Parsonage, 127n.

Vasari, Giorgio, 136
Virgil, 178
Voltaire, 161

Wagner, Richard, 220
Wahl, J. R., 28n.
Ward, Maisie, 26n., 225
Watkins, Charlotte C., 62n., 67n.,
    86n.
Wedderburn, Alexander, 24n., 200n.
Wedgwood, Julia, 27n., 30-31, 202
Whiting, Lilian, 166n., 227n.
Whitla, William, 19n., 47n.
Wilkes, John, 199
Wise, T. J., 20n., 181n., 191n., 245n.
Wollstonecraft, Mary, 183
Wordsworth, William, 76, 169, 228
    "Elegiac Stanzas on Peele Castle,"
    76, 228
    "Intimations Ode," 228
    "Tintern Abbey," 228

Yeats, 30, 161
    "Lapis Lazuli," 161

Browning's Later Poetry, 1871–1889

Designed by R. E. Rosenbaum.
Composed by York Composition Company, Inc.,
in 11 point Intertype Baskerville, 2 points leaded,
with display lines in monotype Deepdene.
Printed letterpress from type by York Composition Company
on Warren's Number 66 text, 50 pound basis.
Bound by John H. Dekker and Sons, Inc.
in Columbia book cloth
and stamped in All Purpose foil.